Daniel Bowles
The Ends of Satire

Paradigms

Literature and the Human Sciences

Edited by
Rüdiger Campe · Paul Fleming

Editorial Board
Eva Geulen · Rüdiger Görner · Barbara Hahn
Daniel Heller-Roazen · Helmut Müller-Sievers
William Rasch · Joseph Vogl · Elisabeth Weber

Volume 2

Daniel Bowles
The Ends of Satire

Legacies of Satire in Postwar German Writing

DE GRUYTER

ISBN 978-3-11-065170-6
e-ISBN (PDF) 978-3-11-035953-4
e-ISBN (EPUB) 978-3-11-038684-4
ISSN 2195-2205

Library of Congress Cataloging-in-Publication Data
A CIP catalog record for this book has been applied for at the Library of Congress.

Bibliographic information published by the Deutsche Nationalbibliothek
The Deutsche Nationalbibliothek lists this publication in the Deutsche Nationalbibliografie;
detailed bibliographic data are available on the Internet at http://dnb.dnb.de.

© 2015 Walter de Gruyter GmbH, Berlin/Munich/Boston
This volume is text- and page-identical with the hardback published in 2015.
Cover illustration: *Ragazza sinistra*, 2005. Lime wood and acrylic paint. 138 × 38 × 32 cm.
© Gehard Demetz. Courtesy of the artist and Jack Shainman Gallery, New York.
Typesetting: Claudia Wild, Konstanz
Printing and binding: CPI books GmbH, Leck
♾ Printed on acid-free paper
Printed in Germany

www.degruyter.com

Table of Contents

Acknowledgments —— **VII**

Introduction | **Satire around 1800: Jean Paul** —— 1

1. Prolegomena —— **3**

2. The Case of Jean Paul: Unreadable Writing, Unwritable Readings —— **16**

Part One | **Inversion**

3. The Carnivalesque in Mikhail Bakhtin's *Rabelais and His World* (1965) —— **45**

4. Perspective and Repetition in Thomas Bernhard's *Woodcutters* (1984) —— **62**

5. Destructive Negativity: Thomas Bernhard and *Extinction* (1986) —— **80**

Part Two | **Mythification**

6. Between Theory and Literature: Roland Barthes' *Mythologies* (1957) —— **101**

7. Elfriede Jelinek's Mythic *Lust* (1989) —— **119**

8. Viennese Paradigms in Elfriede Jelinek's *The Piano Teacher* (1983) —— **136**

Part Three | **Citation**

9. From Stage to Page: Judith Butler and *Gender Trouble* (1990) —— **157**

10. Performing Theory in Literature: Thomas Meinecke's *Tomboy* (1998) —— **170**

11. Infinite Paradise of the Infinite Text: Thomas Meinecke's *Music* (2004) —— **192**

Conclusion | **Satire after Satire** —— 207

Bibliography —— 217

Index —— 227

Acknowledgments

I offer my heartfelt gratitude to all who, with their expertise, counsel, suggestions, critical eye and ear, and intellectual community, have made this scholarly endeavor a little less solitary and have thereby improved it (and me). I delight in naming a few of these special people. My deepest gratitude goes to my friend and teacher, Oliver Simons, for his untiring mentorship, his unflagging, fathomless patience, and his inspirational intellectual companionship. Thank you, Oliver. I am ever indebted to those who read drafts of this project at various stages, including Paul Fleming, Rüdiger Campe, my anonymous peer reviewers, Oliver Simons, Judith Ryan, Eric Rentschler, and Alexander Kluger. They supplied just the right mix of validating praise and constructive criticism, and this book is the better for them and would not have come about without them. I am also very grateful to (and for) my colleagues in German Studies at Boston College – Agnes Farkas, Rachel Freudenburg, Geraldine Grimm, Ursula Mangoubi, Hanni Myers, Michael Resler, and Ruth Sondermann. Their enthusiastic support of my work and kind encouragement are an invaluable motivation. To Caz Novak, for his assistance in preparing the manuscript for publication, and to Kenneth Brummel, for his unparalleled critical acumen and sage advice, I offer sincerest thanks. And one final debt of gratitude I will always be unable to repay is the one I owe my family. As a most modest token of my thanks, I dedicate this book to them.

Chestnut Hill, Massachusetts
August 2014

A remark on translations: unless otherwise noted, all English translations from the German are my own.

Introduction | **Satire around 1800: Jean Paul**

1. Prolegomena

To speak of satire is to invoke a long history of confusion, ambiguity, and uncertainty. This history consists in the myriad attempts to define the contours of a term at once considered a genre,[1] a form, a mode of writing,[2] a technique of corrective criticism,[3] a kind of literary parasitism,[4] a manner of perception [*Empfindungsweise*],[5] "a quite openly aggressive literary mode of expression" but also a creative method,[6] and a negative figure of the "inverted world,"[7] among others.[8] Just as numerous are the approaches taken towards constructing this definition. Exploits in etymology accompany journeys through the history of literature back to the ostensible origin of satire in antiquity[9]; studies of literature in

---

1 Frank Palmeri, *Satire, History, Novel: Narrative Forms, 1665–1815* (Newark: University of Delaware Press, 2003), 11–15; This particular conception of satire as genre has lost significant currency in satire studies and is, judging from recent critical literature, considered outmoded. Palmeri himself writes alternately of satire as genre and form without distinguishing between terms. Helmut Arntzen marks the decline of this understanding of satire "at the very latest since Schiller." See Helmut Arntzen, *Satire in der deutschen Literatur: Geschichte und Theorie* (Darmstadt: Wissenschaftliche Buchgesellschaft, 1989), IX.
2 Brian A. Connery and Kirk Combe, eds., *Theorizing Satire: Essays in Literary Criticism* (New York: St. Martin's Press, 1995), 9.
3 Friedemann Weidauer, Alan Lareau, and Helen Morris-Keitel, "The Politics of Laughter: Problems of Humor and Satire in the FRG Today," in *Laughter Unlimited: Essays on Humor, Satire, and the Comic*, ed. Reinhold Grimm and Jost Hermand (Madison, Wis.: University of Wisconsin Press, 1991), 56.
4 Dustin H. Griffin, *Satire: A Critical Reintroduction* (Lexington, Ky.: University Press of Kentucky, 1994), 4. Griffin's take on satire is more nuanced and carefully considered than others', but in rejecting or deconstructing extant approaches to satire, he neglects to position himself clearly, making it difficult to delineate his perspective. For him, satire is parasitic, but it also plays host to parody, which he seems to view as a textual infection or, less metaphorically, a type of textual resignification.
5 Friedrich Schiller, "Über naive und sentimentalische Dichtung," in *Theoretische Schriften*, vol. 8, *Werke und Briefe* (Frankfurt am Main: Deutscher Klassiker Verlag, 1992), 748.
6 "[E]ine ganz offen kämpferische literarische Ausdrucksweise." Georg Lukács, "Zur Frage der Satire," *Internationale Literatur* 2, no. 4/5 (1932): 149, 139.
7 Klaus Lazarowicz, *Verkehrte Welt: Vorstudien zu einer Geschichte der deutschen Satire* (Tübingen: M. Niemeyer, 1963); Arntzen, *Satire in der deutschen Literatur*.
8 Jürgen Brummack adds his own series to the list: "a historical genre, but also an ethos, a tone, an intent, as well as the in many respects highly variegated works shaped by them." "Zu Begriff und Theorie der Satire," *Deutsche Vierteljahrsschrift für Literaturwissenschaft und Geistesgeschichte* 45 (May 1971): 275.
9 Many general historical overviews of satire begin with attempts to unearth the term's originary meaning by reverting to its etymological derivation. For a thorough introduction to the history of

its social, political, and biographical contexts invite forays into hermeneutic text explication, merely leading into a thicket of work-specific definitions of satire without a common terminological basis.[10] That satire is "irritatingly ambiguous" is clear.[11] As one critic writes, satire is "the most problematic mode to the taxonomist, since it appears never to have corresponded to any one kind."[12] A seemingly endless array of theorists and critics has indeed thrown up its hands in despair at the taxonomic difficulties, claiming that no single conception of satire may or should exist.[13]

But critics are even uncertain about the proper term to substantiate. Can we speak of *a* satire, or is the word so fraught with abstract complexity that we must necessarily resort to writing about the satiric, a quality whose nominalized formulation nonetheless fails to skirt the issue of what it means? Should one consider satire a kind of practice or textual operation – that of satirizing – that alters a text in some fundamental way yet to be described? No general agreement exists, and the panoply of different terminological problems remains a gadfly for any

---

the term, see Otto Weinreich, *Römische Satiren: Ennius, Lucilius, Varro, Horaz, Persius, Juvenal, Seneca, Petronius* (Zürich: Artemis-Verlag, 1949), VII–XXIII; other studies not dealing exclusively with the satires of antiquity also mobilize the etymological roots of the term to shed (spurious) light on its history. See also Brummack, "Zu Begriff und Theorie der Satire," 275–286.

10 Gilbert Highet, *The Anatomy of Satire* (Princeton, NJ: Princeton University Press, 1962); Robert C. Elliott, *The Power of Satire: Magic, Ritual, Art* (Princeton, NJ: Princeton University Press, 1960); Lazarowicz, *Verkehrte Welt: Vorstudien zu einer Geschichte der deutschen Satire*; cf. especially Frank Palmeri, *Satire in Narrative: Petronius, Swift, Gibbon, Melville, and Pynchon* (Austin: University of Texas Press, 1990).

11 Brummack, "Zu Begriff und Theorie der Satire," 275.

12 Alastair Fowler, *Kinds of Literature: An Introduction to the Theory of Genres and Modes* (Cambridge, Mass.: Harvard University Press, 1982), 110; Hegel concurs, noting that satire is the artform "to which common theories have been unable to do proper justice because they remain in perplexity about its classification." *Aesthetics: Lectures on Fine Art*, vol. 1 (Oxford: Clarendon Press, 1975), 514.

13 "The definition of satire cannot be codified." Arntzen, *Satire in der deutschen Literatur*, X; "More so than other conceptions of genre, [the notion of satire] has become so complex over the course of its history that it can no longer be defined." Brummack, "Zu Begriff und Theorie der Satire," 275; "[...] we should view with suspicion or skepticism any universalizing claim about the nature of satire [...]." Griffin, *Satire*, 185; "Our intention is not to engage in the folly (and, on occasion, the knavery) of solving the dilemma of what satire is or ought to be." Connery and Combe, *Theorizing Satire*, 13; "In light of the colorful variety of methodologies, it would be senseless to speak of a fixed definition of satire or to aim for one." Harald Kämmerer, *"Nur um Himmels willen keine Satyren—": Deutsche Satire und Satiretheorie des 18. Jahrhunderts im Kontext von Anglophilie, Swift-Rezeption und ästhetischer Theorie* (Heidelberg: Universitätsverlag C. Winter, 1999), 4.

serious discussion of satire, most of which (including this one) begin by recounting precisely this definitional conundrum.

Whatever the solution to this intractable issue of nomenclature and definition, it is not likely to lie in understanding the (arbitrary) word itself, especially after a century of rigorous post-Saussurean thought on the linguistic sign. In seeking some common thread among these studies, in penetrating through the layers of signification to expose the signified, we must first answer several fundamental questions. To what extent is satire a textual phenomenon? What are ultimately the structural and formal qualities that constitute and legitimate satire, lending it its historical function? Through these questions we can direct the discussion away from essentialist assertions about the meaning and purpose of satire and reorient it around measurable, empirically observable formal characteristics – textual practices and strategies, for example – that acknowledge the historicity of the term through their varied combination while displaying distinct phases of accretion and thus historical developments and shifts.

To comprehend satire and its history, we might do better thus to conceive of a nuanced combination of forces that creates the illusion of a homogeneous concept of satire – since attempting to expose the signified is a fallacious endeavor that always relies on an illusory sense of finality. Put differently, it behooves the critic to seek the general recipe for the observed phenomenon rather to lose himself in the specificity of pragmatic interpretations; individual meanings are less important in formulating a theory of satire than recognizing what, in general, makes satire tick. Such an undertaking inevitably exposes the notion of satire to be the realm of intertextual operations and many different media – textual, visual, and aural – both explaining satire's dogged resistance to a single, coherent reading and accounting for the shifts, alterations, and inversions of meaning accorded to it.[14] It is, in short, not a matter of semantics; it is a matter of semiotics.

Indeed, it is the semiotics of the satiric that has served as the tacit common denominator in almost all previous studies of the phenomenon, irrespective of literary tradition, time period, or whatever shape the Protean notion of satire has taken: the manipulation of signs, be they linguistic or non-linguistic. And yet the ways these signs have been manipulated to produce something called satire or

---

14 That satire is not purely a literary phenomenon makes matters at once more interesting and more vexing. Indeed, satire has seemed to find fecund soil in contemporary visual culture, especially in television. For the purposes of consistency, however, the scope of this book shall remain definitively circumscribed by linguistic signs, with the hope that a semiotics of the satiric in literature would be at least partially transferable to studies of the satiric in other media.

the satiric has scarcely been the focus of any large-scale study, much less of one in German Studies.[15]

A second, related concern is the virtual absence of satire in serious academic studies of twentieth-century and postmodern literature in general. Already in the nineteenth century, G. W. F. Hegel effectively banishes satire from the realm of aesthetics with a single taciturn sentence, thereby robbing satire of signifying potential and placing it on uncertain terrain with regard to its status as literature.[16] More than a century later, Fredric Jameson echoes this pronouncement by way of analogy to a related practice – parody – by claiming that pastiche has supplanted parody in the period of late capitalism.[17] For Jameson, pastiche is parody defanged, "amputated of its satiric impulse,"[18] and thus both incapable of some undefined instrumental function but also, and more importantly, the skeleton of satire's former vessel. What Jameson describes in the new era of postmodern literature is thus a postsatiric age; indeed, satire frequently only appears as a point of comparison for parody, a form that Jameson marks as absent from contemporary post-

---

15 Long the red-headed stepchild of literary studies, satire rarely makes an appearance in aesthetic theories and only occasionally appears in Baroque or Enlightenment poetics. Studies of satire do not even have their own library classification, lumped together instead with wit, humor, and parody, among other miscellany, as if library scientists with the Library of Congress blushed with embarrassment at the prospect of ascertaining satire's proper place among arts and letters. As for literary studies, most major contributions to studies of satire in German cover historical ground only through the eighteenth century, with the exceptional few focusing on cabaret or political resistance movements in the Third Reich or the GDR. See Lazarowicz, *Verkehrte Welt: Vorstudien zu einer Geschichte der deutschen Satire*; Frank Wilhelm, *Literarische Satire in der SBZ/DDR 1945–1961: Autoren, institutionelle Rahmenbedingungen und kulturpolitische Leitlinien* (Hamburg: Kovač, 1998); see also Arntzen, *Satire in der deutschen Literatur*. Arntzen's book, enticingly subtitled *Band 1*, traces the history of satire through the Early Modern period; no second volume ever followed. Lazarowicz likewise contributes only "preliminary studies" that examine satire in eighteenth-century German literature, largely from a biographical point of view.
16 "These days satires no longer seem to succeed." Hegel's understanding of satire as a "transition to a higher mode of configuration" also undermines the notion of satire as a viable form unto itself. *Vorlesungen über die Ästhetik II*, ed. Eva Moldenhauer and Karl Markus Michel, vol. 14 (Frankfurt am Main: Suhrkamp, 1970), 125; *Aesthetics*, 1:516, 512.
17 Fredric Jameson, *Postmodernism, Or, The Cultural Logic of Late Capitalism* (Durham: Duke University Press, 1991), 16. In tracing the publication history of satire studies in German, one finds that the serious critical and theoretical discussion of satire in German literature effectively ceases with Karl Kraus and Robert Musil. And yet precisely this caesura, noted by Jameson, marks the point beyond which satire vanishes from the literary landscape.
18 Fredric Jameson, "Postmodernism, or The Cultural Logic of Late Capitalism," *New Left Review* I, no. 146 (1984): 65.

modern literature anyway.[19] If satire has gradually disappeared from the literary scene, having been demoted to a secondary or tertiary entity in studies of humor and parody, what has prompted this disappearance? Or, perhaps more aptly, to where did it vanish? Where is it hiding? If satire in a traditional sense no longer obtains, might it not exist in the postmodern era under an alternate guise and participate in an alternate history of writing? In the following pages, the notion of an age of satire after satire – of a new understanding of the satiric effect and an investigation into the ubiquity of its practices – takes center stage.[20] Before I proceed, however, a word on methodology.

First, by deriving from the fragmented history of satire a set of semiotic textual strategies that constitutes the satiric effect – a term I will use to circumvent the problem of employing a specific terminological category *a priori* – I focus more intently on the textual, formal aspects of satire that exist independently of the historical, political, and social context of the work. That is not to say that satire is not involved with historical, political, or social matters – in the case studies to follow, precisely these elements not immanent to the text will creep back into the picture surreptitiously – nor is it wise to exclude context from interpretive consideration.[21] In this heuristic stage, however, identifying purely textual practices that give rise to satire both tests the hypothesis that satire is a textual phe-

---

[19] The prevalence of studies on parody in the past thirty years needs no elaboration, but the relative lack of theories of satire is surprising by comparison. See, for instance, Margaret A. Rose, *Parody//Meta-Fiction: An Analysis of Parody as a Critical Mirror to the Writing and Reception of Fiction* (London: Croom Helm, 1979); Linda Hutcheon, *A Theory of Parody: The Teachings of Twentieth-Century Art Forms* (New York: Methuen, 1985); Margaret A. Rose, *Parody: Ancient, Modern, and Post-Modern* (Cambridge: Cambridge University Press, 1993); Linda Hutcheon, *Irony's Edge: The Theory and Politics of Irony* (London: Routledge, 1994); Simon Dentith, *Parody* (London: Routledge, 2000); Margaret A. Rose, *Parodie, Intertextualität, Interbildlichkeit* (Bielefeld: Aisthesis, 2006).

[20] Whatever the case may be, the aim of this project is not to rehabilitate satire as a viable genre – it is not a genre – nor is its purpose, to paraphrase Gérard Genette on parody, merely "to censure the abuse of the word ['satire'] (since, in effect, that is what we are dealing with) but only to point it out and – because it is impossible to clear up this lexical area effectively – at least provide its users with a conceptual tool enabling them to check and focus with greater swiftness and accuracy what it is they are (probably) thinking about when they (haphazardly) utter the word [satire]." *Palimpsests: Literature in the Second Degree*, trans. Channa Newman and Claude Doubinsky (Lincoln: University of Nebraska Press, 1997), 26.

[21] Since the foundation of this project thus lies in the semiotics of the satiric effect rather than in a hermeneutics of satires, the focus on satire as a textual phenomenon will thus not be at cross-purposes with the inclusion of context in the hermeneutic enterprise; they tackle different issues and answer different questions, and my focus derives from an interest in the former and addresses the latter secondarily.

nomenon and provides the basis for a new understanding of satire from which to trace its history to the moment it allegedly vanishes from the literary landscape. One dual benefit of this approach lies in determining whether there is or has ever been an adequate basis for speaking of satire as a coherent entity with clear discursive boundaries, and in suggesting the boundaries and limits of satiric discourse.

Second, with an established semiotics of satire, a diagnosis of the satiric effect is possible with the aid of its constitutive practices and without recourse to a limited cache of formal shapes as paratextual identifiers. For the period following the Second World War, when pastiche's star rises and satire's falls, this methodology shows the tacit links between the history of satire and the prevalence of intertextual practices that have become emblematic of postmodern writing, both literary and theoretical. Indeed, in an interesting corollary, the boundaries between literary and theoretical writing in the postwar, postmodern period become porous, especially when one considers the apparent congruence between this semiotic theory of satire and extant theories of intertextuality. It is this crucial relationship between satiric and intertextual practices that structures the narrative of satire's disappearance in the twentieth century – and its reappearance elsewhere. What's more, the ways in which this relationship between satire and intertextuality amalgamate processes of writing and reading allow for a formulation of an overarching theory of satire as a mode of reading. Satire, in other words, may be found at one intersection of the practices of writing and reading.

Understanding satire as a mode of writing *and* reading constituted by a set of semiotic practices, furthermore, sets satire apart from other terms to which it has historically been related, such as the ridiculous, wit, humor, the grotesque, parody, and irony. To offer a comprehensive categorization here and attempt to clarify these terminological matters once and for all certainly extends beyond the scope of this project; others have undertaken more thorough studies elsewhere that address these concepts and differentiate them from satire.[22] But with a conception of satire as a semiotic construct, the ridiculous, wit, humor, and the gro-

---

[22] For elaborations on the poetics of the ridiculous, wit, and humor, see Jean Paul, *Vorschule der Ästhetik*, ed. Norbert Miller, vol. 5, *Sämtliche Werke*, 1. Abteilung (München: Wissenschaftliche Buchgesellschaft, 2000), 102–124, 124–144, 169–207; Jean Paul, *Horn of Oberon: Jean Paul Richter's School for Aesthetics*, trans. Margaret R. Hale (Detroit: Wayne State University Press, 1973), 71–87, 88–103, 120–147. Maximilian Bergengruen's insight into Romantic humor is particularly helpful in distinguishing between satire and humor. See *Schöne Seele, groteske Körper: Jean Pauls ästhetische Dynamisierung der Anthropologie* (Hamburg: Felix Meiner, 2003), 212–228. For a history of the grotesque and its relation to satiric writing, compare Wolfgang Johannes Kayser, *Das Groteske: Seine Gestaltung in Malerei und Dichtung* (Oldenburg: G. Stalling, 1957). Linda

tesque can be understood as resultants of the combination of satire's strategies, not as part of its semiotic makeup: as effects of satire or as metaphors to describe the dominant strategy (see below). If parody is, as Jameson argues, merely pastiche with a "satiric impulse," then it too emerges from the interplay of satiric practices, here as a formal descriptor, not as an effect. Irony is another matter, however.

Unlike satire, irony has been embraced by literary studies as a central device in semiotic analyses of literature that aim to uncover multiple layers of meaning, especially in the twentieth century.[23] Through semantic stratification or oscillation, texts and utterances employing irony demonstrate the complexity of signification through ostensibly fixed signs, and in this way, irony is an important point of comparison for satire, for it provides a model for using satire in an analogous manner: as an organizing construct for an alternate history. It also helps us understand the slippages in meaning that occur with citational palimpsests and thereby more deeply intertwines satiric signification with intertextuality. In this regard, irony is distinct from satire; it refers to one of the ways by which satire signifies, but is not identical with satire or its constituent practices.

In the following pages, we first turn to a cross-section of works by Johann Paul Friedrich Richter (Jean Paul) to find three dominant textual practices – epistemological inversion, mythification, and citation – that make up the repertoire of the satiric. These textual procedures, though to a degree ahistorical in their own right and not exclusive to satire, show historical variance in their combination. The dominance of certain practices over others at a given point in time illustrate the historical development of the satiric as a phenomenon comprised of different textual practices. The degree to which these very practices become entangled in the discourse of intertextuality, as it is theorized from the mid-twentieth century, likewise shows the great extent to which strategies of satire are both inscribed into the text and point beyond it. Like irony, intertextuality provides a model for rethinking satire not as a form *per se*, but as a complex interplay between texts.[24] It is this reorientation of the satiric as an effect of textual relationships that will shape satiric practices in more contemporary times.

Hutcheon's studies of parody and irony, finally, are excellent resources for these notions and their relations to satire: *A Theory of Parody*; *Irony's Edge*.
23 Hutcheon, *Irony's Edge*, 55.
24 Satire is not coterminous with intertextuality as the latter is merely one aspect of the former. Other satiric practices affect the signifying potential of textual relationships, such as figures of inversion and mythification.

To illustrate this shift, I will examine each of the primary semiotic strategies of satire – epistemological inversion, mythification, and citation – within the framework of a series of case studies. A reader of Jean Paul himself, Mikhail Bakhtin, with his study of the carnivalesque in *Rabelais and His World* (1965), will serve as the first node in an analysis of the figure of inversion in theoretical and literary writing. Read from a literary perspective, the carnivalesque denotes a narrative strategy anchored in literary history that inverts a cognitive order of knowing and effectively turns the order of things on its head. Discursive rules are suspended, allowing different narrative voices, hitherto suppressed, to come to the fore. Bakhtin's own writing employs this epistemological procedure, while the novel, he argues, is the primary modality through which the carnivalesque subverts a prevalent mode of thought. This ostensibly literary procedure nevertheless reappears as a leading practice in contemporaneous theoretical thought, particularly in theories or theoretical approaches, such as Deconstruction, feminisms, and Marxist criticism, in which the subversion of dominant discourses plays a central role in the function of argumentation; the very figure of carnivalesque inversion they employ has a history within the discourse on satire, intertwining certain kinds of theoretical and literary writing together in a relationship with satiric practices that has gone unnoticed.

That the practice of epistemological inversion is an element of both theoretical and literary writing will become evident in a further examination of two novels by Thomas Bernhard, *Woodcutters* [*Holzfällen: Eine Erregung*] (1984) and *Extinction: A Novel* [*Auslöschung: Ein Zerfall*] (1986).[25] In Bernhard's works the carnivalesque appears as an element of style and as a formal characteristic of each novel's unconventional narrative structure. The oft-maligned hallmark of Bernhard's style, the monomaniacal first-person narrator, concentrates the narrative perspective at a vantage point of cultural and political critique that exposes Austrian and Viennese society, though at first glance normalized, as an unanchored ship of fools drifting about on a sea of the carnivalesque. Bernhard's writing echoes this foregrounding of the carnivalesque by upsetting conventions of narrative teleology, syntactical clarity, and literary variation, preferring instead to bask in a stagnation, even stultification, of narrative progression. Lan-

---

[25] Neither English translation of Bernhard's works maintains the curious subtitle of each, which defy typical publishing conventions in labeling the texts "novels." In the case of *Woodcutters*, the subtitle translates roughly as "an arousal," "an agitation," or "an uproar," in keeping with the narrator's increasing irritation. "Ein Zerfall" means "a collapse," "a decay," or "a disintegration," also more illustrative of the text's narrative arc and perhaps a tangential reference to another long text about a family's ruin: Thomas Mann's *Buddenbrooks*, subtitled "Verfall einer Familie" ["Decline of a Family"].

guage in Bernhard becomes a playground for labyrinthine grammatical and syntactical structures and repetition. Oddly, the conservative position of Bernhard's narration, whereby the narrating protagonist imputes a kind of unreason or madness to his context, is itself criticized as a novelistic exercise in madness.

Taking up the mantle of procedural and methodological criticism of literature and culture, Roland Barthes' *Mythologies* (1957) will inaugurate the second phase of this project. In turning away from epistemological inversion to mythification, we find that Barthes' diagnosis of a zero degree of literature is predicated upon the notion of the disappearance of style, of a collapse of the axes of style and language, which had grown separate in nineteenth-century writing in the development of literature as a phenomenon unto itself. Literature, Barthes argues in *Writing Degree Zero*, amounts to nothing more than one possible resultant of a historical development in the manipulation of written language. The return to the axial origin, to the zero degree, is thus both an endeavor of twentieth-century writing as well as the eradication of literature *per se*; to conflate or collapse style and language is to pull the proverbial rug out from under the institutionalization of literary *écriture*. This effacement of literature effectively amounts to an effacement of style or, put differently, to a mythifying relationship with language. But mythical relationships are never unproblematic. By attempting to show the unmediated emergence of writing from language, defined as "a corpus of prescriptions and habits common to all the writers of a period,"[26] Barthes points to an erasure of agency; style, he argues, is a functional relationship between the writer and his or her language: idiomatic, interruptive, and irruptive, and thus a product of agency. To eliminate this authorial dimension through mythification is to make do with a language not yet individuated, one that consists only of its generic ahistorical paradigms and clichés; "to imitate," writes Gérard Genette, who employs Barthes' notion of *écriture* in his own study of hypertextuality and imitation, "is to generalize."[27] This mode of writing, however, insofar as it engages in mythification, amounts to nothing more than pastiche: an imitation of genre. Whether the pastiche is successful in generalizing well – by which I mean imperceptibly, thereby concealing its own status as imitation, as pastiche – is a matter of interpretation or reading. In reanimating and deploying certain paradigmatic signifiers of writing, as Barthes himself shows in his *Mythologies*, this mimetic dynamic effectively mythologizes literary writing, elevating its constitutive elements to the level of a second-order sign.

---

26 Roland Barthes, *Writing Degree Zero*, trans. Annette Lavers and Colin Smith (New York: Hill and Wang, 1968), 9.
27 Genette, *Palimpsests*, 85.

Elfriede Jelinek's novels *The Piano Teacher* [*Die Klavierspielerin*] (1983) and *Lust* (1989) employ this same theoretical dynamic, but they do Barthes one better. Lying in the intermediate space between pastiche and critique, Jelinek's two novels are constructed from remnants of Viennese paradigms, thus mythologizing a discursive context subverted on the narrative level. They manage, in their asymptotic approach toward the zero degree, to retain a stylistic sleight-of-hand that undermines these paradigms and exposes them as hollow, contingent second-order signs. *The Piano Teacher* and *Lust* can thus be read as pastiches that nevertheless have a surreptitious satiric effect, mobilizing a satiric practice – mythification through imitation – whose conscientious application exposes the crumbling discursive decay beneath the gilt sheen of Old Vienna. That Jelinek's novels can be read as theoretical responses to Barthes – that Jelinek herself is engaged as a theorist of myths – is evident not only from the novels, but from her direct critical engagement in "Endless Innocence" ["Die endlose Unschuldigkeit"] (1970).[28]

In this essay, Jelinek expounds and builds upon Barthes' model of the myth as a semiological system, a critical stance she employs in the writing of her novels. Their status as pastiche thus amounts to a deployment of a second-order sign. Pastiche as a signifier for neutral generic imitation becomes a sign of its own with political significance, a mark of the conservatism of the very paradigms Jelinek imitates, the stifling conservatism of Vienna. This unexpectedly critical use of mythification as a satiric practice comes about when the mimetic act itself signifies something beyond the mere practice of imitation. In a way, Jelinek's use of mythification exposes pastiche as an ideological operation that is never empty of meaning and that never leaves the mimotext (to use Genette's term) untouched. Pastiche may in fact have superseded parody in the postmodern era, as Jameson has argued, but in the shift from a textual operation that privileges an individual work (parody) to one that exploits an entire genre (pastiche), one does not necessarily witness a concomitant eradication of critical inversion. On the contrary, this displacement of emphasis from a discrete work to a category of forms merely testifies to a historical epistemological shift: that of the intertextual turn.

With intertextuality in the proverbial crosshairs, we come to the third and final satiric practice, which arises precisely from this intertextual turn: citation. In her work on political feminism in *Gender Trouble* (1990), Judith Butler has become, perhaps unwittingly, the standard bearer for a theory of performance that relies on discursive citation for the production of meaning. Divorced from their historical contexts and reorganized in a (frequently) non-linguistic, gestural array

---

28 Elfriede Jelinek, "Die endlose Unschuldigkeit," in *Trivialmythen*, ed. Renate Matthaei (Frankfurt am Main: März-Verlag, 1970), 40–66.

of signs, signifiers in performance can be employed to subvert hegemonic, dominant discourses in an endeavor to form a subjective identity unconstrained by phallogocentric, binary models of, for example, gender. This procedure of citation is constitutive for Butler's theory of performance but also, interestingly, suffuses her own writing. While any theoretician or scholar presumably uses citational practices to link his or her work to or differentiate it from extant models or schools of thought, Butler's writing (and *Gender Trouble* in particular) stands out as a paradigmatic example that mobilizes multiple disciplines and histories to present its argument. Citing psychoanalytic and sociological models of identity formation, Deconstructionist perspectives on subversion, linguistic (structuralist) notions of meaning-making, and feminist perspectives on the place of women in society, *Gender Trouble* has epistemological underpinnings in the very notion of performance it propounds; the referential procedures it deploys resemble the performative citations used to undermine the binary models of gender introduced by a masculinist language. With citation Butler acknowledges the eternal ineluctability of hegemonic discourse – language itself – while offering a theory of performative signification that uses the very tools of this hegemony against itself. Butler's theory of performance works from within language to subvert language's clandestine aim to perpetuate its phallogocentric order.[29] This deconstructive (not necessarily Deconstructionist) effect of citation follows from the satiric effect, which both jars meaning through contextual disjunction and points to a genuine intertextual relationship between discrete works. This latter point reveals a curious corollary in the implicit assumption – not only in Butler's theory, but also in the use of citation as a semiotic practice – of an intertextual episteme. What once accounted for a deficient application of aesthetic practice in its fundamental claim of the interdependence of texts – and thereby the disavowal of a model of the independent, self-contained work – is now a foundational model for all writing. In this way, intertextuality is a symptom of satire. Owing to its reliance on citation as a semiotic practice, which in turn is also a component of *satiric* practice, Butler's theory of performance tacitly both reveals its roots in the history of satire and attests to the ubiquity of satiric practice in writing predicated on citational procedures (and, by extension, on an intertextual episteme).

In a similar vein, the contemporary German author Thomas Meinecke employs citational practices as the central formal element in his recent novels

---

[29] This may be why her theory has found arguably greater resonance among literary theorists and semioticians than among feminists working through the political establishment.

and writings.[30] *Tomboy* (1998) and *Music* [*Musik*] (2004) in particular are suffused with extensive quotation – be it direct or anonymous citation, attribution, or allusion, formal or otherwise – which forms the basis of his relation with Judith Butler and *Gender Trouble*. A key source of Meinecke's citational practices, Butler's theory of performance, specifically as it pertains to gender identity, figures prominently in the narrative of both novels. What is less evident but more significant for the history of satiric practices, however, is the degree to which Butler's theoretical framework and narrative style, if I may indeed call it that, serve as templates for Meinecke's own narrative structure and writing, furnishing both the story and its stylistic idiosyncrasies with ample material. In a grand act of intertextual borrowing, *Tomboy* incorporates Butler into its content and form by highlighting her theories as a motivating factor for a novelistic excursus on gender theory and gender identity, and by mimicking a distinct theoretical style punctuated by dense, jargon-laden prose, hypotactic sentences, and a penchant for rhetorical interrogatives. In citing *Gender Trouble* as a primary intertext, Meinecke's novels establish a close textual and stylistic relation with academic writing. That they deploy Butler's own narrative strategies further underscores the narrow threshold between literary and theoretical modes of writing. What *Tomboy* and *Music* ultimately demonstrate is the close generic relationship of these two kinds of writing through textual practices common to both, their indebtedness to theory, and the capacity of literature to function as theory. Beyond this we see in these two representative novels by Meinecke a narrative deployment of theory: an adaptation of Butler in a novelistic guise that seeks to stage the abstractions of performance theory in a concrete manner. Supplementing theory with a pragmatic focus on the exigencies of identity formation as explored through narrative, Meinecke's quasi-pastiche of Butler thus goes beyond its model, superseding it. His is the bridge between theory and (narrative) praxis. By the same token, the saturation of Meinecke's texts with citational procedures raises questions about the possibility of literary originality and authorship, revealing a close alignment of narrative and metanarrative; both exalt a notion of signification beholden to derivation through discursive citation rather than authorial creation *ex nihilo*.

---

30 Indeed, in recent years, Meinecke has turned ever more radically to citational procedures as the constitutive hallmark of his writing. To the amusement and bemusement of his listeners, for example, Meinecke delivered the 2012 Frankfurt Lectures on Poetics as a series of quotations about himself and his work from secondary sources: no original material. This performance of his poetics, in the spirit of Judith Butler, was arguably a more profound statement about Meinecke's aesthetic process than any traditional lecture might have been. The published version of his lectures bears the apt title *I As Text*. See *Ich als Text: Frankfurter Poetikvorlesungen* (Berlin: Suhrkamp, 2012).

Where then does satire figure into performative discourse? And to what extent can one consider these texts – theories and novels alike – satiric in general? For one, this project of examining satire from a semiotic perspective locates satire through a genealogy of its constitutive practices, thereby identifying hitherto unseen and uncommented relations between satire and practices commonly used in theoretical and literary writing. What this book thus aims to trace is how satiric practices like epistemological inversion, mythification, and citation have come to be deployed through mainstream literary and theoretical constructs, particularly intertextuality. Insofar as intertextuality is an episteme that assumes a general circulation or "copresence of texts," as Genette defines it, we see that satire, once declared defunct by Hegel and disregarded by aesthetic theories since its ostensible heyday in the eighteenth century, lives on in an epistemological sense via writing practices that have become commonplace. Unmarked and arguably unmarred by paratextual traces like a subtitle of "satire," these works by Bakhtin, Bernhard, Barthes, Jelinek, Butler, and Meinecke all share textual procedures rooted in the history of satire and nevertheless bear its mark. To read these works as satires themselves offers a new perspective on their relationship with other texts in literary history and with each other. A corollary of this comparison allows us to read theory and literature as modes of writing that can, through certain paradigmatic satiric practices, be brought into fruitful dialogue with one another as writing with similar modalities of signification. Indeed, in the course of these pages, we are necessarily compelled, by the semiotic perspective, to read satire as a mode of signification-through-writing that also implies a particular mode of reading. In attempting to define satire more specifically, we find, ironically, a more general and appropriate definition of satire as a habitus of writing and reading.

2. The Case of Jean Paul: Unreadable Writing, Unwritable Readings

When Jean Paul's *School for Aesthetics* [*Vorschule der Ästhetik*] first appeared in 1804, it contained in its preface a brief, almost offhand concessive statement identifying what in light of the celebration of originality by *Sturm und Drang* thinkers some decades earlier (and, more contemporaneously, in light of the abiding fascination with the figure of universal genius in Weimar Classicism) might be termed an epistemological shift. "I have nothing to say," Jean Paul writes of his theoretical project, "about the aesthetics presented here, except that it is at least more my own work than that of others – insofar as a man can say the word *mine* of any idea in an age of printed paper, when a desk stands so close to the bookcase."[1] Aesthetics, he asserts matter-of-factly, is a matter of personal practices, not one of categorical validity.

While Jean Paul's statement denies a Kantian notion of reasoned, universal aesthetic principles, it succeeds in bringing three pertinent issues to the fore. In lending his era such an appellation, first, Jean Paul elevates the status of texts, and certainly among them the periodicals he so assiduously read and excerpted,[2] to one of prime significance for the very character of the period; it is the age of a proximal, reciprocal relationship between reading and writing printed texts (the second issue at stake), "when a desk stands so close to the bookcase," which, thirdly and finally, has ramifications that call into question then-current notions of authorship and originality.[3] When can one claim ownership of a thought in an era of such textual circulation, "in an age of printed paper"? How might we conceive of authorship and originality in an age predicated on such intimate proximity between reading and writing? With a mode of literary production based largely on excerpting passages from his reading, Jean Paul all but announces a new epoch: the intertextual era.[4]

---

1 Jean Paul, *Horn of Oberon*, 11; Jean Paul, *Vorschule der Ästhetik*, 25.
2 Dorothea Böck, "Die Taschenbibliothek oder Jean Pauls Verfahren, das 'Bücher-All' zu destillieren," in *Masse und Medium: Verschiebungen in der Ordnung des Wissens und der Ort der Literatur 1800/2000*, ed. Ingeborg Münz-Koenen and Wolfgang Schäffner (Berlin: Akademie Verlag, 2002), 28; Michael Will, "Jean Pauls (Un-)Ordnung der Dinge," *Jahrbuch der Jean-Paul-Gesellschaft* 41 (2006): 79.
3 Magnus Wieland, "Parasitärer Paratext: Die 'Hand in margine' in 'Des Feldpredigers Schmelzle Reise nach Flätz,'" in *Am Rande bemerkt: Anmerkungspraktiken in literarischen Texten*, ed. Bernhard Metz, Sabine Zubarik, and Thorsten Bothe (Berlin: Kulturverlag Kadmos, 2008), 202.
4 That this was also an age in which satire itself was changing is made clear by Maximilian Bergengruen. *Schöne Seelen, groteske Körper: Jean Pauls ästhetische Dynamisierung der Anthropolo-

To date the advent of intertextual practices to Jean Paul's time would of course be fallacious. That Jean Paul was nevertheless one of the first German authors not only to incorporate his *Lesefrüchte* so directly into his writing, but also to comment so openly on this methodology as constitutive of his literary production is no far-fetched claim.⁵ Indeed, his excerpt books are legendary.⁶ A numerical summary is as impressive as it is overwhelming; over 44 years Jean Paul used 112 notebooks of varying size, filling over 10,000 manuscript pages with more than 71,000 excerpts, most not exceeding three lines in length.⁷ The sheer volume of material, combined with the broad array of topics he excerpted, lend the impression of a constructivist bent towards authorship; *bricolage avant la lettre*, a combinatorial tinkering with source material and learned discourse, supersedes universal aesthetic principles that guide the creation of original works *ex nihilo*. "Scarcely any other author of his age," one critic notes, "developed a sensibility comparable to Jean Paul's for the intertextual dependency in the production of literature and continually gave poetological account of this fact, and especially by way of the striking mise-en-scène in his texts."⁸

Even before this aesthetic pronouncement in the *School*, Jean Paul formulates his claim of proximity between reading and writing by explicating the methodological procedure of excerpting within a literary framework. To his friend Theodor Christian Ellrodt's *Almanac for Instructive Entertainment for the Young and Their Friends for the Year 1796* [*Taschenkalender zur belehrenden Unterhaltung für die Jugend und ihre Freunde auf das Jahr 1796*] Jean Paul submits a short text, "The Pocket Library" ["Die Taschenbibliothek"], that confounds the boundary between essay and *Erzählung*. The first-person narrative revolves around an encounter with an extraordinarily intelligent dance instructor, Aubin, whose learnedness amazes the narrator. The secret to Aubin's knowledge – and, ironically, the reason for his weak memory – is the pocket library, his compendium of excerpts from diverse sources. "Initially I caught two or three oddities from each book, like butterflies," he explains to the narrator, "and fastened them in my excerpt book with ink. I conscripted my recruits from all areas of study. To each

---

gie, 12–15.

5 For a review of the relevant sources in Jean Paul's work that reflect on this methodology, see Götz Müller, "Jean Pauls Privatenzyklopädie: Eine Untersuchung der Exzerpte und Register aus Jean Pauls unveröffentlichtem Nachlaß," *Internationales Archiv für Sozialgeschichte der deutschen Literatur* 11 (1986): 73–76.

6 For a cogent summary of the nature of Jean Paul's excerpt books and a discussion of his copious citations, see Müller, "Jean Pauls Privatenzyklopädie"; Böck, "Die Taschenbibliothek."

7 Will, "Jean Pauls (Un-)Ordnung der Dinge," 84.

8 Wieland, "Parasitäter Paratext," 193.

curiosity I allotted three lines of space, no more. [...] The principal issue is that I make excerpts from my excerpts and bottle up the spirits yet again."⁹ This continual concentration of knowledge from varied disciplines into ever smaller droplets of information bears a striking resemblance to Jean Paul's own practice of excerpting, both formally and practically. Notwithstanding the irony that this procedure presages the ruination of Aubin's memory (and Jean Paul's?), the narrator recommends to his readership this unquenchable thirst for knowledge and the distillation of it: "I had to press to my heart the man whose heart burns for all knowledge and confess to him that I have been on much the same path since my 14th year. And you, dear lads, act such that you, too, might be embraced for such a reason someday."¹⁰ What trumps the procedural similarity between narrative and biography is the aesthetic, semiotic issue of the specific practices deployed under this epistemological model. Writing and reading correlate to one another reciprocally: the former as a means of gleaning and condensing the knowledge available in the latter, the latter as the condition for the possibility of the former. The curious procedure of excerpting is propounded as an organizing epistemology in the face of a chaotic abundance of knowledge and information, a way of circumventing the time-consuming activity of hermeneutic reading.

And yet Jean Paul's methodology of excerpting and indexing these excerpts betrays a chaos of its own. Although it is possible to trace the flow of excerpted information into his published works, his process is by no means a systematic one.¹¹ The miscellany and disorder in Jean Paul's excerpt books and their indices would seem to undermine the suggestion in "The Pocket Library" to distill knowledge from manifold sources into a single location for easy reference; the apparent randomness of the excerpts, their sources, and their combination in a register, encyclopedic though it may be, lacks an ordering principle for reference. But as one critic puts it, "this chaos is calculated [*Kalkül*]."¹²

---

9 Jean Paul, "Die Taschenbibliothek," ed. Norbert Miller, vol. 3, *Sämtliche Werke*, 2. Abteilung (München: Wissenschaftliche Buchgesellschaft, 2000), 771–772. Some critics, notably Dorothea Böck, have read this passage as a programmatic statement of Jean Paul's own method. Despite the similarities to his excerpt books in the narrative, the passage is spoken by Aubin to the narrator and, ironically, follows a discussion, topical even today, of the deleterious effect on one's memory of multitasking: "his [Aubin's] memory had become a field sucked dry from his quick, successive reading of things that did not belong together. Naturally, this debilitation of a memory that today gives me nothing but examples of its strength is incomprehensible to me; yet the claim is true that someone who takes up a new science or a new errand every minute ruins his memory" (770).
10 Jean Paul, "Die Taschenbibliothek," 772.
11 See especially Will, "Jean Pauls (Un-)Ordnung der Dinge," 83–93.
12 Müller, "Jean Pauls Privatenzyklopädie," 78.

The preference for disorder essentially upsets a residual dominant paradigm of reasoned, systematic structure still prevailing from the Enlightenment, and it testifies to the "disintegration of an enlightened public sphere."[13] Even the model of the polymath, seemingly embodied by Jean Paul's broad intellectual interests, undergoes an inversion in its function. While the traditional genius still "bundles, orders, and classifies" knowledge, "such an ordering principle is foiled, if not consciously sabotaged, by the principle of randomness in Jean Paul."[14] From this notion of chaos ensues a productive "mutual pollination of realms of knowledge,"[15] a juxtaposition of discourses that results in new metaphors and new ways of signifying. Jean Paul dissolves extant rules and principles of ordered discourse by eliminating hierarchies and emancipating knowledge from classificatory boundaries: "He thereby consciously violates the ordering systems of scholarly disciplines, be they of a juridical, medical, or theological kind. The excerpts mix these domains of knowledge by aleatory, miscellaneous means, regardless of the criticism of their validity."[16]

What results is a poetology of seemingly chaotic knowledge, a poetics undergirded by semiotic practices selected to upset, invert, level, and reorder knowledge. The suspension of an enlightened episteme and its replacement by chaotic excerpts, for instance – the reciprocal cross-pollination of writing by reading and vice-versa – is a constitutive textual practice in Jean Paul's oeuvre.[17] That this figure of epistemological inversion resembles what Mikhail Bakhtin would later call the carnivalesque is no coincidence. Indeed, what might be termed the epistemic carnivalesque in Jean Paul's work is a primary practice developed most fully in his later prose (as we will see in his unfinished 1822 novel, *The Comet* [*Der Komet*]).

Jean Paul's poetics – if one can speak of a single, coherent method or even, to paraphrase the author himself, say the word *his* of any poetics in an age of printed paper – certainly developed from an engagement with late eighteenth-century

---

13 Burkhardt Lindner, *Jean Paul: Scheiternde Aufklärung und Autorrolle* (Darmstadt: Agora Verlag, 1976), 231.
14 Will, "Jean Pauls (Un-)Ordnung der Dinge," 89.
15 Müller, "Jean Pauls Privatenzyklopädie," 78.
16 Götz Müller, "Nachwort," in *Jean Pauls Exzerpte*, by Jean Paul, ed. Götz Müller (Würzburg: Königshausen & Neumann, 1988), 346.
17 Götz Müller's conclusions from his study of Jean Paul's excerpts still stand to scrutiny: "1. The semantic system of the register leads directly to the semantic system of the poetic work. The register preforms central motifs of Jean Paul's writing even after the age of satires. 2. The register articles know no hierarchical pyramid of concerns as the classics of polyhistorism would have sought. 3. The precondition for constructing new relations between things is the total disassembly of conventional and scientific discourse with rules that localize and exclude." "Nachwort," 346.

aesthetic and philosophical thought, particularly his familiarity with Herder, Fichte, and Kant. But this poetological method to his madness also has a history in satire. While Jean Paul's period of activity is frequently divided into two phases, that of the early satires and the later novels, it nonetheless witnesses in this constant technique of excerpting a transposition of "results stemming from problems that had concerned the 'satirist' Jean Paul in the 1780s"[18] to his later narrative works; the early satires thus form the "necessary intellectual precondition" for the "stylistic foundation of the novels."[19]

Yet in spite of the political, philosophical, and aesthetic connections between Jean Paul's early satires and his later prose works, the transfer of semiotic practices from one medium to the other has escaped attention, perhaps because of a historical fluke; Jean Paul's oeuvre spans a threshold, an "epochal shift within the history of satire"[20]; "the age of printed paper" witnesses not just a "discrediting of the concept of satire"[21] as a genre by the Romantics, but a development in notions of authorship and originality. The trend moves away from knowing the world through reasoned cognition, from categorical aesthetic principles, from quasi-creationist images of genius authors composing masterworks *ex nihilo*. The reciprocal relation between writing and reading gains currency, pointing to a circulation, if not circularity, of discourse and discipline; novel poetic practices emerge from tinkering readers of books who collect, collate, cite, and construct excerpted ideas, words, and forms into patchwork encyclopedic compendia. That this moment in literary history displaces satire from its own independent genre to a mode of writing is no coincidence, but the subsequent "deliterarization of the concept"[22] by which the Romantics and their successors cast satire from the pantheon of viable aesthetic modalities poses a new problem. If satire retreats from a category independent of other literary forms, where does it go? Precisely because Jean Paul, "without a doubt the greatest German satirist around 1800,"[23] strad-

---

18 Wolfgang Proß, *Jean Pauls geschichtliche Stellung* (Tübingen: M. Niemeyer, 1975), 2.
19 Proß, *Jean Pauls geschichtliche Stellung*, 7.
20 Jürgen Brummack, *Satirische Dichtung: Studien zu Friedrich Schlegel, Tieck, Jean Paul und Heine* (München: Fink, 1979), 5.
21 Brummack, *Satirische Dichtung*, 5.
22 Wolfgang Weiß, *Swift und die Satire des 18. Jahrhunderts: Epoche, Werke, Wirkung* (München: C. H. Beck, 1992), 17. "In this understanding of literature, the origins of which lie in Classicism and Romanticism," Weiß summarizes, "only such texts were received into the corpus of *belles lettres* that had not cleaved to the historical-empirical reality of their time of origin, but had instead detached themselves from it by creating their own fictional world, and to which, therefore, the creation of their own reality could be attributed and thus the claim to a significance that transcended their own age."
23 Brummack, *Satirische Dichtung*, 82.

dles this threshold between different conceptions of satire, he offers an ideal point of departure as a case study for understanding the semiotic transfer across the epistemological divide.

One constant in Jean Paul's oeuvre, the intertextual method of excerpting used in composing the early and the late works, which has been dubbed "the satiric procedure par excellence,"[24] provides the semiotic framework for investigating these satiric practices. How do procedures of excerpting create a satiric effect? Which strategies used in early satires does Jean Paul deploy in his novelistic texts? To what extent should we ultimately speak of satiric practices rather than satire? And finally how might we formulate a semiotics of the satiric?

To understand how satire survives as the satiric, I turn first to Jean Paul's late unfinished novel *The Comet*, a self-professed "novel of all novels," which helps illuminate which textual strategies are at stake in a phenomenon intractably defined by metaphors without a formal basis (aggression, attack, critique, negativity, humor, et al.). Close readings of exemplary passages will show how satire operates within the narrative and allow us to distill from these episodes a set of semiotic practices that constitute literary satire after 1800.

That Jean Paul himself is not an unproblematic figure within literary history and German studies, however, must first figure into the equation. Whether his linguistic "first-degree provocations"[25] have indeed rendered his works unreadable, as some suggest,[26] or untranslatable, detracting from his Anglophone readership and reception,[27] Jean Paul has most certainly not enjoyed the primacy of place in the canon accorded to his contemporaries Goethe, Schiller, and Kleist. Regardless of the increasing disinterest in his works shown by the German reader-

---

24 Weiß, *Swift und die Satire des 18. Jahrhunderts*, 29.
25 "Contemporary readers and critics lament the unreadability of his books, take umbrage at the excess of scholarly allusions, comparisons, and metaphors. Even today, the manifold knowledge unleashed in his works has its deterrent effect and overshadows their reception." Hans-Walter Schmidt-Hannisa, "Lesarten: Autorschaft und Leserschaft bei Jean Paul," *Jahrbuch der Jean-Paul-Gesellschaft* 37 (2002): 42.
26 Wolfgang Harich, "Satire und Polemik beim jungen Jean Paul," *Sinn und Form* 19, no. 6 (1967): 1488; Schmidt-Hannisa, "Lesarten: Autorschaft und Leserschaft bei Jean Paul," 42; Christian Sinn, *Jean Paul: Hinführung zu seiner Semiologie der Wissenschaft* (Stuttgart: M & P, Verlag für Wissenschaft und Forschung, 1995), 61–62.
27 Within the last twenty years, a scant three monographs have been published: Paul Fleming, *The Pleasures of Abandonment: Jean Paul and the Life of Humor* (Würzburg: Königshausen & Neumann, 2006); Erika Reiman, *Schumann's Piano Cycles and the Novels of Jean Paul* (Rochester, NY: University of Rochester Press, 2004); Catherine J. Minter, *The Mind-Body Problem in German Literature, 1770–1830: Wezel, Moritz, and Jean Paul* (Oxford: Clarendon Press, 2002).

ship "for generations"[28] – doubtless partially due to the linguistic challenge of reading his writings – Jean Paul is a historical outlier whose difficult relation to those traditional periodizations bookending his life, Classicism and Romanticism, was even noted by the likes of Heinrich Heine.[29] The scholarship on Jean Paul has also been hesitant to subject individual works, especially later texts, to the scrutiny of close reading,[30] focusing instead on implicit theories,[31] the use of humor and satire,[32] his understanding of subjectivity,[33] or his place in history.[34] Considering Jean Paul's oeuvre in its abundant modalities as part of a unified whole has helped contextualize his overlooked work within the broader spectrum of German literature and its periodizations, but reading the author's texts distantly, without regard for their particularities (or with the use of infelicitous terminology like "Jean Paul's entire output"[35] or "Jean Paul's satire"[36]) amounts to a reductionism that has hampered more nuanced understandings of his poetics.[37]

---

[28] Harich, "Satire und Polemik beim jungen Jean Paul," 1488; nevertheless, there has been a recent revival of interest, perhaps no better in evidence than in the new critical edition under preparation by scholars at the Universität Würzburg. "Jean-Paul-Portal: Neue Werkausgabe," accessed June 1, 2014, http://www.jean-paul-portal.uni-wuerzburg.de/neue_werkausgabe/.

[29] Wulf Köpke, *Erfolglosigkeit: Zum Frühwerk Jean Pauls* (München: W. Fink, 1977). See in particular the discussion of "the eternal question regarding Richter's attitude toward Classicism and Romanticism," 404.

[30] To be sure there are exceptions, among them, to name one example, Uwe Schweikert, *Jean Pauls "Komet": Selbstparodie der Kunst* (Stuttgart: Metzler, 1971).

[31] Monika Schmitz-Emans, *Schnupftuchsknoten oder Sternbild: Jean Pauls Ansätze zu einer Theorie der Sprache* (Bonn: Bouvier, 1986); Sinn, *Jean Paul*; Dirk Otto, *Der Witz-Begriff Jean Pauls: Überlegungen zur Zeichentheorie Richters* (München: Utz, 2000).

[32] Renate Grötzebach, "Humor und Satire bei Jean Paul: Exemplarische Untersuchungen mit besonderer Berücksichtigung des Spätwerks" (Berlin: Freie Universität Berlin, 1966); Harich, "Satire und Polemik beim jungen Jean Paul"; Köpke, *Erfolglosigkeit*; Brummack, *Satirische Dichtung*; Fleming, *The Pleasures of Abandonment*.

[33] Peter Sprengel, *Innerlichkeit: Jean Paul: oder, Das Leiden an der Gesellschaft* (München: C. Hanser, 1977); Herbert Kaiser, *Jean Paul lesen: Versuch über seine poetische Anthropologie des Ich* (Würzburg: Königshausen & Neumann, 1995); Minter, *The Mind-Body Problem in German Literature, 1770–1830*.

[34] Proß, *Jean Pauls geschichtliche Stellung*; Lindner, *Scheiternde Aufklärung*.

[35] Albert Béguin, *Traumwelt und Romantik: Versuch über die romantische Seele in Deutschland und in der Dichtung Frankreichs* (Bern: Francke, 1972), 206.

[36] Brummack, *Satirische Dichtung*, 90–97.

[37] Understanding the relationship between Jean Paul's aesthetic writings and his narrative works also has also been prickly business. During the revival of scholarly interest in Jean Paul in the 1960s and 1970s, scholars lamented the unreflective practice of "interpreting [...] the oeuvre on the basis of the theory" as a given, of reading, for example, his *School for Aesthetics* as a "key to the intention of [his] novels." To read his theoretical works on their own terms seems to have

2. The Case of Jean Paul: Unreadable Writing, Unwritable Readings — 23

The primary problem beleaguering Jean Paul's exemplary role in understanding the semiotics of the satiric, however, involves the seemingly irresolvable question of the relation between Jean Paul's early satiric writings and his later novelistic creations. The caesura between his early works in the 1780s and 1790s – explicitly labeled satires – and the later novels (with *The Invisible Lodge* [*Die unsichtbare Loge*] as a point of departure) arises naturally, it would seem, from chronology. While the author turned toward longer narrative only in the 1790s, the sharp generic division between the "age of satires"[38] and the novelistic period – during which Jean Paul incidentally also wrote aesthetic, philosophical, and political texts – has stifled a discussion about a relation or carryover in writing practices between the two.[39] Recent critical work has focused on Jean Paul's procedures of excerpting and their relation to his early and later work, but the link between such a methodology and a satiric manner of writing is still outstanding.[40] Partially responsible for this missing critical dialogue are the outmoded conceptions of satire employed in Jean Paul scholarship in general.

To be sure, most scholars engaging with both Jean Paul and satire draw few distinctions between satire and other categories delineated to a certain degree in Jean Paul's writings, such as humor, wit, and polemic – which may at best be

---

become accepted practice in the interim. Schweikert, *Jean Pauls "Komet": Selbstparodie der Kunst*, IX; Burkhardt Lindner, "Satire und Allegorie in Jean Pauls Werk: Zur Konstitution des Allegorischen," *Jahrbuch der Jean-Paul-Gesellschaft* 5 (1970): 55; in her study of fantasy and the system of excerpts, for instance, Annina Klappert argues exclusively with the *School for Aesthetics*, with the conclusion that its implicit poetics activates a poetics of visibility in Jean Paul's oeuvre. Annina Klappert, "Jean Paul intermedial: Phantasie und Exzerptsystem als Medien der Sichtbarmachung," *Zeitschrift für deutsche Philologie* 128, no. 2 (2009): 207–217; Monika Schmitz-Emans likewise takes care to note in her introduction the problematic applicability of Jean Paul's theoretical writings to his literary works. She proceeds, however, not by gleaning a theory of language from the literary works themselves, but by affirming theoretical claims with literary evidence, leading to a dubiously tenable theory. *Schnupftuchsknoten oder Sternbild*, 9–10.
38 Müller, "Jean Pauls Privatenzyklopädie," 92.
39 Götz Müller has convincingly argued that the procedure of excerpting, which began in Jean Paul's youth and was constitutive for his satiric writings, laid the groundwork for narrative strategies in his later prose. "Jean Pauls Privatenzyklopädie," 99; Andreas Kilcher's study of encyclopedic modes of writing in Jean Paul, makes important contributions toward understanding Jean Paul's *modus operandi* with excerpts. "Enzyklopädische Schreibweisen bei Jean Paul," in *Vom Weltbuch bis zum World Wide Web: Enzyklopädische Literaturen*, ed. Waltraud Wiethölter, Frauke Berndt, and Stephan Kammer (Heidelberg: Winter, 2005), 129–147; Michael Will's updated take on the procedure of excerpting is likewise relevant. See "Jean Pauls (Un-)Ordnung der Dinge."
40 In his seminal study, Max Kommerell does link Jean Paul's later works to the earlier satires, though he views the latter more in terms of a maturation away from satiric writing. See *Jean Paul* (Frankfurt am Main: Vittorio Klostermann, 1957), 366.

regarded as subjective epiphenomena of the satiric effect, but cannot be said to be formally constitutive satiric practices – and rely instead on ostensibly self-evident notions of satire and sociological or political attack or critique.[41] Later critics within Jean Paul scholarship who take up this conception of satire, not as a literary term, but as a means of extraliterary political commentary, link satire in Jean Paul to critical metaphors of humans as machines suffering from "deficient subjectivity."[42] Attempts to read satire as an aesthetic or semiotic category in its own right, a proposition revived only in twentieth-century satire criticism,[43] has seldom found favor in Jean Paul scholarship.[44] Instead, critics have relied on pithy but malleably vague definitions of satire that have perpetuated the confusion inherent in equating a mode of writing with an affect (aggression), affording themselves a subjective buffer to interpret satire intuitively.[45]

---

[41] Grötzebach, "Humor und Satire bei Jean Paul"; Harich, "Satire und Polemik beim jungen Jean Paul"; in his cogent résumé of satire studies in German and Anglophone criticism, Wolfgang Weiß notes that the "blurring of differences between wit, humor, and satire" dates to Schiller's reformulation of satire to exclude the notion of aggression. Weiß continues, however, in noting that this terminological confusion was eliminated by a British critic in 1928, thus testifying to the outmoded take on satire persisting in German-language criticism nearly forty years later. *Swift und die Satire des 18. Jahrhunderts*, 21–22.

[42] Peter Sprengel, "Maschinenmenschen: Ein zentrales Motiv in Jean Pauls Satire," *Jahrbuch der Jean-Paul-Gesellschaft* 10 (1977): 100; see also Wilhelm Schmidt-Biggemann, *Maschine und Teufel: Jean Pauls Jugendsatiren nach ihrer Modellgeschichte* (München: K. Alber, 1975).

[43] Helmut Arntzen, "Nachricht von der Satire," in *Gegen-Zeitung: Deutsche Satire des 20. Jahrhunderts*, ed. Helmut Arntzen (Heidelberg: W. Rothe, 1964), 6–17; Lazarowicz, *Verkehrte Welt: Vorstudien zu einer Geschichte der deutschen Satire*.

[44] One exception is Maximilian Bergengruen, whose monograph on Jean Paul interprets the late works synthetically as combinations of the grotesque in the early satires and of moral concerns for sensibility. What results is a satiric mode of writing that turns upon itself, that becomes self-reflexive. *Schöne Seelen, groteske Körper: Jean Pauls ästhetische Dynamisierung der Anthropologie*, 212–227. The self-reflexivity of Jean Paul's satiric mode likewise points to the fact that satire itself is a matter of language.

[45] "Satire is social criticism with comic means," or "What is constitutive is the attack." Lindner, "Satire und Allegorie in Jean Pauls Werk: Zur Konstitution des Allegorischen," 8, 11; only the occasional scholar of satire, Jürgen Brummack foremost among them, has ventured into Jean Paul scholarship. But even this cross-pollination by a critic whose long definition of satire is one of the only sustained theorizations in German fails to inject new life (that is, new theories of satire) into Richter studies; Brummack's readings of passages from Jean Paul's *Years as a Lout* [*Flegeljahre*] and *The Airship Captain Giannozzo's Rutter* [*Des Luftschiffers Giannozzo Seebuch*], while commendable for their focus on the texts, aim toward demonstrating a general unity of purpose to Jean Paul's satire while ignoring the countless early satiric writings in the argument. *Satirische Dichtung*; for Brummack's long definition, see "Zu Begriff und Theorie der Satire."

Because no extant connection between the satires and the novels rests on a solid theorization of satire, the semiotic link between the early satires and the later fictional prose must be established by Jean Paul himself. The following pages thus examine his final novel *The Comet, or Nikolaus Marggraf: A Comical Story* [*Der Komet, oder Nikolaus Marggraf: Eine komische Geschichte*], published in installments in 1820 and 1822 and left unfinished upon his death. As an early model in prose of the look of satire within this intertextual episteme, the text is a case study for the state of affairs in satire in the early nineteenth century. The aim here is to distill from close readings of selections that exhibit unusual ruptures or ambiguities in meaning – where the shadow of intertextuality and excerpting seems to loom largest – a set of satiric practices that constitute the peculiarities of satiric signification in a novelistic mode of writing.

The Comet – A Case Study

To read Jean Paul's last novel, however, one must first decide where to begin. Having never met a digression he did not like, the author complicates the physical form of the text with a preface, appendices, pre-chapters, a listing of his works published hitherto, and excursions for the female reader, leaving the reader, male or female, to determine what belongs to the novel proper and what serves an ancillary function. That the narrative itself is punctuated repeatedly by first-person metanarrative commentary merely underscores the overall effects of the various textual appurtenances on the story, namely the delay and interruption of narrative development, an implicit insistence upon digressive reading strategies, the formation of a strong omniscient narrative subject, and the writing of a narrative parallel to the story of Nikolaus Marggraf: the story of the novel's composition and construction.[46] Jean Paul's novel *The Comet* is thus a novel about writing novels: the creation of a narrative work from the reflections on such creation, or to put it differently, the birth of a novel from the spirit of theoretical reflection, "from so many papers, from pamphlets and certificates of redemption – from pastoral letters and the most gracious handwritten epistles – from comedy leaflets and diplomatic reports and concordats, though I'm not even counting the love

---

46 Ralf Simon has pointed out Jean Paul's curious reliance on the phatic code – the foregrounding of the scene of writing itself – as a key poetic mechanism. See "Das Universum des Schreibens in Kuhschnappel (Jean Paul, 'Siebenkäs' – Roman Jakobson)," in *"Mir ekelt vor diesem tintenklecksenden Säkulum": Schreibszenen im Zeitalter der Manuskripte*, ed. Martin Stingelin, Davide Giuriato, and Sandro Zanetti (München: Fink, 2004), 140–155.

letters and bills of fare and pharmacological scrips since they are mere padding [*Bauchfedern*]."⁴⁷ This conglomeration of material excerpted from such disparate discourses shall lift his novelistic patchwork "paper kite" (569) of excerpts as high "as a meteor falls" (572). In a sense, and as Jean Paul's own index of published works shows, *The Comet* stands as the crowning and final achievement of his literary engagement (the final three volumes merely collect diverse shorter journal publications).

Such authorial activity, from the first volume to the final planned fifty-seventh, takes place under the influence of a lifelong engagement with comic literature and satire, beginning with the *Greenlandic Trials* [*Grönländische Prozesse*]. Indeed, in his preface to the first volume of *The Comet*, Jean Paul describes the novel to follow in the second volume – at that point still unpublished – as "my last comical work" (569), expressing his intention "to dance myself out completely with the comic muse just once in my life" (569). These hopes to perpetrate "aesthetic and innocent impertinence after impertinence" (569) under the sign of Rabelais and Cervantes inspire the conception of a work that empties the cornucopia of satiric tricks in one grand novelistic digression (569), a debauchery [*Ausschweifung*] of the highest order – and, incidentally, wordplay on the sweeping tail of the comet, or *Schweifstern*, after which the work is named. Jean Paul explicitly rejects the spurious rumors that he will imitate Cervantes, "a new Don Quixote" (570), pointing to Christoph Martin Wieland's own failure in this regard with *Don Sylvio*. His novel, by way of contrast, has no single narrative model, created as it is from "papers of all kinds [...], papers of lords and papers of kartouwen, gilt-edged papers of grief and state paper and stamping paper" (569), but the influence of prior texts like Cervantes' picaresque romance cannot be denied "since [the author] always had the old Don Quixote in his hands" (570). The direct imitation of a single work in Wieland, running the risk of parody, gives way to an intertextual smorgasbord of excerpts.

To refer to this excerpted material, already in the preface Jean Paul employs footnoting, more often an academic practice, which nevertheless served as a major writing strategy for his earlier prose works as well.⁴⁸ With such external

---

47 Jean Paul, *Der Komet, oder Nikolaus Marggraf: Eine komische Geschichte*, ed. Norbert Miller, vol. 6, *Sämtliche Werke*, 1. Abteilung (Darmstadt: Wissenschaftliche Buchgesellschaft, 2000), 571. Quotations from the novel will be cited by parenthetical page numbers in the text.
48 For a recent, coherent analysis of this practice in Jean Paul's *Schmelzle*, see Magnus Wieland, "Parasitärer Paratext: Die 'Hand in margine' in 'Des Feldpredigers Schmelzle Reise nach Flätz,'" in *Am Rande bemerkt: Anmerkungspraktiken in literarischen Texten*, ed. Bernhard Metz, Sabine Zubarik, and Thorsten Bothe (Berlin: Kulturverlag Kadmos, 2008), 191–208; Christian Helmreich examines the digressive character of Jean Paul's prose more generally, including the use of foot-

references the text engages in autoreferential play, alluding to its interdependence on other texts for the production of meaning, and in a digressive gesture simultaneously pointing the reader beyond its own work-immanent boundaries.[49] A "practice of the secondary,"[50] this explanatory tactic comprises at once both a paratextual and narrative formal element of *The Comet* that multiplies significatory potential through citation and concomitantly establishes a textual palimpsest; footnotes, one scholar writes, trigger "semantic white noise, insofar as they distract from the text and its coherence, but also simultaneously besiege the text with supplements that unleash a semiosis that ultimately produces an unfiltered surplus of meaning."[51] It is the supplementary character of the footnotes coupled with this pseudo-academic rhetorical practice of exophora, a kind of extratextual deixis by footnotes, that constitutes a not insubstantial part of the semiotic program. To be sure, the ambiguity activated by such a semiotic practice also resonates with the semantic interference arising from Jean Paul's use of names as indistinct signifiers – for instance, in the names Nikolaus, Marggraf (similar to *Markgraf*, margrave), Rom (Rome), Hof (Court), Römischer Hof (Roman Court), Pabst (Pope), Nikolopolis, not to mention the various appellations of the painters in Lukas-Stadt. Such polysemy also engenders an intertextual nexus of irresolvable references to historical periods and personages, excerpted works, obscure terminologies, and tangential mini-narratives. Such intertextual white noise continues unabated from the preface, through the pre-chapter [*Vorkapitel*], and into the novel proper. As such it is a strategy that calls attention to the novel as an intertextual construct, to the heterogeneity of its form, and to the inability, at least with this practice as a criterion, to exclude the digressive paratextual appendages from consideration as part of the novel proper. The ubiquitous digression to which the reader is privy (perhaps most noticeable in the footnoting), the text implies, is either tantamount to the narrative or supplants it entirely. Jean Paul thus makes good not only on his prolegomenous promise to write a single, overarching *Ausschweifung*; through this practice he also composes a sustained novelistic digression, *Abschweifung*, which he elevates to an aesthetic and formal principle.

---

notes, by looking at *Siebenkäs* and *Titan* as well as the aphoristic works. "'Einschiebeessen in meinen biographischen petits soupers': Jean Pauls Exkurse und ihre handschriftlichen Vorformen," in *Schrift- und Schreibspiele: Jean Pauls Arbeit am Text*, ed. Geneviève Espagne and Christian Helmreich (Würzburg: Königshausen & Neumann, 2002), 99–122.
49 Helmreich, "'Einschiebeessen in meinen biographischen petits soupers': Jean Pauls Exkurse und ihre handschriftlichen Vorformen," 111.
50 Wieland, "Parasitäter Paratext," 208.
51 Wieland, "Parasitäter Paratext," 198.

If the preface demonstrates the potential multiplication of meaning through digressive practices like footnoting, citation, and extraliterary referentiality, the narrative exhibits further challenges to unambiguous signification through its representation of representation itself, through a literary portrayal of mimetic practices: the portraiture scenes with the painters of Belgian and Italianate schools from Lukas-Stadt. Convinced of his royal parentage – partly through his now-deceased father's insistence, partly through a misreading of his own name by metaphor and pronunciation – Nikolaus Marggraf has abandoned his apothecary in Rom, with the wealth provided by his artificial diamonds, to search for his blue-blooded father and, following his princely upbringing, to assume the rights and privileges accorded him by his alleged royal birth.

With his entourage of traveling friends as advisors bivouacked in his portable encampments of Nikolopolis, the would-be prince apothecary has entered Lukas-Stadt in a second-degree disguise as Graf von Hacencoppen on a side-mission to trail his erstwhile beloved, the princess Amanda, whom he has seen once and whose stolen wax bust he dutifully, if worshipfully, carries in his caravan. In this royal residence the arrival of the incognito Nikolaus is greeted with a flurry of excitement, particularly as his easily exploited penchant for charity manifests itself in a city of artists in need of patrons. With the promise of handsome remuneration, two rival schools of painters, sixteen of the Belgian-Dutch realist tradition and sixteen Italianate utopian portrait artists, vie for his favor, but the apothecary's democratic magnanimity rules the day. To guarantee equal treatment, Marggraf qua Hacencoppen sits for each school on successive days. His acquiescence is not, however, without selfish motivation.

On the one hand, self-representation is a ritual of royalty, in painting and coinage alike, and so he merely plays his part. On the other hand, Nikolaus notes, his aim is more personal: "And since the artists naturally hang their matutinal artworks in the large exhibition together: it is thus highly likely that the foreign princess, who is in the palace, will remember having seen me in Rom beside one of her exalted friends and will notify a lady friend or me of this or that" (936). His thirty-two (!) portraits shall thus grace the halls of a gallery and, if his plan succeeds, lure the appreciating eye of his father and his immortal beloved, Amanda, thereby triggering her memory of their fleeting encounter more than a decade before. Depicted in both styles, he hopes to increase his chances at recognition.

The baroque scheme nevertheless runs afoul of the apothecary-prince-count's uneducated young assistant, Stoß, whose reasoned bewilderment takes issue with the necessity of such elaborate measures: "*Ciel*! [...] they'd be damned lively and know right away whom they had before them if Your Highness came and showed up yourself" (936). Why trouble oneself with representations if the real thing is available? Why employ signifiers in place of the referent? Stoß' objection points to competing epistemologies and modes of signification. The prince apothecary, "who, as was mentioned, saw everything only when it was reflected and heard everything only when it was echoed" (936), relies on a conventional mode of knowing the world through representations of it, an insistence upon mediated knowledge and experience. That Amanda has already seen him is irrelevant within this frame of reference; the aestheticization of his self-representation – his self-styling in other words – intensifies the meaning of his very appearance, adding a supplementary rhetorical flourish; Nikolaus aspires to be a simulacrum of himself.

The absurdity of his position reveals itself not in its contrast with his assistant's rational exhortations to trust in direct experience, however, but in his own admission of an extraneous farce: "my incognito here is only feigned as it is, and everyone knows quite well who I am" (937). The mediation of representation and the creation of such aestheticized simulacra amount to procedures of identity formation: a consciously alienating performance of royalty. By distancing himself through successive degrees of disguise from his birth identity as Nikolaus Marggraf – the narrator refers to him by novel's end almost exclusively as Hacencoppen, which is already a pauper's disguise of his more noble identity – Jean Paul's protagonist demonstrates the inconsistencies of establishing an identity by ever more accurate approximations of truth. Through his actions Nikolaus exposes the alienating effects of the very attribution of a proper name as a marker of identity. While seemingly individualizing, the act of naming and thereby the assumption of an identity involves ever increasing degrees of distance from the referent through added layers of signifiers.

With a conception of satire as critique, one might read this passage as a satire of the nobility, a hobbyhorse of Jean Paul's early satiric and political writings.[52] What manifests this satiric effect on the semiotic level, however, is the inversion of a conventional epistemology of signification. In this passage of *The Comet*, Jean Paul illustrates the orphaning of the referent through the valuation of the signifier. Simulacra – "my portrait," "my likeness" – gain currency as second-order signs themselves, and quite literally; Nikolaus links the significatory power of the image to the symbolic value of currency. As a metonymic seal of state authority and monetary authenticity, the embossed visage of the ruler legitimates coinage and its circulation as a means of exchange: "Were I to have sixty thousand likenesses of myself made, some in silver, or even in gold at that, and were I to pass the portraits around: verily, no one would be able to get enough of them"

---

[52] See in particular Sprengel, "Maschinenmenschen: Ein zentrales Motiv in Jean Pauls Satire"; Schmidt-Biggemann, *Maschine und Teufel*.

(935). But Nikolaus confounds the metonymic symbolic power of his likeness with the metaphoric semiological value of precious metals. His botched conclusion in this chicken-or-egg game – which invests which with meaning and thus value, the likeness or the gold? – underestimates the semantic potential of the medium of representation and reveals the underlying epistemological inversion mentioned above. Nikolaus insists upon the replacement of the real with signifiers in an endless chain of representation; his solution to the problem of the referent is merely to eliminate it from consideration. Indeed, the protagonist's fetishization of portraiture, on canvas or coinage, elevates the abstraction of symbolic signification to an ordering episteme of superficiality and appearances, of semblance. For Nikolaus the act of representation supersedes the object or medium of representation. Therein inheres the epistemological inversion.

Involved in a complex nexus of the representation of currency and wealth, silver and gold circulate as part of a second-order semiological system, as a quotidian myth, to speak with Roland Barthes. The likeness of a monarch as a metonym for the state may likewise be understood as a complex sign. But Nikolaus' persistent valuation of the signifier causes a rift between the signifier and the signified, much less the referent, which he ignores outright. What remains is a semiotic system of floating signifiers divorced from the reality they are to represent; Jean Paul depicts representation for its own sake without the Kantian thing-in-itself. The critical thrust of this depiction lies in the untenable implicit claim that meaning and value proliferate with a multiplication of the signifiers that ostensibly carry them. Thus, Nikolaus orders thirty-one portraits (an engraver, the thirty-second portraitist, tags along with the Italian school) and speaks in his numismatic musings of the tens of thousands of coins he could mint with his profile struck on the obverse. Resting before sitting for the painters, he even has "one of the most glorious dreams," musing in a grotesque reversal "that he saw himself with 16 bodies and 32 arms all interwoven in an agreeable group, sitting for a painter" (937). In its inversion of the numbers of painters and subjects, the reverie of the monstrosity of body echoes the grotesque inversion of an episteme of representation and signification, making Nikolaus' multi-limbed frame the site of unnatural representation. From the abundance of portraits in the gallery and the princely act of self-representation through portraiture (and by extension artistic patronage), Nikolaus hopes to effect an identity shift from a rags-to-riches apothecary merely acting the part of nobility – to nobility itself. A catalyst for such a metamorphosis, the recognition from Amanda's noble gaze will finish what the fetishization of representation through mere performance had begun.

On the following day Nikolaus sits for the Belgian school, "as the Dutch school there called itself" (923), a group of painters whose stylistic hallmark is the precise rendering of their subjects in realistic, minute detail. The innkeeper

Pabst – whose pontifical name, like much wordplay in *The Comet,* never quite resolves its resonation between proper name and metaphor – leads into the hall a bevy of Dutchmen who themselves suffer from a problem of identity and illustrate the inverted order of representation with their names. "The greatest Dutch masters in all of Lukas-Stadt, a Denner, a Potter, an Ochs [ox], an Esel [ass], a Laus [louse] et cetera, marched up the stairs with their work boxes, the innkeeper Pabst at the head, as their Leo X. – as their *monte di pietà* and general creditor – as their *Oberhofmarschall* who would introduce them to the count" (937–938). As the narrator explains, the appellations of this shabby bunch are not their birth names. Instead, in a reversal of genealogical order, they are christened "as fathers by their children" (923): by their painting styles, their subjects, or their best work.

Again, Jean Paul confronts the reader with a disruption in the usual path of metonymic representation. As Nikolaus' visage legitimates the precious metals on which it is embossed, so too does the painters' work lend them their names rather than vice-versa. Thus, like Denner's relation to the eighteenth-century Balthasar Denner (923), Potter bears his name not due to any relation to seventeenth-century painter Paulus Potter, but from his imitation of the Baroque Potter's painting of a urinating cow: "the Lukas-Stadt Potter placed beside the evangelist Luke a pissing ox of such perfection that one not only forgot the evangelist on account of his animal (the reverse of which often happens in the legends of the saints), but also conferred onto the painter the name of the creature" (941). The amusement of Jean Paul's use of the indefinite for the definite article aside – "*ein* Ochs, *ein* Esel, *ein* Laus [my emphasis, DB]" – the other members of the artistic entourage likewise derive their names from their most recognized subjects or masterworks: "Other Belgian masters, e. g. a Hase [rabbit], a Sau [sow], a Laus [louse], named themselves after their pieces and went around in normal life on the conventional heels of the prize animals on which they, like Muhammed on the donkey, or in Rome like the souls of the caesars from the funeral pyre on an eagle released aloft, would be carried to the heavens. Other masters the innkeeper had brought to paint portraits, e. g. the so-called Säufer [drunkard], the Bettler [beggar], the Fresser [glutton], let their masterworks of these names christen them, as fathers by their children [...]" (923). The derivative nature of this naming procedure underscores the significance accorded to the act of representation itself. The act alone confers meaning by constituting identity, even recursively altering the very identities of the painters whose masterfully executed beggar or louse, for instance, rebaptizes them accordingly; children christen their fathers in this inverted episteme.

The epistemological distortion becomes increasingly evident in the session that follows. To save time and display impartiality, Nikolaus sits simultaneously for all sixteen painters, each of whom would otherwise require an hour. Naturally the spatial logistics involved for the portraitists are not inconsiderable – "making space and sharing light caused much distress" (938) – and necessitate the hanging of a mirror so that those to his rear may see his face. With the modest media at the artists' disposal and the sixteen portraits taken from sixteen different perspectives, Nikolaus proudly hopes to surpass the threefold immortality Emperor Karl V had claimed to receive through Titian's three portraits of him: "[Nikolaus] might perhaps count on even more manifold immortality" (938). The grandiosity of the rhetoric that elevates him beyond emperors into godlike immortality allows him to witness in this scene of self-representation an act of divine creation: "for the six days of his face's creation were compressed into a single morning" (939). Through metaphor the narrator continues the monstrous imagery of Nikolaus' oneiric vision the previous night of himself as "sixteen-headed" with "sixteen brows" and eventually "sixteen noses" (939). In his exhortations to the painters to remain unwaveringly accurate in their renderings of his pock-marked countenance, Nikolaus reveals an ingrained confusion between representation and reality. "He stated how much their school in particular satisfies the connoisseur who has his or someone else's portrait painted because from them he does not in fact receive a mock image of himself, but a true one, nothing brushed in, nothing brushed out, nothing glossed over, just precisely that which he himself is" (939). In such realistic portrayals of identity that aim to be "merely true to art, merely obedient to nature" (940), one may discover the real, as the prince apothecary makes no distinction between sign and referent.

One's self, Marggraf argues, may thus be derived from one's likeness. The link made earlier between identity, likeness, and portrait is recapitulated here, both with the metaphor of numismatic portraiture – now considered deficient because of the "beautifying artificiality [*Schönkünstelei*]" involved (939) – and a supplementary extratextual allusion; Jean Paul relates Nikolaus' appreciation for the representation of imperfections to a similar regard for them by three authors: Jonathan Swift, René Descartes, and Jean-Jacques Rousseau. The sign-referent problem, one may thus surmise, is a literary-philosophical problem and, in its epistemological inversion, a satiric one. The juxtaposition of the most prominent Anglo-Irish satirist with a French Enlightenment scientist-philosopher of the self and a Swiss philosopher-novelist is surely no coincidence; after all, the satiric practice of epistemological inversion distorts an Enlightenment episteme of self-identity and signification with literary means. As if to underscore the relationship among satire, philosophy of the self, and literariness, Jean Paul continues the comparison with a peculiar image. While sitting for his portraits, Nikolaus requests that Balthasar Denner, an artist known for including in his own self-portrait a microscope "through which one was able to glimpse the finest and most invisible features quite visibly and enlarged" (940), paint a magnifying glass over his portrait so that one might see the equivalence of art with nature: "under the microscope everything ought to have the same effect it does in nature [...]" (940). To verify the reality of the representation, Denner must inscribe a scientific instrument into his portrait, carrying the game of perceptual duplicity further. Hacencoppen's confusion of empirical reality with representational reality – with simulacra – thereby affects even the capacity of science to differentiate fact from fiction. In Nikolaus' episteme there exists no concept for *trompe-l'œil* although it is an ordering principle for all depictions and imitations. Indeed, in light of their meager talents and generous remuneration, the Belgians promise to revise and improve the verisimilitude of their initial work to the extent "that one should recognize him [Hacencoppen] at the exhibition from thousands upon thousands of paces away" (943). In this inversion the proliferation of simulacra does not dilute the meaning of the original but, through the very act of representation, multiplies it in a signifying gesture that ennobles the object of representation; Nikolaus now gains *Doppelgänger* and credence for his purported nobility.

If the Belgian school hewed toward verisimilitude of representation in order to create a perfect simulacrum of the original, then the beautifying tendencies of the Italians, "the Latin [*welsche*] School" (953), would contrast with that careful copying. A closer look at the second round of portraiture nevertheless shows a similar epistemological dynamic at play despite methodological differences in the manners of representation. For one, the naming conventions of the Italian painters accords with those of the Belgians, maintaining the inversion of order encountered earlier: the christening of the father by the child, to employ Jean Paul's metaphor. Named after the most renowned proponents of their styles, the Italian painters – "a Titian, Fra Bartolomeo di S. Marco, a Da Vinci, a Kauffman (probably Kauffman Angelika)" (954) – are themselves simulacra, mere stylistic repetitions of their predecessors. Unlike their Belgian compatriots, however, the (Renaissance) Italians more properly deploy classical techniques of painting derived from antiquity: mimesis rather than imitation. "Art as such always ennobles;" Nikolaus declaims in his somewhat revisionist opening remarks, "it is not a mere silhouette board for the face or an English copying machine for figures, but rather a birthing Madonna – it ought to be more than a mere plane mirror for the face that one hangs everywhere, it ought to be a sublime mirror that enhances [...]" (954). Parroting his audience's own artistic principles, Hacencoppen emphasizes this time the exalting gesture of portraiture. Yet the rhetorical flourish of his pronouncement cannot disguise a similarity in his conceptions of painting.

If the Belgians were concerned with surface renderings, the Italians ought instead to capture "the sacred eternal interior" and thus "paint the true, genuine silvery gaze through the portrait" (954). This mode of representation, he argues, is no mere mechanical reproduction but a divine act of creation in its own right, a virgin birth. Here, too, the signifier bears exceptional import in its substitutability with the referent. The glorification of inner life "without offending similarity" (954) makes the subject "to a Bird of Paradise," exalting the ideal through the "painterly pruning of lips, ears, and flesh" (955). As the Greeks did with the busts of antiquity, so too do the Italians artists attribute to the resulting artwork "a suitable name of a singular being [*Einzelwesen*]," specifically the name of its subject (955). Through this representation of Nikolaus' ideal face as interpreted through his inner spirit, the Italian portraitists ironically assert his uniqueness as an *Einzelwesen* despite the mimetic multiplication of his image. The finest of these paintings comes from the brush of the engraver and painter of saints whose work proceeds "through double distance from the original image [*Urbild*]" (955), i. e. with a mirror, underscoring the representational character of Nikolaus' features. The distance provided by the mirror seems somehow more real than the primal image: his own face. Given the invisibility and ambiguity of the inner life to be painted, Nikolaus himself becomes a floating cipher, a signifier with variable but repeatable meaning. Indeed, "the Nikolaus almost invisible in the mirror" (955) notices his own shifting significance when viewing the engraver's work, so much so that "Hacencoppen hardly looked like himself anymore and came to find he more resembled the picture he had painted in his childhood of his name saint" (956). Through the Italian master's hand at painting icons, Nikolaus begins to look more like his holy patron than himself. The power of representation thus alters the significatory capacity of the object of representation.

Which, then, is the referent and which the sign? Jean Paul's *Comet* suspends this distinction by toppling a framework of signification that gives primacy to signs that draw meaning from bracketed referents. By eliminating the notion of a real referent and thus essentially freeing signs from any anchoring in a fixed referential system, Jean Paul inverts the epistemological hierarchy that gives preference to the signified. This inversion occurs within a narrative of an infinitely contingent system of meaning-making. While signifiers circulate in their pure difference, the responsibility for ordering this sign system and avoiding pure chaos falls to the act of representation itself. Likened to painting portraits, the minting of currency, or alternately a divine birth, the creation of new signs within Jean Paul's novel thus lends legitimacy to new signifiers, even if they are nothing more than simulacra of extant signifiers. This confusion of simulacrum with signifier is of interest because it sets in motion a peculiar use of signs – the naming conventions are perhaps the most visible symptom of it – and undermines a dynamic of identity and subjectivity.

One minor consonant shift away from nobility, Nikolaus Marggraf surely demonstrates the traversable gap between bourgeois and blue blood by playing the part of the latter: adopting the habitus of a prince and shifting discourses, settings, and appearances. But by donning a new identity with such ease, Nikolaus also points to the performativity of identity and the perilous footing of subjectivity. As in a hall of mirrors, mere images of himself multiply, redefine, and shift his identity, demonstrating the slippage between subject and object in a semiotic system where there is little difference between the two. The powerful subject who controls his identity by altering appearances thus elides with the subject of a portrait: the mutable object of representation, the Protean cipher of the onlooker. Indeed, that Nikolaus himself shows a clear preference for the idealistic approximations of the Italian school over the imitative exactitude of the Belgian school indicates a preference for mimesis over imitation, for art over nature, and ultimately for interpretability over fixed meaning. Although Nikolaus does not hide his pleasure at Denner's and Ochs' renderings of him, the disappointment in the results that ended his first sitting yields to delight in the second. He bids the Italians farewell "with the most heartfelt joy," begging them for "speedy completion and duplication of their sacred works" (957). The exhortation to the Italian painters to duplicate their works, omitted from the first session, shows a clear preference for their more utopian renderings of his likeness. In attributing sanctity to their works, moreover, Nikolaus references not only the Italians' hagiographic expertise, but also his significatory drift toward his saintly namesake and the divine act itself of creation through representation. For Hacencoppen mimesis is a godly operation that elevates his social standing, legitimates his birthright, and destabilizes his identity.

This interpretability of Nikolaus himself points to a further ramification of the signifying episteme in this passage of *The Comet*. Through the exponential proliferation of his image by doubling the "house of counts or princes of sixteen Nikolausian visages" (955), Hacencoppen seeks to establish his countenance not merely as a sign and placeholder of himself, but as a sign of the power of this mimetic gesture, a symbol of his ascension through the social ranks. During the portraiture sessions the use of mirrors and the parity of perspectives reveal an implicit equivalence between Nikolaus' "primal image" – his own face – and his reflection. What is painted has less import than the manner in which it is painted. Nikolaus' concern with the end result of each sitting thus stems less from narcissistic pride than from an interest in the quality of the artists; princely patronage, especially at his level of generosity, can well afford to represent itself in the best light. The mundane twelve pock marks, long one of his distinguishing features, become grotesquely exaggerated at the hands of the shabby Belgian artists, whereas the Italians wash away impurities of appearance so well "that you could swear afterward you had someone else's head before you" (955). Even if "everyone had depicted [*getroffen*] something different about him," Hacencoppen finds himself pleased with the difference: "He did not conceal from himself that he looked like the sixteen faces at once" (957). Ultimately he prefers doubling through mimetic evocation rather than mechanical mimicry; idealistic resemblance thus trumps unforgiving precision as the approximations of the apothecary's face transform him into a shifting signifier, a man without qualities.

By instrumentalizing his approximate likeness through artistic representation, Nikolaus, flush with anticipation, hopes to exercise the memory of his beloved Amanda (with the help of her friends). "How of course the latter picture [by the painter of saints] would take hold of the foreign princess and bestrew her with hundreds of memories from the Rom days of springtime just now past when it stood in the gallery and Amanda's friend stood with joy before it [...] – Nikolaus could hardly wait to experience all this the day he sat for the Italian masters" (957–958). The platoon of faces in the gallery, he plans, will serve as a proxy for his own with the added heft of princely signification. While each portrait is a substitute for Nikolaus, his sea of likenesses also has a secondary semiological function; the portraits self-reflexively signify his wealth and standing. In investing portraiture with this second-order meaning, Jean Paul mythologizes, to speak with Roland Barthes, the act and product of aesthetic representation. The novel thus presents the reader with a myth of nobility through its own artistic portrayals of itself. On the one hand, this mimetic procedure perpetuates the paradigms of self-representation, portraiture, and aesthetic depiction in circulation around 1800. On the other hand, however, the complex nature of signification in such self-representation – its semantic stratification – exposes the way these paradigms overburden aesthetic signifiers with meaning as markers of identity and as substitutes for it. Here, too, the ambiguity of meanings resonates between extremes: between self-styling as both a sign of royal birth and a sign of a cheap mimetic trick, between the establishment of the subject and his eradication, between the creation of signs and their subsequent confusion with the real. This irreducible surplus of meaning points to a second major satiric practice Jean Paul deploys in *The Comet*: mythologization through mimesis.

If sitting for the painters reveals an implicit model of signification in Jean Paul's novel predicated on epistemological distortion and a transformation of signs into second-order semiological systems, three other key passages of *The Comet* show a congruity with and expansion of these semiotic practices. The scene in which Marggraf transforms himself into Count Hacencoppen – his second identity shift since his days as a struggling apothecary in Rom – concentrates the ubiquitous breach of naming conventions into a short span of text. The oscillation of Rom with Rome, *romisch* [of Rom] with *römisch* [Roman], Marggraf with *Markgraf* [margrave], Nikolaus with the eponymous saint, and Pabst with *Papst* [pope], to name but a few of Jean Paul's clever uses of aural palimpsests, shows a play with signifiers that stretches through the novel from beginning to end. Indeed, as Nikolaus lacks proof of his royal birth except through his father's dying words and his faith in them, the polysemous name alone must suffice in amassing a powerful surplus of meaning to offset its contingency. In one of his countless metanarrative reflections, the narrator ponders Nikolaus' impending entrance to Lukas-Stadt: "Could the prince enter as a prince; especially since he could not or would not give the princely name of his lord father?" (889). The impossibility of this occasions a council of his traveling court wherein Peter Worble advises the prince apothecary of "the boundless advantages [...] that traveling princes have derived since time immemorial from traveling incognito" (890). Like portraiture previously, traveling under a disguise signifies to Nikolaus – at least with Worble's evidence of emperors who downgrade their own status – his innate nobility. What is most striking about this passage, however, is the replacement of Nikolaus' lacking documentation and pedigree with the trappings of an assumed noble identity: with more meaningless signifiers, in other words. But by implementing these counterfeit markers of identity, the novel legitimates them; their real presence, despite their dubious provenance, imbues them with meaning. Of primary significance for Nikolaus is the choice of name, only secondarily the "trifle" (891) of its documentation by a token signet. Worble's suggestion to revive the name of an extinct dynasty leads him to a peculiar speaking name and back to Jean Paul's excerpts.

Worble suggests "Hasencop" (892), an orthographic variant of a name derived from a genealogical volume printed the year before the novel's action. Jean Paul does not fail to footnote the work (with further bibliographic detail provided by Worble himself), entitled *Listings of Noble Heraldry* [*Nachrichten von adelichen Wapen*] by Christian Friedrich August von Mering (1786), whose entry on "Hasenkopff" Jean Paul copies verbatim from the first volume. The precision of the citation triggers a series of identity crises. Like Jean Paul himself rather than the eponymous narrator, Peter Worble practices excerpting. Concerned with the possession of his rare signet, he "thus copied for [himself] from Mr. von Mering's Listings of Noble Heraldry the notes on the von Hasenkopff family (336th section, in the 1st volume), a little page that I have here" (892). The overdetermined source – the narrator even provides the correct page number and full title in a footnote – lists no fewer than seven spellings of the name. Nikolaus may thus travel "as a mere count von Hazenkoppen or Hacenkop or Hasecop or Hasencopp or Hasenkopff" (893), though he ultimately adopts the older, more distinguished title Hacencoppen. When an argument erupts over the proper heraldry – accompanied incidentally by a proliferation of footnotes to Mering's text – the theology student inadvertently insults the notion of a rabbit [*Hase*] on Hacencoppen's seal, prompting a rejoinder from Worble. "[O]ur meteorological prophet and seminarian Richter," he notes, had placed a similar pseudonym "beneath the preface of his glorious 'Selections from the Devil's Papers': J. P. F. Hasus" (896). Names, however, are never what they may seem in *The Comet*.

The clever, self-congratulatory intertextual reference might lead the reader, if he had not already done so after an earlier admission (834), to equate the theology student with the narrator and author himself, but the novel resists this easy identity as well, the narrator's admissions notwithstanding. "It is this name Hasus," the narrator explains in a footnote, "which is not to be denied all taste, that the same author gave himself back then in his essays for Archenholz' Studies of Literature and Peoples and in the German museum; – about which one may read further under his name in the 'Encyclopedia'" (896). Despite the overlap, the implication remains that the narrator and Richter are two separate figures.[53] The narrator's consistent reference to Richter in the third person, ironic or not, creates an unresolved tension between the two names: the Jean Paul Richter as theology student and the Jean Paul Fr. Richter of the two signed prefaces (573, 710). This ironic self-referential stance multiplies the meaning of a single sign and overloads it with competing referents, in a manner analogous to that of the naming conventions of the Lukas-Stadt painters. When seminarian Richter attempts to justify his choice in pseudonyms with reference to an old Latin text, his boredom with the book and perplexed wondering "why I even list it here" (896) prompts the narrator to respond in a footnote in a moment of dubious self-commentary: "I have the very same issue" (896). Through this constant recursion of self-reference, Jean Paul creates a *mise-en-abîme* that unsettles the reader's perception of a single sign repeated again and again. Governed by the same sign, the narrator and his textual *Doppelgänger* are nevertheless incommensurate with each other. What the theological candidate notes in reference to the deliberations on a choice of city names for Nikolaus – "as one can of course give two and more names just as easily to a city as to a child to be christened, which Byzantium and Constantinople and Stamboul not so much attest as attests" (867) – here experiences its converse; the naming conventions of Jean Paul's novel, by contrast, dictate that one name refer to multiple people, places, and things. To identify anything using seemingly simple signs, to rely on the proper name, inevitably leads to confusion.

Precisely this difficulty, however, leads to a narrative interruption in Jean Paul's text, a brief excursus on identification that employs a pastiche of Jonathan

---

53 Jean Paul's sketches for the novel likewise always refer to the *Kandidat* in the third person, despite the author's bestowal of his own name upon the character. See Jean Paul, "Studienhefte zu dem Roman 'der Komet,'" in *Jean Pauls Sämtliche Werke: Historisch-kritische Ausgabe*, ed. Eduard Berend (Weimar: Verlag Hermann Böhlaus Nachfolger, 1996), 412–507.

Swift's *A Modest Proposal*. "*Brief Faint Praise of Today's Higher Science of Passports*," in a nutshell, questions whether "the police could – after the first confession, for instance – brand general passports onto the backs of all those of legal age, as a second baptismal certificate, with place of birth, parents, etc. in such a way that it would be more seen than felt" (902). "Such quick tattooing of passports" (902), he argues, would save scribe fees while battling counterfeiting and crime. "My passport would, as much as I, too, have imitated and stolen from Swift and Sterne, distinguish even my closest imitators and thieves from me" (901). Drawing Jonathan Swift and Laurence Sterne into the heady debate on identifying procedures in *The Comet* amounts to more than a mere passing reference; by employing Swift's own structure of argumentation from *A Modest Proposal* (1729) in his own, Jean Paul explicitly weaves Swift into the intertextual fabric of the novel and juxtaposes his own writing with the more historically prominent tradition of eighteenth-century Anglophone satire. Just as Swift's solution to overpopulation, famine, and other social issues in Ireland is the (infant) body itself, so too does the body in Jean Paul serve as a panacea for the beleaguering of identity. The branding of identifying information onto the body constitutes an attempt at reforging the broken bond between sign and referent. This brief digression, set off both formally and rhetorically from the narrative, brings into focus the problem of signification in Jean Paul's novel. The connection between sign and referent having been rent asunder, the signifier increasingly drifts away from its alienated signified. Jean Paul's social criticism couches itself in satiric textual practices that operate, as it were, as a semiotics of satire.

Perhaps the most notorious passage in *The Comet* – Nikolaus' encounter with Kain – may give us a final look at the intricate workings of Jean Paul's last novel. The specter of this Adamitic figure in the concluding chapters of the third volume [*Bändchen*] haunts the novel's narrative cohesion as well as the handful of studies of Jean Paul's final work. Just as shocking as Kain's beastly appearance, his emergence in the text serves as a moment of irruption in Nikolaus' pursuit of his father and is, furthermore, emblematic in the scholarship of the direct influence of Jean Paul's excerpting on his novelistic writings.[54] What larger narratological role Kain might have played within the fabric of Jean Paul's finished text will always remain uncertain, but his gradual introduction by the narrator certainly takes the plot by surprise. Nikolaus' first fleeting encounter with him occurs during his fogged-in procession into Lukas-Stadt. "A fleshless, sallow man, stretched tall and dressed all in leather, with hair like horns and a long black beard" (911) emerges from the thick fog, announcing himself to a servant who confuses him

---

54 Müller, "Jean Pauls Privatenzyklopädie," 80–81.

with the Wandering Jew. "I am Kain," he rejoins, "do you not see the snake?" (911). Unlike Nikolaus, this curious figure clothed in ape leather bears the mark of his identity inscribed on his body: a red serpent, ready to strike, drawn on his forehead; he is sign and referent in one.

In this sense Kain represents that to which Nikolaus aspires – a subject whose fixed identity needs no external determiners – but his horrific appearance and heretical allegiance to the "Prince of the World" (911) over earthly authority conflict with Nikolaus' more explicit aspiration to assume his own princely power and status. Kain's invasions of Nikolaus' unquiet dreams after their initial meeting soon become a physical invasion of Nikolopolis with torch in hand. Having adopted Nikolaus as his foil, the otherworldly Leatherman [*Ledermensch*] sends him a charred, rotting coffin plank with the inscription "for I am Lord and none other" (965) as if to challenge Nikolaus' pretensions to his own ostensible throne. Taken from a nearby cemetery, the plank serves as "a letter" (965), a sign, like its sender, whose referent is inscribed in its physical substance. Hacencoppen's presence – and Kain sees through his disguise, incidentally – somehow directly threatens his opponent as he becomes the preferred target of Kain's continual molestations. Indeed, just as Kain penetrates Nikolaus' masquerade as Hacencoppen, so too does his unrelenting, seething enmity for the prince apothecary resemble his hatred for "all Habels oder Abels whom I wished to slay altogether, just as he, according to his belief, as Kain had killed the first Habel" (967). That Marggraf bore the name "Happel" in Jean Paul's sketches points to a deeper, extratextual relation between the characters.[55] Given the absence of this information in the text, the remarkable opposition between Marggraf and Kain develops more as a result of their use of signs and their relation to their respective princes rather than from any residual fratricidal animosity. His relentless aggression counterbalances Nikolaus' subtlety much as an outmoded notion of satire does a novelistic one. While Kain's jeremiad to Hofprediger Süptitz betrays an eloquence "that the psychologist finds more frequently among men driven and inflamed by a fixed idea" (971), it amounts to a monomaniacal hysteria lacking in the polysemous wordplay and name games in Nikolaus' episteme. Süptitz's response to Kain's charges effectively disassembles the latter's existence into a series of excerpts – a dictionary entry of Pierre Bayle, biblical speculation by Jacques Sau-

---

55 Sabine Eickenrodt, "Horizontale Himmelfahrt oder poetische 'ars volandi': Die optische Metaphorik der Unsterblichkeit in Jean Pauls 'Komet,'" *Jahrbuch der Jean-Paul-Gesellschaft* 35/36 (2001): 275; cf. also Jean Paul, "Studienhefte zu dem Roman 'der Komet.'"

rin, commentary by Johann David Michaelis – a mere cipher ultimately derived from the early excerpt books of the young satirist Johann Paul Friedrich Richter.[56]

Jean Paul's late work thus illustrates a dynamic by which this new novelistic notion of satire does battle with the old one, stepping away from it, as the protagonists do Kain, "with revulsion" (1004). "The end simply must always be satire or instruction," Jean Paul writes.[57] In keeping with this self-admonition in these last notes on *The Comet*, the author embeds the exposed satire of his youthful work into a complex novelistic structure by transferring its semiotic practices into a new form. In this new conception, Jean Paul exposes these practices, embodied at times by his protagonists – Nikolaus, Worble, Richter, Süptitz, and even Stößer – as the channels of encyclopedic intertextual discourse and the agents of satire after satire.

In these five varied but representative passages from his 1822 novel *The Comet or Nikolaus Marggraf*, Jean Paul deploys three primary semiotic strategies that adapt satire to a mode of novelistic writing. From the preface to the first volume, the portrait scenes, the Hacencoppen disguise, the "Science of Passports" digression, and Nikolaus' encounters with Kain, we may glean a consistent inversion of epistemology, a mythologization of signs through mimetic procedures, and a proliferation of citational practices.

For brevity's sake the first of these may be dubbed epistemological dissonance. Its figure of inversion resonates sharply with previous (sociological) conceptions of satire as an "inverted world" or as "the inverted."[58] As the following pages show, this practice remains a dominant semiotic device in German-language satire after the Second World War. Indeed, as satire lost its contours in the centuries since Jean Paul and made a transition from genre to textual operation, this epistemic procedure becomes a constitutive part of twentieth-century intellectual history and fictional prose. With case studies of Mikhail Bakhtin and Thomas Bernhard, both avid readers of Jean Paul's novels,[59] Part One traces this filiation of epistemological dissonance in postwar writings. Bakhtin's *Rabelais*

---

56 Müller, "Jean Pauls Privatenzyklopädie," 80–81.
57 Jean Paul, "Studienhefte zu dem Roman 'der Komet,'" 506.
58 Cf. Lazarowicz, *Verkehrte Welt: Vorstudien zu einer Geschichte der deutschen Satire*; Arntzen, *Satire in der deutschen Literatur*, IX.
59 *Siebenkäs* is among the narrator's five quintessential works in *Auslöschung*, and in his study of the *Bildungsroman* (and elsewhere, too), Bakhtin numbers Jean Paul's novels, especially *Titan*, among the "major examples" of the novel of education. See "The 'Bildungsroman' and Its Significance in the History of Realism (Toward a Historical Typology of the Novel)," in *Speech Genres and Other Late Essays*, ed. Caryl Emerson and Caryl Michael Holquist, trans. Vern W. McGee (Austin: University of Texas Press, 1986), 20, 22.

and His World (1965) and Thomas Bernhard's novels *Woodcutters* (1984) and *Extinction* (1986) serve as exemplars for the literary function of this satiric procedure within modalities of writing theoretical and novelistic.

The procedure by which Jean Paul creates second-order signs through a mimetic recycling of paradigms likewise settles into differing modes of writing in more recent history. This practice, mythification, to adopt Roland Barthes' nomenclature from *Mythologies* (1957), infects a different strain of novelistic writing in Elfriede Jelinek. With Barthes' text, her 1983 masterwork *The Piano Teacher* and her subsequent 1989 novel *Lust* act as case studies for this particular satiric practice; in Barthes' case, the procedure operates self-reflexively and illustrates the affinity of such theoretical formulations with satiric textual practices.

The final satiric device, essentially derived from modes of writing akin to Jean Paul's encyclopedic excerpting, citation may be the most visible of the three. Be it through quotation, reference, allusion, footnote, parenthesis, borrowing, or pastiche (among others), citational practices invoke the intertextual episteme from whence they sprang by overtly linking the text that deploys them to a circulation of textual discourse. The notion of the closed work against which Jean Paul so playfully and formally reacted no longer obtains among so much postwar literature and theory insistent upon establishing rhizomatic connections to other works, disciplines, and discourses. For the final part of this study, Thomas Meinecke's novels *Tomboy* (1998) and *Music* (2004) are put into dialogue with Judith Butler's *Gender Trouble* (1990) for their respective use of citation. In exposing the debt owed by contemporary literary and theoretical modes of writing to satiric practices, these case studies also uncover an affinity between satire and intertextuality more generally.

Part One | **Inversion**

3. The Carnivalesque in Mikhail Bakhtin's *Rabelais and His World* (1965)

It is no secret that the belated publication in 1965 of Mikhail Bakhtin's *Rabelais and His World* came on the heels of decades of storied academic conflicts, manuscript revisions, a heated dissertation defense, political maneuvering and intervention, and a prior exile in Kazakhstan.[1] Active in Soviet academic life since the 1920s, Bakhtin was 70 years old when his Rabelais book, initially intended as a doctoral thesis and containing "some of his most exciting and controversial writing,"[2] finally appeared in print. When in 1967 a young Bulgarian scholar in Paris extolled Bakhtin's theories of dialogism and the carnivalesque as the basis for a notion of intertextuality,[3] the Russian academic's reputation in the West was cemented, buttressed by his critic's own rising star among the various constellations of French structuralist (and nascent poststructuralist) thought.[4] In fact, Julia Kristeva's study of Bakhtin and the carnivalesque constitutes one of her first forays into criticism. Her development of the notion of intertextuality and the special significatory possibilities of dialogic poetic writing, with the help of set theory and mathematics, are remarkable in their own right, but so too is Kristeva's perspicacious determination of the liminal position occupied by Bakhtin's writing.

Neither entirely theoretical, nor purely literary, Bakhtin's writing, she attests, is comprised of a patchwork of textualities that each approach the issue of structural readings of literature: "Bakhtin shuns the linguist's technical rigour, wielding an impulsive and at times even prophetic pen, while he takes on the fundamental problems presently confronting a structural analysis of narrative."[5] On one hand, Kristeva diagnoses in her subject a lack of rigorousness that has always

---

[1] Sylvia Sasse, *Michail Bachtin zur Einführung* (Hamburg: Junius, 2010), 157–160; Katerina Clark and Michael Holquist, *Mikhail Bakhtin* (Cambridge: Harvard University Press, 1984), 139–145.
[2] Simon Dentith, *Bakhtinian Thought: An Introductory Reader* (London: Routledge, 1995), 65.
[3] Julia Kristeva, "Bakhtine, le mot, le dialogue et le roman," *Critique* 17, no. 239 (1967): 438–465; Julia Kristeva, *Semeiotike: Recherches pour une sémanalyse* (Paris: Éditions du Seuil, 1969). In the following I will cite the analogous chapter from her first book, a slightly adapted form of the 1967 essay, as the former was generally more widely accessible to both French and English audiences than the article in *Critique*.
[4] "[...] [I]t is possible to see the intellectual history of Paris as following, at a forty-year interval, the intellectual history of Mikhail Bakhtin, and indeed being partly prompted by it." Dentith, *Bakhtinian Thought*, 89.
[5] Julia Kristeva, "Word, Dialogue and Novel," in *The Kristeva Reader*, ed. Toril Moi (New York: Columbia University Press, 1986), 35.

plagued the "efficacy of scientific approach in 'human' sciences."[6] Others, too, have conceded rather matter-of-factly that Bakhtin "is a wide-ranging, imaginative and suggestive writer, but he is not a systematic one."[7]

On the other hand, Kristeva inveighs against imputing scientific and systematic qualities to the humanities because the latter obey a logic of poetic language that involves a different set of practices and claims than purely scientific scholarship. In this regard, Bakhtin serves as Kristeva's case study for an attempt "to elaborate a model that would be isomorphic to this other logic, that is, isomorphic to the elaboration of poetic meaning, a concern of primary importance to contemporary semiotics."[8] Bakhtin's lack of linguistic rigor, then, may be understood in light of his participation in this semiotic project of investigating the specificities of poetic signification.

Yet precisely this straddling of linguistic and semiotic discourses, of hermeneutic and socio-cultural approaches, has come to be understood as his greatest (ostensible) deficit – especially in *Rabelais and His World*, which in "an ironic decrowning of authoritative discourse [...] has come into greater and greater disrepute in recent years among *seizièmistes* as well as partisans of the great Russian theorist himself."[9] The reasons for such skepticism of the claims in Bakhtin's "most popular, most heavily criticized, and most cited book"[10] range from the concerns of specialists who debate "the values of theoretical versus historicist methods for interpreting Rabelais' mammoth and unwieldy texts"[11] to the charge that his engagement with Rabelais is merely a cover for an "apocryphal examination of Stalinist culture."[12] Indeed, as his biographers have intimated, Bakhtin lays claim to hermeneutic exceptionalism by virtue of his intertextual commensurability with Rabelais, that is, in their shared conflict between repressive official culture and the inversions and legal abrogation of carnival culture.[13]

---

6 Kristeva, "Word, Dialogue and Novel," 35.
7 Dentith, *Bakhtinian Thought*, 88.
8 Kristeva, "Word, Dialogue and Novel," 35.
9 Paul Allen Miller, "The Otherness of History in Rabelais' Carnival and Juvenal's Satire, Or Why Bakhtin Got It Right the First Time," in *Carnivalizing Difference: Bakhtin and the Other*, ed. Peter I. Barta (London: Routledge, 2001), 141.
10 Sasse, *Michail Bachtin zur Einführung*, 157.
11 Miller, "The Otherness of History," 141.
12 Sasse, *Michail Bachtin zur Einführung*, 157–158.
13 Bakhtin and Rabelais are "born out of a similar uniqueness. Each springs from an age of revolution, and each enacts a particularly open sense of the text. Bakhtin can hear Rabelais' laughter because he knows how to read Rabelais' book, and he demonstrates this capability in the act of writing his own book." Clark and Holquist, *Mikhail Bakhtin*, 297.

Such a relationship between the two texts, Kristeva submits, gives rise to the notion of a semantic double-speak, a stratification of signification that she calls intertextuality and that Gérard Genette will refer to under the sign of the palimpsest. "Yes," she explains, "what appears as a lack of rigour is in fact an insight first introduced into literary theory by Bakhtin: any text is constructed as a mosaic of quotations; any text is the absorption and transformation of another. The notion of intertextuality replaces that of *intersubjectivity*, and poetic language is read as at least *double*."[14] The ironic doubling of meaning in Bakhtin's work – his own self-reflexive use of the carnivalesque and dialogism – has three key ramifications for the history of satiric practices.

First, the primary semiotic operation of Bakhtin's concept of the carnivalesque is one of inversion, a constitutive practice of satire and the means by which the social and cultural notion of the carnivalesque, derived as it is from the Saturnalian suspensions of official order in medieval carnivals, becomes literary. Indeed, one of the primary challenges in reading Bakhtin arises from the tricky negotiation of the dialogism he both discusses and employs – from mapping a systematic terminology onto the social, political, cultural, and semiotic schema Bakhtin describes with the word carnivalesque, and distinguishing between the ways in which the carnivalesque refers exclusively to extraliterary cultural phenomena and the ways in which the carnivalesque may refer meaningfully to literary practices and strategies.[15] With its history in Menippean satire, the carnivalesque ultimately enters literary praxis through satiric novelistic writing.[16] And

---

14 Kristeva, "Word, Dialogue and Novel," 37.
15 But how to conceive of literature or the literary? One might approach this terminological hornet's nest in one of two ways. With Bakhtin, the literary is merely the first term in the distinction between written, narrative discourse and non-written discourse – a gap *Rabelais and His World* attempts to bridge by transferring the carnivalesque from social discourse to writing. In these pages I also occasionally juxtapose the term with its (false) opposite – theory – a distinction by which I refer to a traditional division between narrative and metanarrative discourse. Throughout the course of this study, however, the latter distinction dissolves as narrative elements in theory and metanarrative elements in literature make this opposition obsolete.
16 By Menippean satire I understand a historical genre of Classical satire in prose. This term may be contrasted with the Roman verse satires of Juvenal and Horace, which have been more exhaustively studied, partially due to the fact that nearly all Menippean satires of antiquity have been lost. For the elements of Menippean satire, distilled from Bakhtin's own discussion, see Renate Lachmann, "Bakhtin and Carnival: Culture as Counter-Culture," trans. Raoul Eshelman and Marc Davis, *Cultural Critique*, no. 11 (1988): 141.

Bakhtin's example for this writing in times more recent than Rabelais? – Jean Paul and his novels.[17]

Second, Bakhtin's text has a dual function as a treatise describing the entry of carnival culture into novelistic writing, and as a literary text in its own right. By this I do not mean to imply that *Rabelais and His World* should be interpreted as a novel. Instead, his study of carnival and grotesque realism might be read productively as a work that undermines the systematic nature of its argument precisely by employing the practice it describes as inherently novelistic. This performative act of doubling on a metalevel what it illustrates on the textual plane effectively allows Bakhtin's work, like its subject, to transgress the prohibitions of theoretical writing by suspending the hierarchies of systematic language. From this perspective one may see in Bakhtin's use of the satiric practice of the carnivalesque the dialogism[18] he had described in other works,[19] which Kristeva had linked explicitly with the carnivalesque.[20] The intertextual layering that occurs with the dialogical discourse of the carnivalesque between literature and theory spawns an epistemological dissonance, a simultaneity of multiple modes of perception that, by dint of the figure of inversion, conflict with one another.

Through this inherent epistemological tension, third and finally, the carnivalesque reveals its lineage in the history of satire. Bakhtin himself links the carnivalesque with early Menippean satire, and it is from this genre tradition that the

---

[17] Bakhtin connects Jean Paul directly (and repeatedly) with Laurence Sterne and traditions of irony and laughter (an epiphenomenon of hyperbolic irony) as well as with carnivalesque and the traditions of satire. Mikhail Bakhtin, "From Notes Made in 1970–71," in *Speech Genres and Other Late Essays*, ed. Caryl Emerson and Caryl Michael Holquist, trans. Vern W. McGee (Austin: University of Texas Press, 1986), 135, 141.

[18] Simply put, with dialogism Bakhtin refers to the dynamic communicative relationship of influence and signification between intertexts. In the case at hand, dialogism would denote the significatory connection between *Rabelais and His World* and Rabelais' *Gargantua and Pantagruel*; in adopting the practice of carnivalization that Rabelais uses, Bakhtin links their works. Rabelais thus inflects the meaning of Bakhtin's study while Bakhtin's work refracts the meaning of the centuries-old novel. With the concept of the dialogic, Bakhtin circumvents the postulate of anteriority and fixed meaning since signification always takes place anew in light of the dialogic relationship.

[19] In particular Mikhail Bakhtin, *The Dialogic Imagination: Four Essays*, ed. Michael Holquist, trans. Caryl Emerson and Michael Holquist (Austin: University of Texas Press, 1981); for a critical engagement with this work, which lies outside the scope of this study, see Tzvetan Todorov, *Mikhail Bakhtin: The Dialogical Principle*, trans. Wlad Godzich (Minneapolis: University of Minnesota Press, 1984).

[20] Kristeva, "Word, Dialogue and Novel," 43.

carnivalesque as a novelistic *practice* – no longer as a genre – might trace its history. As a semiotic practice available to both theoretical and literary writing, carnivalization spans and links theory and literature. Conversely, by elucidating this historical connection, we can see how a foundational text of postwar literary theory, particularly with regard to the structuralist and poststructuralist filiation we see with Julia Kristeva's reception of the carnivalesque, helped give rise to a tradition of theoretical writing with its roots in the history of satire. Indeed, even as carnivalization may be seen as "a purely literary phenomenon," the continual "reinterpretation and renewal of the carnivalesque mode of writing and its motives" likewise suggest a continual development of its modalities to the present day.[21] From the social practices of the medieval carnival to the novelistic devices of François Rabelais, we bear witness to the entry of carnivalization into the sphere of writing and representation and, in its reception in the twentieth century, from literary writing into theoretical writing. That the carnivalesque and satire have both historically been relegated to the lower rungs of an aesthetic hierarchy of genres[22] suggests that satiric strategies, carnivalization among them, have only hesitantly or surreptitiously been incorporated into literature; they do not, it would seem, belong exclusively to literature. Rather, they perpetually defy genre-specific categorization, moving from one modality of written culture to another and expanding, one may surmise, beyond writing into other manners of sensual and perceptual representation, be they visual, aural, or kinetic.

In serving as a model for his own theory of carnivalization, Bakhtin provides a template for novelistic writing to make use the satiric practice. Although he was by no means actively engaged with structuralist and poststructuralist discourses, the Austrian author Thomas Bernhard, for example, takes up this practice of carnivalization in his own novelistic writings. His novels *Woodcutters* (1984) and *Extinction* (1986) serve as parallel examples of the 'contamination' of writing by the dissociative elements of satire, which, in both Bakhtin and Bernhard, undermines the law of their respective genres. In suspending the order of scientific-theoretical and novelistic writing, the carnivalesque acts as a central medium of satire, particularly via the figure of inversion. A closer discussion of Bernhard's novels follows an examination of the figure of the carnivalesque and the figure of inversion in Bakhtin.

---

21 Sasse, *Michail Bachtin zur Einführung*, 174.
22 Sasse, *Michail Bachtin zur Einführung*, 162.

Bakhtin and the German Tradition

As an attempt both to rehabilitate François Rabelais as a writer of note and to grapple with the Protean notion of carnival, "this half-forgotten idiom,"[23] Mikhail Bakhtin's *Rabelais and His World* (1965, English translation 1968) takes a peculiar tack. In tracing the history of carnival forms through and since Rabelais, the author relies heavily upon not the French, but the German early modern and Enlightenment traditions. For him Hans Sachs, Johann Fischart, Hans Jakob Christoffel von Grimmelshausen, and Ulrich von Hutten are the indispensible progenitors of the practice of rendering the carnival literary (11, 14); the latter represent in medieval humor with Erasmus the "final and complete expression at the highest level of the Renaissance" (14), while J. M. R. Lenz, Friedrich Maximilian Klinger, Ludwig Tieck, Theodor Gottlieb Hippel, E. T. A. Hoffmann, Friedrich Schlegel – and notably Jean Paul – developed the (Romantic) use of the grotesque in literary writings, effectively transforming and perverting carnivalesque forms with Romantic individualism (37).

The very theoretical foundation of Bakhtin's study, moreover, is predicated upon the renewed attention given to the carnivalesque by way of the *Hanswurst* figure (which Bakhtin calls Harlequin). The revival of this debate in German discourse subsequently gave rise to a reactionary response against Enlightenment stricture, which Bakhtin witnesses in the appropriation of the grotesque by German writers. Theoreticians of the grotesque emerged from this German renaissance of carnival, particularly Justus Möser and Carl Friedrich Flögel (35–36), whose late-eighteenth-century rehabilitation of the grotesque as an object of study provided an understanding of the carnivalesque that helped solidify Bakhtin's repeated insistence upon the "festive laughter" (11) of carnival (which he contrasts, somewhat misguidedly, with the somber, destructive potential of satire). Later aesthetic conceptions of laughter and the grotesque likewise draw almost exclusively on German sources; Friedrich Schlegel's *Dialogue on Poetry* is juxtaposed with Jean Paul's *School for Aesthetics* (41–42), while G. W. F. Hegel's and Kuno Fischer's aesthetic writings contrast with Heinrich Schneegans' *History of Grotesque Satire* [*Geschichte der grotesken Satire*] (44–46).[24] Incorporated into Bakhtin's text after the initial drafts, a critical response to Wolfgang Kayser's *The Grotesque in Art and Literature* [*Das Groteske: Seine Gestaltung in Malerei und*

---

23 Mikhail Bakhtin, *Rabelais and His World*, trans. Hélène Iswolsky (Bloomington: Indiana University Press, 1984), 11. Subsequent references to Bakhtin's Rabelais text shall be noted parenthetically with page number.
24 Heinrich Schneegans, *Geschichte der grotesken Satire* (Strassburg: K. Trübner, 1894).

Dichtung] likewise forms the basis for an engagement with more recent writings on the grotesque.²⁵

Bakhtin's reading of Rabelais aside, his engagement with and theorization of the carnivalesque has German roots through and through. In anchoring a history of the carnivalesque in the German tradition, Bakhtin betrays a deep knowledge of German-language works and conventions even while simultaneously attempting to define carnival as a practice that defies national borders. Mention is made of Shakespeare, Cervantes, and Sterne, but Rabelais seems to be an outlier, a figure whose own literary tradition otherwise fails to engage recurrently and explicitly with carnival. For Bakhtin's text, the German tradition fulfills this purpose in its theorizations, be they historical or contemporary. This reliance upon Germanic notions and treatments of the carnivalesque is all the more striking in light of Bakhtin's initial emphasis on situating Rabelais within the context of a pan-European literary tradition, of securing "his place in history among the creators of modern European writing, such as Dante, Boccaccio, Shakespeare, and Cervantes" (2), none of whom was German or wrote in the language. And yet, in the historical exposé of the Middle Ages and in the readings of *Gargantua and Pantagruel*, Bakhtin's text proposes a conception of carnival whose acme may be found in the German Baroque and whose gradual endangerment and downfall comes about with the rise of Herder and (German) Romantic solipsism (4). Before we turn to Bakhtin's text, which unlike the others in this study explicitly and oppositionally addresses satire, let us first situate it in the context of contemporaneous understandings of satire.

In using satire as a counterweight to the carnivalesque, Bakhtin draws a distinction that reveals a common conception of satire since at least 1800. Described frequently as destructive, negative, polemic, or aggressive, satire, as noted earlier, had come to represent less an aesthetic than a socio-critical or political phenomenon. Its formal shapes multitudinous and continually proliferating since antiquity, satire was understood as an entity – if one even deigned to speak of it as a single category, or to speak of it at all – incongruent with the ever more frequent attempts to systematize theories of art and poiesis since the Enlightenment. Topical and thematic analyses of satire discounted the possibility that it might achieve aesthetic autonomy in its own right through certain idiosyncratic literary or aesthetic principles; indeed, historical difficulties in systematizing ancient Roman satire into a coherent genre had led critics to focus instead on satire's use of topical commentary and extraliterary deixis. As a consequence of this seeming lack of aesthetic closure, satire was equated with a kind of social criticism and,

---

25 Kayser, *Das Groteske: Seine Gestaltung in Malerei und Dichtung*.

thus bound to its historical and social context, considered incapable of aesthetic viability and autonomy. It was subsequently omitted from most serious attempts to develop an aesthetics after the age of the Enlightenment.

Bakhtin, it should be noted, does not develop a theory of satire in concert with his theory of the carnivalesque, nor does he note his sources for the conception of satire he employs tangentially; satire was all but absent from the aesthetics of the day since the early nineteenth century anyway. Nevertheless, his frequent references to satire in opposition to the carnivalesque and the grotesque[26] – for Bakhtin the literary *mise-en-scène* of the carnivalesque – allow the reader to reconstruct an implicit conception of satire from certain points of overlap and difference.

One similarity lies in their omission from aesthetic theories. That Bakhtin addresses with grotesque realism a phenomenon ignored or underestimated by aesthetic theories suggests a certain kinship with satire, which his understandable attempts to draw hard and fast terminological boundaries for the grotesque overlook. In fact, the history of the grotesque since Romanticism parallels that of satire, which it was admittedly not Bakhtin's mission to describe. After Hegel and Fischer in the mid-nineteenth century, for example, Bakhtin diagnoses a continuous decline in serious engagements with the grotesque, which "in the further development of philosophical aesthetics up to our times [...] has not been duly understood and evaluated; there was no room for it in the system of aesthetics" (45). The very same argument, in fact, could be made for satire. While parallel aesthetic histories are of course insufficient reasons for establishing a semiotic kinship between the grotesque and satire, the resulting equation of the grotesque with "a peculiar form of satire, directed against isolated, purely negative objects" (45), an erroneous assertion according to Bakhtin, does imply a deeper link.

How the two might relate to one another is not part of Bakhtin's aim for the Rabelais book, and indeed his definition of the grotesque against the negative backdrop of satire provides a convenient, if obscurantist, straw man for his discussion. What distinguishes satire from Bakhtin's notion of the carnivalesque is, foremost, the attribution of universality and a rejuvenating, restorative function to the "festive laughter" of carnival – and by contrast an individual, destructive function imputed to the "pure satire of modern times": "The satirist whose laughter is negative places himself above the object of his mockery, he is opposed to it. The wholeness of the world's comic aspect is destroyed, and that which appears comic becomes a private reaction. The people's ambivalent laughter, on the other

---

[26] In the text, Bakhtin generally does not distinguish between satire and parody, essentially using the terms interchangeably as points of negative comparison with the carnivalesque.

hand, expresses the point of view of the whole world; he who is laughing also belongs to it" (12). That the vehicle of comparison between satire and carnival is laughter remains a curiosity of Bakhtin's text.[27] Despite the initial intent to investigate the "culture of folk humor in the Middle Ages and the Renaissance" (4), laughter as such is neither the focus of Bakhtin's analysis, nor is it necessarily a reaction ascribed to the reader. Be it in relation to folk humor in general or to Rabelais in particular, laughter is instead a metaphor Bakhtin employs for the quintessential thrust of carnival: a gesture of inversion whereby earnestness is suspended through humor and playful, universal mockery, albeit only through the relativizing participation of an entire community. It is, in a sense, a metaphoric, social release of tension through ambivalence. Along with the regenerative effect of laughter, this communal, universal aspect of the carnivalesque is most significant.

On the one hand, Bakhtin's insistence upon the universality of carnival laughter bespeaks the historical exigencies of his time and situation; in the Soviet Union of Stalin the carnivalesque finds its *raison d'être* precisely in its roots as a revolutionary phenomenon of the people: of the undifferentiated masses among whom class difference is meaningless because it is nonexistent. On the other hand, Bakhtin uses the notion of undifferentiated carnival experience as an antipode to what he perceives as the individuated, even solipsistic nature of satire. Satire, he argues, lacks what he identifies as the "universal spirit" of carnival, which attends to "the world's revival and renewal" through its laughter (7). To him satire and parody, specifically that of his own period, amount to pure negativity ("[b]are negation") and are thus diametrically opposed to the carnivalesque, which is to say "completely alien to folk culture" (11). The opposition Bakhtin erects between the carnivalesque (via the grotesque) and satire, however, is predicated upon nothing but apodictic claims about semiotic capabilities, which he does not analyze in detail.

Throughout he places the emphasis not on semiotic or formal elements of carnival (nor, in his comparisons, on satire), but instead on the thematic aspects of it and their social, anthropological ramifications. For Bakhtin, Rabelais' *Gargantua and Pantagruel*, for example, serves largely as a repository of grotesque tropes that he both uncovers and interprets in light of their function within soci-

---

[27] That he conceded to laughter the status of an epiphenomenon of satire is evident from published notes written several years after the publication of *Rabelais and His World*. What to make of such backpedaling – whether it marks a true shift in his thinking or is merely an inconsistency redolent of his oft-criticized unsystematic thought – is another question entirely. See Bakhtin, "From Notes Made in 1970–71."

ety; in the end, *Gargantua and Pantagruel* is simultaneously a masterwork of the European novelistic tradition and a case study, a nodal point at the intersection of social, political, and anthropological discourses about a certain cultural practice in the Middle Ages and Renaissance. Seen from this perspective, neither the carnivalesque nor satire attains aesthetic or literary autonomy for Bakhtin. They are symptoms of a social practice that links literature with society. In essence, his treatment of these phenomena derives from a functionalist position vis-à-vis literary writing – namely, that literature fulfills a certain social function – although, as we shall see, with the carnivalesque he attempts to show how a social practice became literary.

Carnival, Literature, Inversion, and Satire

In Bakhtin's extensive study of how *Gargantua and Pantagruel* represents an outsider folk perspective on official culture – a subversive element that was never subsumed under hegemonic discourse – the long introduction serves as an exemplary passage for examining the transfer of carnival forms into literary practice. Here, the aim is twofold: first, to bring to light what is literary about the carnivalesque, which Bakhtin claims "belongs to the borderline between art and life" (7) and thus sits astraddle two distinct realms of inquiry; second, to demonstrate that the figure of inversion, that quintessential device of the carnivalesque, is a constitutive element of the fabric of *Rabelais and His World*. By introducing the concept of a marginal, subversive element that arises from the people and opposes official culture,[28] Bakhtin develops a narrative that both counters the history of received ideas about Rabelais and, in an extratextual move, simultaneously expresses an ambivalence about the cultural and political situation of its own inception. He thus offers an example of a literary modality for the carnivalesque, which in turn links his project with the deployment of the carnivalesque: as a satiric practice in other modes of writing and as a mode of political critique.

In his introduction Bakhtin makes far-reaching promises. Faced with the challenge of interpreting a seminal work of world literature that has been misunderstood through "shortsighted" modernizations, he takes a different tack to explain "[Rabelais'] peculiar language, that is, the language of the culture of folk humor" (58). In jettisoning the centuries of scholarship on his topic, Bakhtin travels a solitary path of academic opposition that lays claims to hermeneutic excep-

---

[28] Cf. Sasse, *Michail Bachtin zur Einführung*, 168.

tionalism by criticizing "the wide beaten roads followed by bourgeois Europe's literary creation and ideology during the four hundred years separating him from us"; "[a]lthough during these four hundred years there have been many enthusiastic admirers of Rabelais, we can find nowhere a fully expressed understanding of him" (3). At the same time, however, Bakhtin excises Rabelais from the canon of world literature precisely by mystifying him as a hermeneutic enigma belonging to popular carnival culture rather than officialdom. Rabelais "correctly understood" thus requires, as the text notes, a critical reconstruction, renunciation, and revision: a series of all-encompassing regenerative negations of past findings and research that culminates in an exploration of an alternative space of inquiry, "a sphere as yet little and superficially studied, the tradition of folk humor" (3). That folk humor and the carnival tradition form the hermeneutic key to understanding Rabelais, however, is little more than a bald assertion of certitude. The examination of Rabelais' language, which is Bakhtin's stated primary aim, must thus proceed from this *a priori* link of the text to carnival spectacles and acts in medieval and ancient societies; it is the function of the introduction to trace the history of carnival forms and show how they made the transition from social practices to literary strategies. Throughout his introduction, Bakhtin maintains the narrative dynamic of inversion, negation, and repetition of mostly unsupported claims.[29] The tenability of these claims notwithstanding, Bakhtin's writing employs the same devices as the carnival forms he describes and thus "reproduces, within its own structures and by its own practice, the characteristic inversions, parodies and discrownings of carnival proper."[30]

Indeed, a hallmark of Bakhtin's writing style in his introduction is the opposition of his own perspective on Rabelais to that of the "eyes of the new age" (58), which misinterpret him by modernizing him (18). In an oft-cited antinomy to the carnivalesque, Bakhtin pillories the standards "of modern times," be they of parody (11), literary norms in general (18), or analysis (45, 58), while evincing a nostalgia for a bygone time – "the early stages of preclass and prepolitical social order" (6) – in which the serious and the comic were undifferentiated, a time that provides the key to understanding folk humor. "The problem of the grotesque and of its aesthetic nature," he writes, "can be correctly posed and solved only in relation to medieval folk culture and Renaissance literature" (51). This exclusionary perspective particularly opposes the extremism of Romantic strains of the

---

[29] Craig Brandist argues that Bakhtin ignores historical research and develops the notion of the carnivalesque as "a sort of 'proto-genre' described in terms of anthropology." *The Bakhtin Circle: Philosophy, Culture and Politics* (London: Pluto, 2002), 137.
[30] Dentith, *Bakhtinian Thought*, 65.

grotesque in the early nineteenth century, which introduced to the world "with the angry eyes of satire" "a terrifying world, alien to man" (38). This terror resonates with his invocation of modernity and the contemporaneous historical context of his study.

Such a nostalgia has three consequences of particular interest here. First, Bakhtin posits an epistemological split between the worlds in which and about which he writes. Ultimately beholden to a nineteenth-century tradition of realism, the oppressive Socialist Realist regime under which Bakhtin writes does not, he implicitly claims, possess the epistemological means for understanding Rabelais. Like their twentieth-century successors, the Romantics too "were incapable of revealing [Rabelais'] essence and did not go beyond enraptured surprise. [...] The vast majority [...] simply do not understand him. In fact, many of his images remain an enigma" (3). Precisely this claim constitutes the great political inversion of Bakhtin's text: the notion that the Communist episteme cannot account for the restorative carnivalesque humor of a prepolitical society and has instead rendered carnival a "half-forgotten idiom, in so many ways obscure to us" (11). The prevailing body of scholarship and the scholarly establishment are thus rendered obsolete in a rhetoric of carnivalesque relativism.

The nostalgia Bakhtin's text demonstrates for a "preclass and prepolitical" age also situates his argument in opposition to the Stalinist socio-political landscape of his time, the second of these ramifications. In so claiming an exceptionalist understanding of Rabelais on epistemological and hermeneutic grounds, Bakhtin effectively levels criticism against the interpretive wherewithal of the dominant cultural and political apparatus, which "can be read as a subversive attack on the perverted concept of folk culture that prevailed in the Stalin era, a culture that was decreed from on high and that in reality offered no alternative to the official one."[31] This layer of the text does not so much manifest itself in words – it certainly would not have passed muster by the censors – but is a constitutive part of the historical understanding of the text. Indeed, the veiled attack on the Soviet establishment in *Rabelais and His World* proceeds from a notion of the carnivalesque that is both beyond the reach of Communist understanding and supplementary to the hegemony of Stalinist culture. Outside Soviet statutes and at a historical remove, the carnivalesque provides a safe mechanism for social critique that arises, ironically, from the ostensible vehicle of Stalinist Communism: the people.

The third and final implication of Bakhtin's Renaissance–modernism antinomy is more problematic. In locating the roots of the carnivalesque in a suspen-

---

31 Lachmann, "Bakhtin and Carnival," 118; see also Dentith, *Bakhtinian Thought*, 71.

sion of social hierarchies that can only ever be comprehended politically, Bakhtin also links what I have termed a satiric practice to the political. Divorcing satire irrevocably from the political is, it would thus seem, impossible, but it points to a development in the notion of satire we will witness in the coming pages. To be sure, the explicitly political nature of the carnivalesque links the modality of satire practiced by Bakhtin to a more traditional notion of satire as political polemic or critique. The function of the carnivalesque as a figure of semiotic inversion may still be maintained, but the extraliterary, political aspect refuses to vanish. What differs in my estimation, however, is the fact that the carnivalesque, true to its doubling nature, straddles extraliterary and literary domains. In other words, in Bakhtin's use of the carnivalesque, we see a mode of satiric writing that translates into practices of written discourse while maintaining a historically socio-political character. The political dimension of satire will continue with Thomas Bernhard although, as the following chapters show, it gradually diminishes in importance as an element of satiric discourse as the carnivalesque becomes a less dominant practice of writing.

For now, a closer look at the way Bakhtin develops the notion of the carnivalesque will help reveal this dynamic of satire and politics. In reconstructing a culture of folk humor, to begin, Bakhtin narrates a parallel history of life in the Middle Ages and Renaissance whose various forms "offered a completely different, nonofficial, extraecclesiastical and extrapolitical aspect of the world, of man, and of human relations" (6). In this "second world" (6), Bakhtin asserts, there existed an alternative order that defied the hegemony of the organizing institutions of culture, be they the political establishment or the Church. By virtue of its very opposition to official culture, this doubled order invariably takes on a subversive quality insofar as it "provides a malleable space, in which activities and symbols can be inflected in different directions"[32] in opposition to established authority. On a parallel plane, carnival "celebrated temporary liberation from the prevailing truth and from the established order; it marked the suspension of all hierarchical rank, privileges, norms, and prohibitions" (10). Such transgressive potential is all the more powerful since Bakhtin links it with an anthropological claim to universality; carnival was sanctioned because it belonged to no group, but to everyone (7). To a certain degree such a conception of the carnivalesque merges a utopian, falsely nostalgic yearning for classless society with the unrealistic assumption of social homogeneity. For Bakhtin, the historical distance of classic carnival culture, which he traces from Roman antiquity through the Mid-

---

[32] Dentith, *Bakhtinian Thought*, 75.

dle Ages, allows him to make this claim with impunity, but it also provides an unassailable ideal for developing his notion of the carnivalesque.

What he describes as the carnivalesque in Rabelais has limited scope, however. Rabelais is at once the acme and the endpoint of the development of carnival laughter in literature, "which has found in his works its greatest literary expression" (4, see also 62). The reasons for this are less because the literary practices of the carnivalesque changed during the course of ensuing epochs than because of the changes in carnival imagery, the connotations of it as interpreted by contemporaneous theorists, and Bakhtin's notions of (modern) satire and parody, to which he opposes the regenerating effect of the carnivalesque. Yet how does Bakhtin describe carnivalization as a literary practice? And to what extent can we in fact see an affinity on the semiotic level between the carnivalesque and the satiric?

To transfer carnival forms into literary practices, Bakhtin names a literary style that renders into writing what carnival had rendered as visual performance, parodic works, or expletives. For carnival forms, the vehicle of laughter, he writes, is comic imagery, and this imagery enters the literary imagination by way of a mode of writing that might somehow capture the universal festivity and distorting inversions of carnival culture; the suspension of hierarchical laws and orders must be copied on the linguistic level – but how? To describe a style of literary writing that conveys the extreme corporeality of comic carnival imagery Bakhtin employs the term "grotesque realism" (18).

Like carnival culture, grotesque realism aims to portray a bodily materiality that is universal, unindividuated, festive, classless, regenerative, and ambivalent (19–21). In maintaining a semantic aperture, carnival laughter connotes through excess, which allows it to function primarily "by way of the paradoxical and deferring use of the comparative and of dislocation, as well as by way of deforming hyperbole and the use of the superlative"[33]; "It asserts and denies, it buries and revives" (12), primarily through exaggeration, hyperbolism, and excessiveness (303). In his reception of Schneegans, Bakhtin reluctantly points to the "peculiarities of Rabelais' images and verbal style" as holdovers from a tradition of satire he rejects (and elaborates one-dimensionally): "excessiveness, superabundance, the tendency to transgress all limits, endless enumerations, and accumulations of synonyms" (306).[34] Bakhtin himself does not explicitly reject these

---

[33] Sasse, *Michail Bachtin zur Einführung*, 162.
[34] To be generous, one might see in this interpretation of satire the basis for understanding it as semiotic excess, as having multiple semiological layers, which Bakhtin indeed addresses in his treatise on dialogism and heteroglossia. "Discourse in the Novel," in *The Dialogic Imagination:*

rhetorical qualities in Rabelais and in the nature of the carnivalesque, but his distaste with Schneegans' appropriation of them in what he perceives as a misguided account of the grotesque as satire is palpable.[35]

In her own interpretation, by contrast, Julia Kristeva approaches Bakhtin's carnivalesque as a particularly prolific type of dialogic, and thus intertextual, discourse. "Figures germane to carnivalesque language," she writes, "including repetition, 'inconsequent' statements (which are none the less 'connected' within an infinite context) and non-exclusive opposition, which function as empty sets or disjunctive additions, produce a more flagrant dialogism than any other discourse."[36] In her diagnosis, Kristeva identifies a specific rhetoric of the carnivalesque whose dialogism – whose ambivalence – derives from intertextuality. If one chooses to follow her logic, the rhetorical devices of the carnivalesque include repetition, incomplete logic or a lack of teleology, and oppositional utterances. Here the translation-into-writing of ambivalence and the carnivalesque suspension of law appear more grounded. The strategies of an abrogation of hierarchy and order, along with an indeterminacy of denotation, correlate well with a general practice that can be rendered through image, metaphor, grammar, syntax, structure, form, perspective, or epistemology. It is through the figure of inversion that the carnivalesque allows the reader "to enter a completely new order of things" (34), that the gestures of the grotesque body foreground "the inside out and upside down" (353, see also 11), that madness escapes pathologization as the order of the day (39).

Indeed, inversion captures the quintessential operation of the carnivalesque, be it on the level of discourse or the level of form. The term, moreover, accords well with an understanding of satire as a representation of a world turned upside down or inverted. The advantage of imbuing inversion with such significance in this regard, by relating it to both my conception of satire and an outmoded notion that ignores the semiotics of satire, lies in the ability of inversion to refer

---

Four Essays, ed. Michael Holquist, trans. Caryl Emerson and Michael Holquist (Austin: University of Texas Press, 1981), 414–422.

35 One of the deficits of Bakhtin's text as a theoretical work is the continued emphasis upon grotesque imagery as a distortion or exaggeration of a norm he does not more closely define; it remains forever a tacit, ahistorical convention. Bakhtin describes as its fundamental ambivalence the essential doubleness of the grotesque, its combination of temporal spheres (old/new, past/present, death/birth) and suturing of disparate elements, but how this translates into literary writing other than through imagery does not figure into his study; only through negating the propositions of, for example, Schneegans does Bakhtin suggest the formal contours of the carnivalesque.

36 Kristeva, "Word, Dialogue and Novel," 49.

to both this metaphoric spatial transformation as well as a semiotic practice. Inversion thus need no longer be employed metaphorically.

Furthermore, the practice is no stranger to those used to bolster Bakhtin's argumentation and to structure his narrative of carnival and Rabelais' place in its history. As I have previously argued, the fundamental narrative of *Rabelais and His World* proceeds from the apodictic – and ambivalent – assertion of Rabelais' uniqueness in the history of the novel. Both a highpoint and an outlier, Rabelais is for Bakhtin the sole progenitor of true carnival forms since all who follow him pollute the fundamental characteristics of such forms, obscuring the historical roots of carnival in the festive laughter of the Middle Ages. If the work is read from a purely hermeneutic perspective, we might speak of a narrator who posits himself as an impersonal corrective to the misunderstandings that pervade research on Rabelais. Hyperbolic attestations of the shortcomings of such criticism nullify centuries of scholarship in one claim of exceptionalism; only by examining Rabelais through the lens of folk humor, or so the logic goes, may he be truly understood, a claim accompanied by a study that purports to renew this comprehension through the act of its creation. Only a few works, most of them of German derivation, guide the narrator's orientation around the terrain of critical discourse. "But all this enormous bulk of literature," Bakhtin writes towards the end of his introduction, "with only a few exceptions, is devoid of theoretical pathos. It does not seek to make any broad and firmly established generalizations. The almost immeasurable, carefully selected, and scrupulously analyzed material is neither unified nor properly understood" (54). In a suspension of the hierarchical order of received ideas, the voice of the scholar as narrator consequently declares the domain of Rabelais studies "unexplored" (54).

Traversing the landscape of the carnivalesque in literature and theory since Rabelais, Bakhtin maintains the insufficiencies not only of all theoretical approaches – most of which hinge on what is here argued to be a fallacious and facile understanding of satire as pure negation – but also of literary adaptations of it. What he narrates is a story of the birth of the carnivalesque from the spirit of Rabelais. Within the logic of carnival, however, birth is simultaneously death; in tracing the development of carnival from its disintegration in Fischart's *Geschichtklitterung* (1575) to the Enlightenment, from debates about the *Hanswurst* to the Romantic turn away from the universality of carnival laughter, Bakhtin narrates its demise *and* rebirth in his study. His text thus illustrates the ambivalence it purports to ascribe to the carnivalesque, an ambivalence described by Kristeva as dialogic or intertextual and which I see as of a piece with satire.

What ultimately hinders Bakhtin from accepting the parallel trajectories of the history of the carnivalesque and the history of satire – what ultimately prevents his establishing a link between the two phenomena – is a repeated claim of satire's destructive negativity (62) and mockery, and thus its perversion of the positive festivity of carnival. Such tenacity is blind to the complexities of a practice (satire) with its own history and with its own means of signification. Critics have noted in this rhetorical hardheadedness a characteristic "competition between an ideological and a cultural-descriptive approach"[37] that prevents the systematic coherence of his argumentation. Tensions arise, for example, when Bakhtin mounts an offensive against satire as a mode of writing social criticism while comparing it to the grotesque as a mode of writing culture; the terms are incommensurate with one another.

Nevertheless, the text develops a conception of the carnivalesque predicated on simultaneous negation and affirmation, on an ambivalent, all-encompassing negation through inversion. In what follows, I argue from the premise that this is no fundamentally different from a dynamic of satire understood from a semiotic perspective. In other words, the superimposition of the carnivalesque and the satiric shows considerable compatibility between the terms when the point of comparison is at the level of signification; the carnivalesque is essentially a satiric semiotic practice. Bakhtin himself concedes the emergence of carnival forms from early Menippean satire, which he mentions in greater detail in his book on Dostoyevsky and keeps separate from the "pure satire of modern times" (12). In his early work, Bakhtin also notes the dominance of heteroglossic writing after 1800, which is predicated largely on the second of two stylistic lines: "the parodic epic, the satire novella, the picaresque novel."[38] In her early reception of Bakhtin, Kristeva pointed presciently to this overlap of carnival, satire, and the novel. Unlike the monologic discourse of officialdom, "*dialogical discourse* includes carnivalesque and Menippean discourses as well as the polyphonic novel. In its structures, writing reads another writing, reads itself and constructs itself through a process of destructive genesis."[39] It is this very process of carnivalesque, destructive genesis through inversion that we turn to in the following chapters on two novels by Thomas Bernhard.

---

[37] Lachmann, "Bakhtin and Carnival," 128.
[38] "It could even be said that in the nineteenth century the distinctive features of the Second Line become the basic constitutive features for the novelistic genre as a whole. [...] [I]n it, the novel became what it in fact is." Bakhtin, "Discourse in the Novel," 414.
[39] Kristeva, "Word, Dialogue and Novel," 47.

4. Perspective and Repetition in Thomas Bernhard's *Woodcutters* (1984)

Publicly insulted by the Austrian minister of education during his acceptance speech for a literary prize in 1968, Thomas Bernhard was no stranger to scandal, memorializing this incident in particular in both *Wittgenstein's Nephew* [*Wittgensteins Neffe*][1] and *My Prizes* [*Meine Preise*].[2] The 1984 publication of *Woodcutters*, however, unwittingly stoked a further brouhaha in the press and in the courts when the composer Gerhard Lampersberg, having obtained a precirculated review copy of the novel, filed a lawsuit against the author "for defamation, vilification, and ridicule."[3] Once associated with Bernhard in the 1950s, Lampersberg claimed to recognize himself represented in the text as the composer Auersberger, a sloppily intoxicated host of the "*artistic dinner*"[4] that the narrator attends, and whom the latter characterizes variously as "*Auersberger, the lecherous literary Moloch*" (269; 152), "an *unendurable copy* of Webern" (97; 55), and "our snobbish musical dandy from the Styrian sticks" (96; 55).[5] The police confiscated the book, a lawsuit erupted (which Lampersberg ultimately dropped), and Bernhard decreed that his publisher Suhrkamp suspend distribution of all his works within Austria; all these things conjured a flurry of attention that propelled

---

[1] Thomas Bernhard, *Wittgensteins Neffe: Eine Freundschaft* (Frankfurt am Main: Suhrkamp, 1982).

[2] Thomas Bernhard, *Meine Preise* (Frankfurt am Main: Suhrkamp, 2009). This posthumously published volume recounts several other scandals revolving around Bernhard's acceptance of literary prizes and his speeches at the ceremonies.

[3] Eva Schindlecker, "Thomas Bernhard: 'Holzfällen. Eine Erregung': Dokumentation eines österreichischen Literaturskandals," in *Statt Bernhard: Über Misanthropie im Werk Thomas Bernhards*, ed. Wendelin Schmidt-Dengler and Martin Huber (Wien: Edition S, 1987), 14. Schindlecker provides a good chronicle of the scandal as well as a bibliography of press reactions to the confiscation of the volumes, the lawsuit, and Bernhard's legal countermeasures.

[4] Thomas Bernhard, *Holzfällen: Eine Erregung* (Frankfurt am Main: Suhrkamp, 1984), 7; Thomas Bernhard, *Woodcutters*, trans. David McLintock (New York: Alfred A. Knopf, 1987), 3. References to *Woodcutters* in this chapter will appear in the text parenthetically, with dual pages numbers of the German originals and their English translations, separated by a semicolon.

[5] Similarities between real people and fictional characters did not stop with Lampersberg, although his was the most negative reaction. Some have linked the character Jeannie Billroth to the Austrian poet and author Jeannie Ebner and Anna Schreker to Friederike Mayröcker. Daniel Kehlmann, *Lob: Über Literatur* (Reinbek bei Hamburg: Rowohlt, 2010), 15–16; Schindlecker, "Thomas Bernhard: 'Holzfällen. Eine Erregung': Dokumentation eines österreichischen Literaturskandals," 20–21.

Bernhard into the media spotlight, making him the subject of seemingly endless debates in German and Austrian feuilletons.[6]

At its core, this masterfully manufactured scandal involved a clash between implicitly assumed cultural conventions of literary and non-literary writing, between conceptions of what is fictional and non-fictional, and ultimately about the extent to which a text considered entirely fictional by the author might well still have juridical ramifications for him because of its perceived similarities with reality.[7] Whatever the case may be, Lampersberg's perceptions of overlap between the textual world and the real world instigated a heated court battle over a book on precisely these grounds: that literary reality was ultimately subject to Austria's laws against character assassination and that the veil of fiction did not protect Bernhard's right to free speech. Where does one draw the line between the law and literature? How might one legislate and adjudicate the reach of law into the field of aesthetics? Bernhard's largely self-made scandal did not answer these questions conclusively, but the reception of *Woodcutters* once again aroused discussion of Bernhard as "the apocalyptic social satirist"[8] and the nature of satire as a phenomenon at the intersection of representation and represented reality.[9] In fact, Bernhard would seem to make explicit the implicit political critique we

---

[6] See in particular the extensive bibliography of attention to the scandal in print media from beginning to end: Schindlecker, "Thomas Bernhard: 'Holzfällen. Eine Erregung': Dokumentation eines österreichischen Literaturskandals," 40–58.

[7] See Bernhard's own response in the *Frankfurter Allgemeine Zeitung* of 15 November 1984 quoted in Ferdinand van Ingen, "Thomas Bernhards 'Holzfällen' oder die Kunst der Invektive," in *Literatur und politische Aktualität*, ed. Elrud Ibsch, Ferdinand van Ingen, and Anthonya Visser (Amsterdam: Rodopi, 1993), 142–143. "Mr. Lampersberg has nothing to do with my Mr. Auersberger," 142; by contrast, Bernhard maintains the conflation of fiction and reality in his interview with Krista Fleischmann: "Nothing in Holzfällen is fictional," quoted in Bernhard Doppler, "Erregung gegenüber den fünfziger Jahren: 'Holzfällen' und der Tonhof," in *Thomas Bernhard: Traditionen und Trabanten*, ed. Joachim Hoell and Kai Luehrs-Kaiser (Würzburg: Königshausen & Neumann, 1999), 213.

[8] Kehlmann, *Lob*, 19.

[9] Author Daniel Kehlmann addressed this question more recently again in a short essay. To wit: "The narrator decides to morph what is experienced into literature, and precisely through this repeated thematization of such transmutation, the reader is referred back time and again to the fact that this is not just about spinning yarns, but about real people, about extratextual reality. There's nothing problematic about that; literary satire has been doing that for ages, from Juvenal to Voltaire to Karl Kraus. *Woodcutters* is an artwork in prose about reality and its distortion, defined by wit and brilliance, but also defined by uncommon hatefulness and a series of extra-literary ends." Kehlmann, *Lob*, 13. See also Wolfgang Hackl, "Unterhaltung und Provokation: Thomas Bernhard als Satiriker des österreichischen Kulturbetriebs: 'Holzfällen. Eine Erregung,'" *Germanistisches Jahrbuch DDR – Republik Ungarn* 9 (1990): 132–145.

witnessed in Bakhtin and revive the debate surrounding satire as a political instrument.

What kind of text provokes such a reaction? In seeking an answer for what constitutes the satiric elements of Bernhard's text without resorting to extraliterary Schillerian comparisons,[10] I argue that Bernhard employs the figure of inversion, a strategy of the carnivalesque, both as a means of structuring his text formally and syntactically and as a vehicle for critique.[11] Subtitled "Eine Erregung," an arousal or agitation, Bernhard's novel *Woodcutters* organizes itself around a series of repetitive vitriolic recollections at a dinner party that release their pent-up tension in a climactic moment of inversion. The confrontations between past and present, between the fifties and the eighties, between prior judgments and present assessments, between friendship and hate, one critic writes, "could be termed a drama of inversions and revolutions [*Umdrehungen*]."[12] In fact, the encounter which prompts the narrative – the run-in with the Auersbergers on the Graben – itself results from a sudden inversion or reversal:

> Auf dem Graben gehen heißt ja nichts anderes, als direkt in die Wiener Gesellschaftshölle zu gehen und gerade jene Leute zu treffen, die ich nicht treffen will, deren Auftauchen mir auch heute noch alle möglichen Körper- und Geisteskrämpfe verursacht, dachte ich auf dem Ohrensessel sitzend, und ich hatte aus diesem Grunde schon in den letzten Jahren meiner Wienbesuche von London aus den Graben gemieden und bin andere Wege gegangen, auch nicht auf den Kohlmarkt, selbstverständlich auch nicht auf die Kärntnerstraße [...]. Aber in den letzten Wochen, dachte ich auf dem Ohrensessel, hatte ich aufeinmal ein großes Bedürfnis gehabt, gerade auf den Graben und auf die Kärntnerstraße zu gehen [...]. (9)

---

10 Appearing to take the side of those who view the conformity of literary reality with extraliterary reality as a sign of aesthetic value, Kehlmann invokes Schiller's classic definition of satire in order to question the accuracy with which Bernhard represents reality and thus to measure the ostensible literary value of *Woodcutters*. *Lob*, 15–16.

11 Edit Kovács links the figure of inversion to the rhetoric of judgment: "If one were to describe the rhetoric of judgment [*Richten*] in *Woodcutters* with one figure that dominates the entire narrative, then it would have to be that of *inversion*. Inversion, resetting [*Umrichtung*], reversal, dominate both the level of the plot and the narrator's language of judgment. At its basis lies a way of thinking in directions [*Richtungen*] that correlates the discourse of correctness [*Richtigkeit*], frankness [*Aufrichtkeit*], adjustment [*Berichtigung*], and righteouness [*Gerechtigkeit*] with corresponding spatial ideas." It is perhaps in the link between judgment as critique and satire as a form of critique that one might see the rhetorical use of inversion as a common strategy. "Autor und Leser als Richter: Forensische und rhetorische Lektüren zu Thomas Bernhards 'Holzfällen,'" *Germanistische Mitteilungen* 60–61 (May 2004): 114.

12 Kovács, "Autor und Leser als Richter: Forensische und rhetorische Lektüren zu Thomas Bernhards 'Holzfällen,'" 114.

4. Perspective and Repetition in Thomas Bernhard's *Woodcutters* (1984) — 65

> Going for a walk in the Graben, I thought as I sat in the wing chair, means nothing more nor less than walking straight into the social hell of Vienna and meeting the very people I have no wish to meet, people whose sudden appearance brings on all kinds of physical and mental strains. Hence in recent years, whenever I came over from London to Vienna, I had chosen different routes for my walks, avoiding not only the Graben, but also the Kohlmarkt and, of course, the Kärntnerstrasse. [...]. But in recent weeks, I reflected as I sat in the wing chair, I had suddenly felt an urgent need to go to the Graben and the Kärntnerstrasse [...]. (4)

After several months of 'walking therapy' and the very morning he learns of his friend Joana's suicide, the unnamed narrator encounters long-lost and long-loathed friends, the Auersbergers. Caught off-guard in his distress, he unwittingly agrees to attend a dinner party at their home on the day of Joana's funeral. *Woodcutters* begins *in medias res* the night of the dinner party as the narrator sits in his wing-chair perch behind a door in the darkness, grumbling about his hasty acceptance of the invitation, waiting for the arrival of the guest of honor – a Burgtheater actor in Ibsen's *The Wild Duck* – and observing and rendering judgment upon the attendees and whatever else comes to mind. Only when the tardy actor, initially repellent to the narrator, becomes infuriated by a guest's petulant question does the narrator's hateful judgment flip suddenly into qualified support and respect, sending the narrator running through the streets of Vienna in a frenzy of creative, repetitive, literary energy following the calamitous degeneration of the gathering.

Just as Bernhard's last published novel *Extinction*, *Woodcutters* ends where it began: narrating its own moment of creation as a product of the very story it relates. In this case, the occasion of the dinner party and the crescendo of vituperative arousal culminate in a feverish need to write: "I'll write something *at once* about this so-called *artistic dinner* in the Gentzgasse, no matter what – I'll write about this *artistic dinner* in the Gentzgasse *at once*, *now*. *Now*, I thought – *at once*, I told myself over and over again as I ran through the Inner City – *at once*, I told myself, *now* – *at once*, *at once*, before it's too late" (321; 181 [translation amended, DB]). If one is mindful of this narrativization of writing, the novel amounts to a chronicle of its own inspiration. Indeed, this proairetic reference, like the topographical markers of Vienna (Gentzgasse, Graben, Kohlmarkt, Kärntnerstrasse, Währing) and the biographical similarities between literary characters and real-life personages, works toward establishing a link between the text and external reality and between the narrator and the author.

In fact, this assumed link between text and reality (which prompted the literary scandal in the first place) and the invective that serves as the vehicle for forging it constitute the two primary constellations of concern in studies of Bernhard's novel: on the one hand, the problem of extratextual referentiality and its influence on one's interpretation of a text, and on the other hand, the very central device of critique within the narrative. Previous critical engagements with Bernhard's *Woodcutters* have usually centered around one of these two routes of inquiry. Overshadowed by the public scandal caused by the novel's publication, scholars in the first vein explore the presumed autobiographical links between the text as a *roman à clef* and the real figures it purportedly represents, variously elucidating the historical context of Thomas Bernhard's relationship with Gerhard Lampersberg's Carinthian Tonhof, a gathering place of artists in the late fifties where Bernhard began his literary career, or the problem of literature, extra-textual reference, and cultural context.[13] While these explorations of *Woodcutters* make an important contribution to understanding the work as a cultural artifact and as the product of history, they frequently neglect to engage substantively with the text itself. The formal and semiotic aspects of *Woodcutters* thus get lost amid accounts of its function as a catalyst for scandal.

By contrast, those who follow the second model counter this tendency by focusing on a more careful analysis of various aspects of the text, be it the layers of and shifts in narrative perspective,[14] the rhetoric of the narrator's vitriolic judgments,[15] the autoerotic elements of the narrator's gaze,[16] or the literary character of invective.[17] One study attempts to bridge the gap between "an aestheticizing reading that dismisses the referentiality of the text as irrelevant, and a naively realist reading that assumes a direct correlation between word and world," effectively combining both approaches to show that "the text can be seen as a self-justifying response and solution to the shortcomings it criticizes."[18] In this latter

---

[13] Schindlecker, "Thomas Bernhard: 'Holzfällen. Eine Erregung': Dokumentation eines österreichischen Literaturskandals"; Alfred Pfabigan, "Der Platz von 'Holzfällen' innerhalb der Ordnung des Gesamtwerks von Thomas Bernhard," *Études germaniques* 50, no. 2 (1995): 161–173; Doppler, "Erregung"; Christiane Böhler, "Literaturskandal – Literaturtransfer: Eine Studie zur Rezeption von Skandalliteratur im Ausland am Beispiel von Thomas Bernhards Roman 'Holzfällen. Eine Erregung,'" in *Literatur als Skandal: Fälle, Funktionen, Folgen*, ed. Stefan Neuhaus and Johann Holzner (Göttingen: Vandenhoeck & Ruprecht, 2007), 513–523; Kehlmann, *Lob*.
[14] Gerhard Pail, "Perspektivität in Thomas Bernhards 'Holzfällen,'" *Modern Austrian Literature* 21, no. 3/4 (1988): 51–68.
[15] Kovács, "Autor und Leser als Richter: Forensische und rhetorische Lektüren zu Thomas Bernhards 'Holzfällen.'"
[16] Claudia Öhlschläger, "'In den Wald gehen, tief in den Wald hinein': Autoerotische Phantasmen männlicher Autorschaft in Thomas Bernhards 'Holzfällen. Eine Erregung,'" in *Auto(r)erotik: Gegenstandslose Liebe als literarisches Projekt*, ed. Annette Keck and Dietmar Schmidt (Berlin: Erich Schmidt, 1994), 119–131.
[17] Ingen, "Thomas Bernhards 'Holzfällen' oder die Kunst der Invektive."
[18] J. J. Long, *The Novels of Thomas Bernhard: Form and Its Function* (Rochester, NY: Camden House, 2001), 132.

work, the scholar reads Bernhard's *Woodcutters* as employing the referential code to position itself as a critical text while undermining its own ontological status as such with repeated references to its own fictional literariness; "*Holzfällen*," he concludes, "teaches us that referentiality in fiction is a textual effect created by choices made by the narrator and, in the final analysis, the author."[19] Biographical similarities notwithstanding, the referential qualities of the text result from a series of literary strategies that invert the reader's epistemology of a literary work as a closed, fictional, discrete text.

In my own reading of *Woodcutters*, I suggest building from this conclusion, examining the ways by which Bernhard implements this inversion, and reading the novel and this constitutive practice within the context of a history of satire. If we read the text as a "drama of inversions and revolutions [*Umdrehungen*]," we may find the play of the figure of inversion not only in the narrative perspective, but also on the levels of form, discourse, and syntax. From this perspective, the types of inversions one encounters in the novel contribute to a carnivalesque upsetting of order; "The law of inversion," one might argue, "proves, in this text, to be the inversion of the law."[20] We might thus reinscribe satire in the literary text as a medium of inversion that disrupts a conventional mode of reading and the law of literariness, rather than conceive of it solely as a practice of social and cultural critique. What follows is a closer analysis of the deployment of inversion in Thomas Bernhard's *Woodcutters* and of the relationship of this inversion to Bakhtin's theory of the carnivalesque.

Perspectival Inversion

Rather than analyze the text according to the topics of the narrator's screeds, one might divide the long narrative into two parts determined by the narrative perspective. In the first of these, roughly the first half of the text, the wing chair provides cover for the narrator and becomes a site of reflection and voyeuristic power where "in the semidarkness of the anteroom" he could devote himself "to the thoughts and fantasies that occupied [his] mind" (40; 22). From the security of this shadowy panopticon, the narrator renders judgment upon the "consummate performers" (45; 25) who "seemed like figures on a distant stage, like a moving photograph" (54; 31 [translation amended, DB]); "From my vantage point in

---

[19] Long, *The Novels of Thomas Bernhard*, 147.
[20] Kovács, "Autor und Leser als Richter: Forensische und rhetorische Lektüren zu Thomas Bernhards 'Holzfällen,'" 116.

the wing chair I could see the people in the music room without their seeing me" (41; 23). What gives this section coherence is largely the narrative perspective, the insistent repetition and reminder of the narrator's location "in the wing chair."[21]

These passages are largely a meditation on the past, a study in opposing present realities with past realities within a "tripartite time structure."[22] The distant past, the narrator argues repeatedly in the moment of writing, is incommensurable with the narrated present, in spite of the stagnation he diagnoses in the Austrian cultural establishment. Despite the negativity directed towards the Auersbergers and others, "[...] the reader is reminded that the opinions the narrator holds about the Auersbergers today are incompatible with those of his juvenile enthusiasm [...]. Thus there is a constant confrontation between the narrator's current perspective and his perspective as a young man."[23] Physically apart from the action, the narrator engages in introspection, retrospection, and monologic diatribes. The latter provide the reader with the background to Joana's suicide and the narrator's failed relationship with the Auersbergers, while delaying the onset of narrative progression until he moves, at the request of his hosts, into the dining room, "that exquisite Empire monstrosity" (173; 99). Indeed, the stasis of time the narrator witnesses in the Auersbergers[24] is reflected in the stasis of plot in this first part; until his summons to dinner, the narrator does not move from his wing chair, even sleeping through the long-awaited arrival of the actor (173–174; 98–99).

This shift in perspective, however, accounts for a major inversion in itself. The individuated perspective of the narrator in his isolation of personal reflection and cognition – thinking and reminiscing alone in the wing chair – cedes to a perspective from amid the loathsome dinner guests. Beckoned from his wing chair, the narrator begins to participate in the evening's activities, observing the guests during their meal and afterwards in the music room over wine and coffee, always relating and commenting on the conversation.

The solitary wing chair, which has hitherto been the site of narration, if not its medium, yields seamlessly to a different means of prompting narration through the presence of the "*Burgtheater actor*" (173; 98). The actor's monologue,

---

21 In her assessment of Bernhard's reception in Italy, Böhler counts 235 instances of the narrator's *Ohrensessel*. By my own count there are 232, 183 of them referring directly to some variation of "Ich dachte auf dem Ohrensessel." However many there may be, they saturate the first 165 pages of the text and disappear with the change of location. Böhler, "Literaturskandal – Literaturtransfer," 516.
22 Long, *The Novels of Thomas Bernhard*, 138.
23 Long, *The Novels of Thomas Bernhard*, 138.
24 Cf. Long, *The Novels of Thomas Bernhard*, 135.

interrupted only occasionally by the other guests, provides fodder for the running commentary of the narrator, its persistence mirroring the narrator's inner monologue in the first part. Although the apodictic nature of the narrator's damning judgments and the first-person perspective remain constant in the second part of the text – that is, although the narrator continues to be the sole observing subject – the story there is characterized less by personal recollection than by a chronicle of conversation and a continuation of personal reflection on the part of the actor (which is in turn filtered through and reported by the narrator). With the actor's entrance and the narrator's change of location, the inversion of perspective brings an end to the familiar repetition of "I thought, sitting in the wing chair," shifting the character of the text from solitary introspection and reflection to social reportage and judgment. The equally abundant use of the phrase "I thought" in the second part of the narrative, however, links it stylistically to the first while coding the action as a product of the narrator's cognition.

As a result of the inversion in the modality of perspective, there is a concomitant inversion in narrated time. After the arrival of the actor, *Woodcutters* shifts its central focus from the narrated past to the narrated present, from the narrator's distant observation of action to his immersion in it. In this figure of inversion on the level of narrative perspective, the shift maintains "the radically individualized perspective," which for some critics provides a marker of satire due to the degree of polemic it allows.[25] Its inversion of distance and proximity, however, radicalizes the oppositional dynamic between the narrator and what he narrates; the actor's presence amid the dinner guests acts as a catalyst for the narrator's venom, which becomes increasingly reactive to the immediate conversational stimuli. In a word, the Burgtheater actor, in becoming the narrator's foil, also becomes his muse, the reason and justification for his invective. The narrator reports the actor's unmotivated monologue to his captive dinner audience, having substituted the actor's own recollections, digressions, and points of criticism for his own, even if his reliability in relating them leaves something to be desired.[26] Later, too, when the actor declares "*[t]he forest, the virgin forest, the life of a woodcutter—that has always been my ideal*" (302; 170), Bernhard shows a formal sleight of hand in having deferred for nearly the entire book any reference to the enigmatic title, and the totalizing focus of the narrative perspective is at once respon-

---

25 Hackl, "Unterhaltung und Provokation: Thomas Bernhard als Satiriker des österreichischen Kulturbetriebs: 'Holzfällen. Eine Erregung,'" 135.
26 In allowing the narrator to sleep through the actor's arrival, the text papers over the perspectival inversion while downplaying the significance of this key moment promised in the first sentence of the novel.

sible. The apparent repetition of these words for some time went unnoticed by a narrator who had paid "no attention to what the actor was saying most of the time, catching only the odd half sentence, never a full sentence" (303; 171). Such frequent admissions, like Bernhard's repetitive insertion of "I thought," serve to relativize the narration by exposing the degree to which is it mediated. Their presence in the text stages a constant play of inversions through the narrator.

Excursus: Inversions and the Carnivalesque

To speak of inversions on the formal level, let us consider first the ways in which we might define them in a literary text. In the foregoing analysis I have employed the term inversion in one instance to denote a sudden change or shift in narrative perspective, having adapted it as the constitutive figure of Mikhail Bakhtin's notion of the carnivalesque. In that sense, however, inversion involves the abrogation of an established social order, the temporary suspension of a governing regulatory framework. In this carnivalesque paradigm, opposites mingle, and different laws pertain; Bakhtin refers in particular to inversions of order that allow different social classes to assume each other's roles, that admit the juxtaposition of high and low culture and style. In short, Bakhtin's carnivalesque involves the elimination of discursive hierarchies. To transfer the term into semiotic discourse thus requires a metaphoric transformation.

Because social orders in texts are themselves represented through the referential function of language, one must adjust the notion of the carnivalesque as the strategy of political, social, and cultural change it has become[27] to accord with its use as a possible literary device. Literary studies has indeed appropriated the term, even with respect to Thomas Bernhard,[28] but it most often connotes merely the free use of invective or cursing (an activity in which Bernhard rarely engages) or "the simultaneity of the eccentric (or the ill) and the realistic," which

---

[27] Sønke Gau and Katharina Schlieben, eds., *Spektakel, Lustprinzip oder das Karnevaleske?: Ein Reader über Möglichkeiten, Differenzerfahrungen und Strategien des Karnevalesken in kultureller/ politischer Praxis* (Berlin: B_Books, 2008).

[28] In this regard, see especially Adrian Stevens, "Schimpfen als künstlerischer Selbstentwurf: Karneval und Hermeneutik in Thomas Bernhards 'Auslöschung,'" in *Thomas Bernhard: Beiträge zur Fiktion der Postmoderne: Londoner Symposion*, ed. Wendelin Schmidt-Dengler, Adrian Stevens, and Fred Wagner (Frankfurt am Main: P. Lang, 1997), 61–91; Uwe Betz, *Polyphone Räume und karnevalisiertes Erbe: Analysen des Werks Thomas Bernhards auf der Basis Bachtinscher Theoreme* (Würzburg: Ergon, 1997).

equals "the material of grotesque realism"; Bernhard's conception of the body, the argument goes, "decomposes the notions of the ideal and of perfection in the monological, classical, or deductive spirit [...]: it relinquishes norm, beauty, and health as well as a temperate style in favor of 'slaughterhouse scenery' and an exuberant manner of speaking."[29] To be sure, an assessment of Bernhard's prose that witnesses in it the suspension of conventional, normative aesthetic categories is correct. This notion of inversion as an abrogation of norms, however, relies upon an interpretation of Bernhard's writing within a larger, extraliterary discourse of literary norms, an aspect of his work that is doubtless important but that nevertheless does not concern us here.

Of primary interest is rather the representation of the inversions we witness through the carnivalesque within the text itself or, to put it differently, the adaptation of the carnivalesque as a literary device. In order for such suspensions of discursive hierarchies to exist within the text, Bernhard must present the reader with both the normative system of order and its inversion; the text must represent what I termed elsewhere epistemological dissonance: the simultaneous presence of two manners of cognizing the world. In Bernhard's work, this epistemological dissonance through inversion may be found on the level of the narrative perspective as a structuring element that provides formal shape to the whole. We witness how the solipsistic view from the wing chair shifts suddenly, concurrently with the actor's arrival in the text, into an observational mode that also shifts the time of narration from the narrated past to the narrated present. Such an inversion throws into sharper relief the paradoxes of novelistic stagnation (on the part of the narrator's storytelling) and artistic stagnation (in what is related about the Auersbergers and their world) as the ultimate impetus behind literary creation (that which prompts the narrator to write). The (sub-)titular arousal in the text transforms representations of cognitive paralysis and stasis into the necessary conditions for dynamism and progression.

Leaving the narrative perspective aside, what follows will examine how carnivalesque inversion as a satiric practice may also be found in the narrator's propositions, and on the level of syntax and the individual signifier. The novel is thus organized around a series of carnivalesque moments, around inversions that stage the epistemological dissonance so characteristic of satire. With *Woodcutters* Thomas Bernhard delivers a satiric portrait of stagnant artistic life in 1980s Vienna that ultimately functions satirically on the deepest levels of signification and form.

---

29 Betz, *Polyphone Räume und karnevalisiertes Erbe*, 42.

Turned on Its Head

What prompts the narrator's surprising agreement to attend the dinner is unclear, even to himself; he knows only that it was "a grave mistake" (7; 3) to have accepted the invitation and "a piece of monumental folly" (8; 4) to have delivered himself into the hands of his enemies by entering their habitat on the Graben. The circumstances of his acceptance are repeated throughout the text and bear closer analysis as the entire nightmarish evening stems, for the narrator, from an inversion. A stronger character would not have been susceptible to the Auersbergers' entreaties, he claims, "but I'm not strong and I've no strength of character: on the contrary I'm the very weakest person, with the very weakest character, and that's what makes me more or less everyone's victim" (12; 6). Such qualitative oppositions are familiar to readers of Bernhard's prose; this oppositional leap from one quality to its superlative opposite, as we shall see, structures many of the logical claims in *Woodcutters* and constitutes an exaggerated inversion that one encounters frequently in Bernhard's oeuvre.[30]

At first, the narrator makes the repeated claim that he has broken off contact with the Auersbergers for twenty years – "having resolved to have nothing more to do with them for the rest of my life" (13; 6) – but that one moment of weakness and sentimentality is exploited "immediately" (13; 6) by his interlocutors with an "abrupt invitation" (77; 44) that they issue "today and now and here" (18; 9 [translation amended, DB]) which he accepts "at once [*blitzartig*]" (13; 6) and just as abruptly (77; 44). What is remarkable about this recollection, which recurs several times in the text, is the suffusion of modifiers that describe the incredible suddenness with which the encounter and the decision to accept the invitation take place. The narrator recounts an immediate diametric, seismic shift in intention that takes even him by surprise. Even the manner by which he is invited – "they *came up on me from behind*" (13; 7) – speaks to his perception of an ambush and to the peculiarly (and literally) backward circumstances of their encounter which continue to perplex him; "*They came up from behind and spoke to you*, I told myself; they'd probably been *observing you from behind* for some time, *fol-*

---

30 Compare, for example, the swiftly alternating extremes in *Walking* [*Gehen*] or the structuring inversions – the turn in the "opposite direction," for example – in Bernhard's autobiographical volumes *The Cause: An Allusion* [*Die Ursache: An Allusion*] and *The Cellar: A Withdrawal* [*Der Keller: Eine Entziehung*]. Thomas Bernhard, *Gehen* (Frankfurt am Main: Suhrkamp, 1971); Thomas Bernhard, "Walking," in *Three Novellas*, trans. Peter K. Jansen and Kenneth J. Northcott (Chicago: University of Chicago Press, 2003); Thomas Bernhard, *Die Autobiographie*, ed. Martin Huber and Manfred Mittermayer, vol. 10, *Werke* (Frankfurt am Main: Suhrkamp, 2004).

lowing you and observing you, and then *suddenly [blitzartig]*, *when the time was ripe*, they addressed you" (24; 13).

In a telling parallel, however, this way of lurking behind one's interlocutor mirrors the narrator's own voyeuristic method of observation: "We learn a great deal, I reflected in the wing chair, if we observe people from behind when they are unaware of being observed, observing them for as long [as] we can, prolonging our ruthless and monstrous observation for as long as possible without addressing them" (27; 15). Precious little differentiates the narrator's manner of observation from that of the Auersbergers. "They saw that I was the observer," the narrator himself notes, "the repulsive person who had made himself comfortable in the wing chair and was playing his disgusting observation game in the semidarkness of the anteroom, more or less *taking the guests apart*" (83; 47). His analytic gaze is precisely that which the Burgtheater actor, agitated by Jeannie Billroth's indiscreet question, finds repellent among people "who were there only to take you apart, as he put it, *to dissect you into all your component parts*" (295; 166). Given that the relative differences between these perfidious modes of analytic observation may only be determined by the intentions imputed to the observer, the reader must rely exclusively on the characterizations of these intentions by an admittedly unreliable narrator.[31] His voyeuristic observations from the wing chair, one may interpret from his observational perch in the darkness, are on par with passive spectatorship in a theater. On the other hand, as if being followed by predators on the hunt for prey, the narrator speaks of the "ruthlessness," the "monstrous inhumanity" (27; 15) with which his old friends subject him to their hidden observation before striking "quite suddenly [*urplötzlich*]" (77; 44) and "*when the time was ripe*" (24; 13).

Indeed, here as elsewhere, the text bespeaks decisive moments of immediate shifts in direction: either the escape from the deleterious influences of the Auersbergers and their circle (21–22; 11–12), the sudden return to art (89–90; 51), the decisive escape from Vienna and residence abroad as the guarantee of artistic survival (98; 56), the moment of sudden reversal when friend suddenly becomes foe (162–163; 91–92), or the exploitation of (and escape from) others "at the right moment" (220–221; 126). The suddenness of the narrator's acceptance of the

---

[31] If the unreliability of the narrator is not established by the pathological behavior the reader witnesses and the highly individuated and thus subjective point of view, *Woodcutters* demonstrates it through the repeated failure of his logic and his self-contradictions. Towards the beginning of the text, to name but one example, the narrator describes his disgust with the Auersbergers "because they were in every way the exact *opposite* of myself" (76; 43) while conceding later that an opposition between us and those we hate really means that, "if we are honest, we do have dealings with them and are no different from them" (316; 178).

Auersbergers' invitation, the reversal of twenty years of loathing (7–8; 3) and thirty years of entrapment (21–22; 11), constitutes the first inversion, "a classic illustration of the irrational way one reacts under stress [*Kurzschlußhandlung*]" (77), staged by the text. It is a lightning-fast moment of self-negation wherein the narrator admits that he "acted contrary to my nature, and tonight I turned not only my character, but my whole nature, on its head" (32; 18 [translation amended, DB]). The image of having negated and inverted the order of one's identity or belief system – having literally turned everything upside down – is an apt one to represent the ways in which the narrator's subsequent statements, taken as logical propositions, confront the reader with a constant rhetoric of inversion, "a complete about-face" (89; 51 [translation amended, DB]); the initial proposition is overtaken by its negative image: its reversal, its negation, or its opposite.

By citing certain epistemological paradigms in the first-person plural, for example, the narrator both asserts their generality and offers a corrective version with his perception of their actual incommensurability with reality. The result is an "exaggerated discrepancy between the narrator's maxims and the reader's empirical experience of accepted modes of behavior."[32] The inversion from revered friend to hated foe, the narrator argues for example, takes place suddenly and without explanation (224; 123), but the plural "we" by which the text purports to make a valid generalization conflicts with the consistently individuated narrative perspective and the self-imposed isolation of the narrator that dominate the novel. Their hollow ring notwithstanding, the narrator's claims present a clash of paradoxes between perception and reality; "We think we have rights when we have no rights of any kind, I thought. No one has any rights, I thought. There's nothing but injustice in the world, I thought. Human beings are unjust, and injustice prevails everywhere—that's the truth, I thought. Injustice is all we have to hand, I thought" (163–164; 93). Belief and reality, the narrator declares, are opposed to one another. Even in its most egregious of generalizations, however, the text consistently relativizes the purported truth of the narrator's claims by referring it back to the narrative perspective. The phrase "I thought," repeated at the end of each of these five sentences, reveals every one of the narrator's declarations to be nothing but a subjective, individual thought; the punctuation of universalizing claims with references to the cognitive processes of an unreliable

---

[32] Long, *The Novels of Thomas Bernhard*, 145. Long locates twenty-five instances of the narrator's use of the first-person plural in such constructions. For specific page numbers, see his footnote 14.

narrator undermines the veracity of the former. The very figure of repetition and repetitive syntax as a narrative strategy in *Woodcutters* likewise casts doubt on the believability of his assertions.

Repetition as a Mechanism for Inversion

How does the repetition of syntax undermine the truth value of the narrator's claims? To answer this question, one must consider the role repetition plays on the narrative and formal levels of the text. Within the story itself the narrator frequently refers to words and phrases repeated time and again, including the titular woodcutters. These recurrences include snippets of conversation heard from the wing chair – *"death," "suicide," "hanged,"* (43; 24) – but also signifiers recited aloud: "Several times I repeated to myself the word *the artistic world* and *the artistic life*. I actually spoke them out loud, in such a way that people in the music room were bound to hear them—as indeed they did, for all their heads suddenly turned in my direction" (90–91; 52). This is not the last time the narrator cuts a peculiar figure, drawing attention to himself while he sits in the wing chair. Shortly after revealing himself in the darkness behind the guests, the narrator ponders the possibility of his having merely pretended to accept the invitation to the Auersbergers' dinner party. The thought plagues him to the extreme, demonstrating the rhetorical powers of persuasion through repetition: "I pursued this idea to the point at which I finally *believed* it" (106; 60). Setting up a curious parallelism between the pathological nature of both his manner of repetition and that of his intoxicated host, however, the narrator mutters to himself again in an effort to lead his thought to its logical conclusion:

> Ich atmete tief ein und sagte mir und zwar so, daß es die Leute im Musikzimmer hören mußten, *du hast nur ein vorgespieltes Leben, kein wirkliches gelebt, nur eine vorgespielte Existenz, keine tatsächliche, alles, was dich betrifft und alles, das du bist, ist immer nur ein vorgespieltes, kein tatsächliches und kein wirkliches gewesen*. Ich mußte diese Spekulation aber abbrechen, um nicht verrückt zu werden, wie ich auf dem Ohrensessel dachte. (106)

> I drew a deep breath and said to myself, in such a way that the people in the music room were bound to hear it: *You've always lived a life of pretense, not a real life—a simulated existence, not a genuine existence. Everything about you, everything you are, has always been pretense, never genuine, never real*. But I must put an end to this fantasizing lest I go mad, I thought, sitting in the wing chair. (60)

The possibility that the narrator might in fact be insane looms large throughout *Woodcutters* in these and other instances, the vehicle for the expression of which is often repetition, both narrative and formal.

My assessment of repetition in the Bernhard's text is predicated not solely on the narrator. Again and again the narrator points out other instances of repetition, signifiers and phrases repeated aloud, as if only to make noise. These include "*urban quagmire*" and "*rural idyll*" (34; 19), "*Ekdal*" (116–117; 66–67), "*Joana was always an unhappy girl*" (124; 70), "*negligence*" (161; 91), "*Joana—a Spanish name*" (212; 121), "*ideally*" (213; 122), "*how tasteless*" (230, 262; 131, 149), "*you're making yourself ridiculous*" (235; 134), "*someone to paper over the marital cracks*" (268; 152), "*totally pulverized*" (281; 159), "*actually dead*" (283; 160), "*you're right*" (285–286; 161), "*the remaindered goods*" (287; 162), "*this person*" (296; 167), and "*the forest, the virgin forest, the life of a woodcutter*" (311; 170). In several of these cases the text alludes to the bemused reactions of those in earshot and from whom such repetitions elicit either laughter "because his mumbling sounded so comic" (283; 160) or irritation at the negativity of thoughts like "*The human race ought to be abolished*, a pronouncement with which [Auersberger] more than once attracted the attention of the company in the music room, delivering it with rhythmic precision that came from his musical training" (247–248; 141); "But my dear Auersberger, [the Burgtheater actor] said, *what's the matter with you?* [...] *Why do you get so worked up and run everything down when everything is essentially so agreeable and well ordered?* Having said this, he added, *Why do you have to drink yourself almost into a stupor?*" (248; 141). The increasing inebriation of the dinner party's host and his penchant to become fixated on certain words link the repetition of words and phrases in the narrative diegesis to the loss of one's wits, to intoxication. Those who repeat themselves, the text implicitly argues, are untrustworthy or unstable, and this, combined with the link between repetition and madness in the case of the narrator, has further implications for the repetition of the text itself (i. e. the formal level) as well.

Repetition may thus be counted as a mode of pathological behavior, especially with regard to Auersberger and the narrator whose "notorious strangeness and oddity, [...] *dangerous eccentricity*" and "*quite disturbing madness*" (44; 25) draw the attention of the dinner party attendees. "*What a disgusting character you are!* The words were addressed only to myself—no one else could hear them— and I went on addressing myself, working myself into a state of growing agitation," the narrator recounts in pondering his animosity toward Jeannie Billroth, "*You* betrayed Jeannie—*she* didn't betray *you*, I told myself more than once, and I went on repeating it to myself until I was utterly exhausted" (235; 134). Here, unlike before when the narrator aborted his speculations to keep from driving himself mad, repetition leads to exhaustion, to the point of foreclosing further thought, as a kind of self-castigation. That in this instance his whispered admonitions take place at the dinner table among the many dinner guests rather than from the seclusion of his wing chair further estranges him from the banal normality he

4. Perspective and Repetition in Thomas Bernhard's *Woodcutters* (1984) — 77

sees in the other dinner guests whose exhaustion at the late hour guarantees their silence (235; 134). The presence of a judgmental, possibly mad narrator amid the judged – the presence of him who loathes among the loathed – suggests a symptomatic relationship between repetition and an abrogation of order, between Bernhard's primary narrative strategy and the figure of inversion, and thus ultimately between the carnivalesque and the satiric: that the allegedly reasonable mingle with the allegedly unreasonable, the ostensibly healthy with the ostensibly sick, the purportedly sane with the purportedly mad. In suspending an order of logic by repeating oppositional statements, the narrator does not so much erect a new, opposing epistemology; his own questionable reliability undermines his position. "Inversion does not thus set the right circumstances aright," one scholar suggests more generally, "but rather 'maintains' in its instability what has always already been inverted."[33] The repeated signifiers on the narrative level, moreover, establish an association of repetition with cognitive or mental instability that likewise plays out on the metanarrative level.

Just as repetition pervades the story, so too does it dominate the syntactic structure of the text. "Repetition, which is perhaps the most striking characteristic of Bernhard's work," as one critic claims, "plays a constitutive role in organizing the motivic material."[34] To be sure, Bernhard uses repetition to great effect in *Woodcutters* as a means of organizing his text, but its ubiquity in the novel, coupled with its function as a symptom of logical breakdown, has further significance. As the repetition of signifiers served to undermine the truth value of the narrator's claims, so too does syntactic repetition function as a mechanism for ensuring a certain mode of reading. Repeated structures like "I thought, sitting in the wing chair" or Bernhard's penchant for nominalizing strings of repeated verbs and adjectives (and the reverse) – the transformation of "destroyed [*zerstört*]" and "annihilated [*vernichtet*]" into "destroyers [*Zerstörer*]" and "murderers [*Vernichter*]" (20–21; 11), for example, or of "depressing [*deprimiert*]" to "something depressing [*Deprimierendes*]" to "depression [*Depression*]" (93; 53) – lend the text the character of a patchwork of discrete motivic units, to employ a musical metaphor, which the author shifts, distorts, and displaces but nevertheless maintains as the building blocks for the narrative.

Words and phrases highlighted in italics, for instance, pepper the pages of the text, often as fragments of direct quotations the narrator repeats again and again, visually demarcating the text into thematic blocks. These typographic

---

[33] Kovács, "Autor und Leser als Richter: Forensische und rhetorische Lektüren zu Thomas Bernhards 'Holzfällen,'" 115.
[34] Ingen, "Thomas Bernhards 'Holzfällen' oder die Kunst der Invektive," 279.

signposts direct attention to themselves by dint of their visual difference from the text and may serve to indicate a particular narrative tone (emphatic, mocking, parroting) as a medium of an emotive function of language. Such repetitions, be they italic or on the order of a larger syntactic structure, forestall the narrative through recursion to prior structures and formulations. Through this delay and unsettling of narrative progression – that is, of the continuation of plot development – they foreground the manipulation of signifiers and syntax as a means of conveying a metanarrative of instability and stagnation. That unstable, stagnant language is reflected in the ultimate instability of the narrative perspective is of further interest. Bernhard's use of inversion as a dominant semiotic practice in *Woodcutters* has wide-ranging ramifications for both narrative and metanarrative signification, for it affects the formal structure of the narrative and constructs a metanarrative of opposition and instability.

Such narrative stagnation might also be read as a figure of inversion of its own. Given that the text compiles the narrator's recounted thoughts in no discernible overarching order, the subtitle "An Agitation" rather than the more traditional "A Novel" seems provocatively apt. Narrative progression yields to narrative stagnation; mimesis and representation give way to the grotesque. Bernhard thus circumvents genre conventions by providing an inversion of them. What inverts these conventions, practically speaking, are the repetitions of syntax. Aside from the references to his wing chair, the narrator also repeats blocks of thoughts: his notion that he should rather have stayed at home to read Gogol, Pascal, and Montaigne or to play Satie or Schönberg, for example, or the account of his run-in with the Auersbergers in the Graben and their mention of Joana's suicide. These repetitions give the narrative a recursive quality also seen in the repeated syntactic constructions.

Whether in Bernhard's nominalizations or the hyperbolic intensification of language that results from a frequent use of superlatives, the use of repetitive syntax in *Woodcutters* frequently occurs at nodal points in the text. When the narrator finally concludes that his acceptance of the dinner party invitation was "madness" (157; 89), for example, he begins excoriating the Auersbergers in a generalization of the traps laid by patrons rich in material possessions, "and as we ourselves have none of these things, we walk into their trap" (157; 89). In the course of two pages, the phrase "we walk into their trap" occurs in various iterations and permutations thirteen times in successive sentences and clauses, each time with brief expansions. Variations on "pretend [sich den Anschein *geben*]" (164; 93) recur twenty-four times in the course of five pages, perhaps in a rhetorical effort to produce truth through repetition, to persuade the reader that in fact everyone, like the Auersbergers, is merely semblance, not natural reality.

4. Perspective and Repetition in Thomas Bernhard's *Woodcutters* (1984)

In *Woodcutters*, Thomas Bernhard suspends novelistic conventions of narrative progression and questions the reliability of the narrator with his use of repetition in the service of a series of inversions. The established order, the narrator declares, is one of stagnation and lack of productivity. The inversions in this text thus show Bernhard's attempt to counter the stagnation of the Austrian art world, which the narrator criticizes, with a satiric rendering of the agitation this stagnation causes; from the status quo of stultified petrifaction comes the manic, hyperbolic madness of creativity.

5. Destructive Negativity: Thomas Bernhard and *Extinction* (1986)

The very hyperbole and negative rhetoric that comprise the breathless narration in Thomas Bernhard's works also serve as the subject of an interesting, if perplexing methodological question that comes into sharper focus with Bernhard's novelistic swansong, *Extinction*. In reckoning with the narrative strategies in Bernhard's works by way of the narratives themselves, critics refer repeatedly to the destructive negativity of his stories.[1] For some, this ostensible destructiveness constitutes a poetic principle,[2] however vague, while still others see the use of destructive language as a means of foreclosing the possibility of identity formation through narration[3] or, in the particular case of *Extinction*, as complicit in the narrator's endeavor to compose a text that will extirpate everything related to and represented by his childhood home.[4] What is remarkable and simultaneously confounding about this approach to Bernhard's work is the degree to which any actual destructive potential is ascribed to the language in the text.

To be sure, Bernhard's own epithet for himself – "destroyer of stories [*Geschichtenzerstörer*]"[5] – has enticed critics as a sufficient condition for explaining away Bernhard's writing as destructive.[6] Aside from the critical insufficiencies of such an approach to Bernhard, consistent recourse to descriptive metaphors suggests an overarching problem in cognizing Bernhard's hyperbole and nega-

---

[1] As a counter-example, one critic reads the negativity of Bernhard's invective in *Auslöschung* as a sign of its creative engagement with the carnivalesque. See Stevens, "Schimpfen als künstlerischer Selbstentwurf: Karneval und Hermeneutik in Thomas Bernhards 'Auslöschung'."

[2] Anke Gleber, "'Auslöschung. Ein Zerfall': Thomas Bernhards Poetik der Destruktion und Reiteration," *Modern Austrian Literature* 24, no. 3/4 (1991): 85–97; Silke Schlichtmann, *Das Erzählprinzip "Auslöschung": Zum Umgang mit Geschichte in Thomas Bernhards Roman "Auslöschung, ein Zerfall"* (Frankfurt am Main: P. Lang, 1996); Georg Jansen, *Prinzip und Prozess Auslöschung: Intertextuelle Destruktion und Konstitution des Romans bei Thomas Bernhard* (Würzburg: Königshausen & Neumann, 2005).

[3] Sylvia Kaufmann, *The Importance of Romantic Aesthetics for the Interpretation of Thomas Bernhard's "Auslöschung. Ein Zerfall" and "Alte Meister. Komödie"* (Stuttgart: Heinz, 1998), 55–59; Eun-Hee Ryu, *Auflösung und Auslöschung: Genese von Thomas Bernhards Prosa im Hinblick auf die "Studie"* (Frankfurt am Main: P. Lang, 1998), 269.

[4] Martin Schierbaum, "'noch kein Schriftsteller hat die Wirklichkeit so beschrieben wie sie wirklich ist das ist das Fürchterliche': Literatur und Politik bei Thomas Bernhard am Beispiel von 'Auslöschung' und 'Heldenplatz,'" in *An den Rändern der Moral: Studien zur literarischen Ethik: Ulrich Wergin gewidmet*, ed. Ulrich Kinzel (Würzburg: Königshausen & Neumann, 2008), 160.

[5] Thomas Bernhard, *Der Italiener* (Salzburg: Residenz Verlag, 1971), 88.

[6] Long, *The Novels of Thomas Bernhard*, 1–26, here: 2–3.

tivity. In adopting the metaphors Bernhard employs, discussions about them consistently overlook the blind spot of their own metaphoricity, like the frequent impressionism of writing about Bernhard's alleged musical prose, thus betraying what would appear to be a "need to paper over interpretive cluelessness when faced with unconventional texts."[7] Indeed, the narrators of Bernhard's works, particularly in *Extinction*, seem to have the last laugh. Although linguistic repetition on the part of unreliable narrators is one of Bernhard's hallmarks,[8] readers repeatedly slip from the safe vantage point of critical distance and fall prey to the allure of believing the veracity of the apodictic assertions in the texts. Bernhard's metaphors of destruction and negation thus take on a new layer of metatextual meaning by occluding a view to the semiotic workings of his writing. Put differently, the qualitative aspects of Bernhard's hyperbole and negativity join forces with their quantitative ubiquity to appear as narrative devices of actual destruction, as a "weapon against a society and its dominant discourse."[9] Such a conception of the inner workings of Bernhard's writing, of its metatextual organization, attributes to the signifier a power to upset and destroy the discourse of which it is a part. The specific semiotic strategies Bernhard uses to create this effect, I argue, are satiric and constitute a particular mode of writing that engenders a particular mode of reading.

Foremost among these narrative practices is the figure of inversion. Derived from a literarization of the carnivalesque, inversion in Bernhard's *Extinction* assumes many of the same guises it had adopted in his novel *Woodcutters*: epistemological dissonance, the upsetting of norms, logical inconsistencies, and repetition, among others. Here, however, Bernhard's cache of satiric techniques of inversion expands to include a different constellation of narrative perspectives, an intertextual engagement with his own oeuvre, and a resulting dialogic ambivalence that signifies a vestigial presence of carnivalesque forms in his text. Rather than to construct a filiation of ideas and practices that filter from theory into practice, however, the aim here is to demonstrate the genealogy of a satiric practice the legacy of which can be traced through both theoretical and literary writings.

---

7 Irmgard Scheitler, "Musik als Thema und Struktur in deutscher Gegenwartsprosa," *Euphorion* 92, no. 1 (1998): 83–84.
8 Hackl, "Unterhaltung und Provokation: Thomas Bernhard als Satiriker des österreichischen Kulturbetriebs: 'Holzfällen. Eine Erregung,'" 137; Alexandra Barbara Scheu, "'Ich schreibe eine ungeheure Schrift': Sprache und Identitätsverlust in Thomas Bernhards 'Auslöschung,'" *Thomas-Bernhard-Jahrbuch*, 2005, 65.
9 Gleber, "'Auslöschung. Ein Zerfall': Thomas Bernhards Poetik der Destruktion und Reiteration," 89.

In this chapter, Thomas Bernhard's last novel, *Extinction*, serves as a third and final case study for the notion of carnivalesque inversion as a satiric practice. In the foregoing chapters on Mikhail Bakhtin's *Rabelais and His World* and Bernhard's *Woodcutters*, the focal point is how figures of inversion become literary and function semiotically. Here, too, inversion takes center stage: in the carnival elements in the narrative perspective of *Extinction*; in the figure of Gambetti and his laughter as relativizing forces on the grotesque hyperbole of Murau; in the prominent use of repetition as a carnivalesque technique and its role in textual signification; and, finally, in the novel's intertextual nature.[10]

Bernhard's deployment of the figure of inversion does not amount to a wholesale borrowing of ahistorical carnival forms from Bakhtin's elaboration of them. On the contrary, in *Extinction* the reader witnesses the productive tensions that arise between the carnivalesque as a historical element of Renaissance culture and writing on the one hand, and the ways in which Bernhard deploys it in the landscape of late twentieth-century literary production on the other. As a quintessential and unmistakable aspect of Thomas Bernhard's mode of writing, inversion thus ironically invites an ambivalent understanding of its literary function. It operates as a narrative strategy that organizes, alters, disrupts, and obscures the signification of language within a text belonging to traditionally theoretical or literary discourses, and yet inversion may be seen beyond the realm of semiotic practices as a metaphor for the upsetting of social and cultural epistemes and, in Bernhard's case, for the self-understanding of his cultural *métier*. Satire, that is to say, may be understood as a mode of writing that employs specific semiotic devices or, insofar as one may interpret a literary rendering of satire as a social construct, as a political act activated by a particular mode of reading.

"... writes Franz-Josef Murau ..."

As a text narrated in the first person, *Extinction* is no outlier among Thomas Bernhard's literary output.[11] What differentiates it from Bernhard's other novelistic works, however, are matters of layered narrative perspective and framing. Summaries of the text's plot in the critical scholarship are legion and ultimately do not affect the discussion at hand, but suffice it to say, we may identify the primary

---

10 Intertextuality, which will be addressed later in detail, might indeed be considered a satiric practice subordinated to the carnivalesque.
11 Nowhere in his novelistic writing does Thomas Bernhard venture into third-person narration except through reported speech.

narrative voice as a certain Franz-Josef Murau, whose reflections and recollections constitute the majority of Bernhard's longest text. Through his narrative omnipresence Murau also functions as the protagonist of the novel; he reports in hindsight the instigating moment of narration – receiving the telegram that announces his parents' and brother's demise – and, with a series of three photographs of his family to activate his memory, muses upon "the distorted and perverted world"[12] represented as real in their images. Photography, "the devil's art" (243; 121), thus provides a catalyst for remembrance and narration but also acts as a medium for representing reality as a distorted inversion of the real, as "a monstrous falsification of nature, a base insult to humanity" (27; 13). Photographic snapshots distort reality, he attests, by altering human perception through a mutilating act of metonymy. A famous photograph of Albert Einstein, for example, forever transforms the scientist and thinker in his imagination into "that cunning, malignant tongue, stuck out at the whole world, indeed the whole universe" (244; 122), just as Winston Churchill is forever replaced by "his distrustfully prominent Churchillian lower lip" (245; 122 [translation amended, DB]). As one scholar has pointed out, "Murau here offers a radically metonymic reading of photography, which inverts the relationship between photographs and their referents: our access to reality is *mediated* by photographs, rather than being *represented in* them."[13] The narrator's perspective is nevertheless a privileged one capable of perceiving a palimpsest of truth behind the patina of falsification and fakery.

In viewing the images of his family, Murau circumvents the problem of the photographs as a distorting record of reality by attributing to himself a kind of clairvoyant sight that looks beyond the mere signifier: "the longer I look at the distorted images of my parents and my brother in these pictures [...] the more I see the truth and reality of these so-called subjects behind the perversity and distortion. This is because I'm not concerned with the photos as such; I don't see the people portrayed in them as they are shown by the distorting lens of the camera but as I myself see them" (30; 15 [translation amended, DB]). In this highly subjective position, Murau installs himself as the sole arbiter of truth and reality while simultaneously deconstructing a notion of the real as factually given or whole; he brooks no false embellishment: "Only the true, the genuine likenesses.

---

[12] Thomas Bernhard, *Auslöschung: Ein Zerfall* (Frankfurt am Main: Suhrkamp, 1986), 29; Thomas Bernhard, *Extinction: A Novel*, trans. David McLintock (New York: Alfred A. Knopf, 1995), 14. References to *Extinction* in this chapter will appear in the text parenthetically, with dual pages numbers of the German originals and their English translations, separated by a semicolon.
[13] J. J. Long, "'Die Teufelskunst unserer Zeit'? Photographic Negotiations in Thomas Bernhard's 'Auslöschung,'" *Modern Austrian Literature* 35, no. 3/4 (2002): 81.

Only what is absolutely authentic, however grotesque, and possibly even repulsive" (27; 13 [translation amended, DB]). Filtered through photography, reality, Murau notes, is irrevocably altered, but his rehabilitative gaze discerns the authentic truth that nevertheless lies concealed within the distorted perversion of the representation.

What is significant about this seemingly contradictory stance are two things. First, the text reveals through Murau's argumentation a carnivalesque inversion of an epistemology according to which an objective gaze more closely and correctly perceives universal truth. Murau instead radicalizes the notion of individuated perspective and accords it a significance and privilege of perception by arguing that reality as such is always a mere mediated construction. His acknowledgement of its constructedness frees him from the constraints of its order; the proposition of non-individuated reality, that is, of universal truth, dissolves before the radically and insistently individual perspective of the narrator: "Everyone who describes a person sees him differently, I reflected. So many people describing the same person, each looking at him from a different viewpoint, a different angle of vision, produce as many differing views, I told myself" (550–551; 277). Individual subjectivity thus supplants mediated objectivity, in part because it is the only possibility.

One might, like Bakhtin, object to the description of such a figure of inversion as carnivalesque in its shift from universality to individuality, but Bernhard uses literary means to sidestep this objection. While installing Murau as the (partial, opinionated, polemical, subjective) narrative arbiter of reality – and this is the second, significant aspect regarding the novel's assessment of photography – the text simultaneously grants him access to all levels of narrative time. Put differently, Murau reveals the limitations of photographic representation as an ostensibly objective medium by drawing attention to constraints of its mediation and to those of its temporal representation. In fixing a single moment in time, photography falls short of the capabilities of an individual, viewing subject to recount history. Photography may therefore evoke remembrance, but the history of remembrance is not inscribed within the image, only the suggestion thereof. What Murau sees and what his narration ultimately activates from these photographs is the naked truth of past memory, present condition, and future implication. Multiple temporal levels of narration refract his recollections through a layeredness of narrative discourse that suggests, in a Bakhtinian sense, the grotesque simultaneity of past, present, and future: the distant past events in Wolfsegg; the recent past occurrences in Rome and Wolfsegg; the immediate past reflections on the photographs in Rome and his travel to Wolfsegg; the present moment of Murau's transcription of his *Extinction*; the present moment of the minimalist frame story; and the future intimated by Murau's relinquishment and donation of Wolfsegg.

5. Destructive Negativity: Thomas Bernhard and *Extinction* (1986)

The function of photography "to make present that which is absent, and to signal the absence of the thing it stands for"[14] is assumed by the narrative, which conveys the ambivalence of simultaneous presence and absence through narrative recollection of life and death, and through the titular project of eliminating every trace of memory by, ironically, leaving extensive written traces.

The irony that Murau's own project to write a report that will extirpate Wolfsegg bears the same title as Bernhard's novel has not escaped notice[15] and should not be taken lightly.[16] To presume an equivalence between the novel itself and Murau's undertaking, however, is to ignore the complexity of the semantic ambivalence that surrounds the term *Extinction* in the text.[17] Unlike other works by Bernhard in which narrators and protagonists engage in writing within the diegesis (*The Lime Works* [*Das Kalkwerk*], *Correction* [*Korrektur*], *The Loser* [*Der Untergeher*], to name but three examples), *Extinction* positions Murau's project in close semantic proximity to the novel itself, albeit without insisting upon an identity between them. The novel's curious suggestion of a relation between the textual diegesis and itself maintains a narrative ambivalence between reality and representation that does not allow the doubleness – the distinction between the novel *Extinction* and Murau's report – to resolve definitively. Only once in one of the few moments of present-tense narration does Murau provide the reader with an enticingly explicit indexical link to "this work entitled *Extinction*" (651; 326) that would encode the novel through deixis as identical to the narrator's project.[18] This posited identity between report and novel is immediately subverted, however, by the presence, minimal though it is, of an extradiegetic narrator who adds a second level of observational distance, embedding Murau within the narrowest of narrative frames.[19] As one critic suggests, the unnamed frame narrator

---

[14] Long, "'Die Teufelskunst unserer Zeit'? Photographic Negotiations in Thomas Bernhard's 'Auslöschung,'" 90.
[15] Eva Marquardt, "Die halbe Wahrheit: Bernhards antithetische Schreibweise am Beispiel des Romans 'Auslöschung,'" in *Wissenschaft als Finsternis?*, ed. Martin Huber and Wendelin Schmidt-Dengler (Wien: Böhlau, 2002), 88.
[16] To conclude, as some have, that the novel itself is identical with Murau's report is a judgment with which I disagree. To conflate one with the other is to conflate, as Murau warns, the photographic representation with the reality. For an opposing view, see Long, *The Novels of Thomas Bernhard*, 171.
[17] Schlichtmann, *Das Erzählprinzip "Auslöschung,"* 23–27.
[18] The deictic reference to *Extinction* signifies differently in present and past tenses; in the present Murau alludes to its completion while in the past mode of recollection, Murau reflects upon his plans for an as yet uncompleted document.
[19] J. J. Long points out that several critics have mistakenly and without an adequate textual basis argued that the extradiegetic narrator is an editor of Murau's *Nachlass*. He counterargues that the

and framing device itself present Murau's study as a citation of an absent original, the effacement of authenticity, which further distances the reader from the documented extirpation.[20]

Furthering complicating the identity of report and novel are Murau's disparate accounts of his intentions. On the one hand, he attempts with it "to extinguish everything that comes into my head. Everything I write about in this *Extinction* will be extinguished, I told myself" (542; 273 [translation amended, DB]). On the other hand, his plan to undertake such an extirpation of discourse arises from an almost filial desire to carry on the unfinished "*Anti-autobiography*" (188; 94) of his mentor and fellow oppositional figure Uncle Georg: "but since [his Anti-autobiography] no longer exists, it falls to me to take a dispassionate look at Wolfsegg and report what I see" (197; 98). Murau's *Extinction* is thus simultaneously, in the latter case, a sober documentation of autobiographical tribulations and a metaphorical means of extinguishing these from existence by effacing them from posterity. In a carnivalesque move, the promised extirpation – as the negativity of the novel's rhetoric – does not aim so much for destruction as it does for renewal. Relating his intentions to suspend the order of the world as it exists, Murau notes that his student Gambetti shows great fascination when he hears "how the world should be changed, by first radically *destroying* it, by virtually *annihilating* it, and then restoring it in a form that I find tolerable, as a completely new world—[...] since it's impossible to renew it without first annihilating it" (209; 104). Countering critics who have decried the ostensibly destructive rhetoric of the text, Murau's negativity aims for a carnivalesque elimination of hegemonic order *and* for its renewal, "to restore a sense of history."[21] His hyperbolic statements to Gambetti in this regard likewise elicit an infectious laughter that has been shown to be "implicit self-criticism, a relativization of Murau's own conceptual categories and structuring procedures"[22] and "the debunking of all that occupies an elevated

---

more important issue at stake is one of narrative transmission and the problem "that in a novel so concerned with questions of contextualization, he remains utterly uncontextualized" but simultaneously essential and relativizing in claiming over Murau himself "an absolute, self-sustaining legitimacy." *The Novels of Thomas Bernhard: Form and Its Function* (Rochester, NY: Camden House, 2001), 184–185; see also Georg Jansen's monograph which, in its comparison of Bernhard's novel to Kafka's *Proceß*, is predicated throughout upon the notion of the extradiegetic narrator as Murau's editor. *Prinzip und Prozess Auslöschung: Intertextuelle Destruktion und Konstitution des Romans bei Thomas Bernhard* (Würzburg: Königshausen & Neumann, 2005).

20 Gernot Weiß, *Auslöschung der Philosophie: Philosophiekritik bei Thomas Bernhard* (Würzburg: Königshausen & Neumann, 1993), 144.
21 Long, *The Novels of Thomas Bernhard*, 173.
22 Long, *The Novels of Thomas Bernhard*, 176.

position in the hierarchies of power."²³ The vehicle for this unsettling of certainty and earnestness is Murau's interlocutor and a constant presence within the narrative: his student Gambetti.

Gambetti, Hyperbole, and Carnival Laughter

Like the unnamed narrator in the wing chair in Bernhard's text *Woodcutters*, Murau in *Extinction* situates himself spatially and temporally through incessant repetitions of an *inquit*. Variations of the formula "I told Gambetti" recur over 500 times in the first section of the text, entitled "The Telegram," punctuating the narrative with interruptive reminders of reported speech.²⁴ Positioned already as citations by the narrative frame, Murau's written recollections are filtered through layer after layer of mediated subjectivity; the *inquit* both reminds the reader that the narration consists of speech recorded at a temporal distance and structures the text as an alternating, fragmented series of time strata. In the flow of narration – and, more concretely, the visual monotone blocks of text – the reader continually faces the challenge of determining the time of narration which, because of the *inquit* interrupters, may shift from clause to clause.

What may strike an idle reader as an (anti-)autobiographical monologue of undifferentiated disquisitions upon family, state, and self reveals itself formally to have a sophisticated time structure and constellation of narrative perspectives. Murau's repetitive reminders that he is reporting speech once uttered to his student Gambetti function as a carnivalesque satiric strategy of their own, messily relativizing the temporal organization of the novel. In spite of their resemblance to the repetitious *inquit* formulations in other Bernhard novels, these textual markers constitute a unique narrative dynamic in *Extinction* that further relativizes the narrative.

The 'monomaniacal' swells of first-person narration that have so often exasperated the critical establishment²⁵ are subject to a narrative inversion through the

---

23 Long, *The Novels of Thomas Bernhard*, 177.
24 By my count there are 542 occurrences of this *inquit* (or permutations thereof in the preterite) in the first section of the novel and 658 total in the novel. The reader will encounter the first on page eight (page four in the English translation) although the repetition does not begin in earnest until page 103 (in the English: 52). My count, while fastidious, has doubtless missed several other repetitions in the text.
25 See Oliver Jahraus, *Das "monomanische" Werk: Eine strukturale Werkanalyse des Œuvres von Thomas Bernhard* (Frankfurt am Main: P. Lang, 1992), 16–23. Jahraus critically examines the scholarly charges that write off Bernhard's work as monomania.

relationship between Murau and Gambetti, a relationship whose conventional teacher–student hierarchy has already been turned on its head.[26] Rather than function as the central clearinghouse for reported speech, the exclusive mouthpiece for all other secondary narrators, Murau engages with Gambetti as a conversational equal, as a "critical medium of reflection"[27] who responds to his hyperbole with carnival laughter. In a reversal of the usual dynamic in Bernhard, Murau thus recounts "not what another character has said to him, but rather what he has said to another character. By also reporting his interlocutor's reactions, however, he opens up a self-critical perspective, which again calls into question the reliability of his judgments."[28] With the recurrent presence of Gambetti in the text and the repeated instances of his unsettling laughter, the novel is able to turn the figure of inversion upon itself. In his assessment of laughter in *Extinction*, J. J. Long enticingly mentions Bakhtin and the carnivalesque but immediately discounts Murau as a "Renaissance fool."[29] The problems Long diagnoses as a result of the disarming laughter of Gambetti and his teacher, however, merely underscore the presence of carnivalesque inversion in Bernhard's narrative strategies. "By means of laughter," he writes, "Murau criticizes and debunks power, and undermines authority. At the same time, however, the laughter is turned against him, which threatens to divest his critique of any legitimacy it might have possessed. In other words, Murau's own critical standpoint is destabilized by the very techniques he uses to establish that standpoint in the first place."[30] The destabilization of discourse Long sees, however, is precisely a marker of carnivalesque inversion.

As a novelistic figure, Gambetti himself recedes into the background of the story as a minor character, the son of well-to-do Italian parents who hire Murau as Gambetti's non-German German tutor. Gambetti's function on the formal level, by contrast, is much more significant. In his curious relationship with Murau, Gambetti acts as both student and teacher, but in the repetitious *inquit* he takes on the

---

[26] "Gambetti is my pupil, but conversely I am Gambetti's. I learn at least as much from him as he learns from me. We have an ideal relationship: sometimes I am his teacher and he my pupil, but at other times he is my teacher and I his pupil. And there are times when neither of us knows who is the pupil and who the teacher. That is the *ideal situation*" (10; 5).

[27] Andreas Herzog, "'Auslöschung' als Selbstauslöschung oder Der Erzähler als theatralische Figur," in *Thomas Bernhard: Die Zurichtung des Menschen*, ed. Alexander Honold and Markus Joch (Würzburg: Königshausen & Neumann, 1999), 125.

[28] Long, *The Novels of Thomas Bernhard*, 175.

[29] Long, *The Novels of Thomas Bernhard*, 177.

[30] Long, *The Novels of Thomas Bernhard*, 178.

additional role of the addressee of discourse. A large portion of Murau's *Extinction* effectively consists of reportage of remembered disquisitions from his sessions with Gambetti in Rome. An intradiegetic narratee, Gambetti acts as an occasional foil to his hyperbolic tutor, however. Indeed, as a critical countermeasure, his laughter relativizes the exaggerated exasperation of a narrator whose hyperbole knows no bounds. When Murau digresses in his description of Wolfsegg as a marionette theater controlled by his overbearing mother, Gambetti laughs aloud and accuses his teacher of "monstrous exaggeration," calling him a "typical Austrian pessimist with a grotesquely negative outlook" (123–124; 62). Murau initially resists the characterization, but Gambetti's improvised epithet for his teacher, "a *forenoon fantasist*" (128; 65), soon unleashes a joint bout of laughter they both relish (128; 65). The relativizing power of the diegetic laughter reorients Murau's narration and "keeps both Wolfsegg and its exaggerated carnivalesque representation from congealing into one-sided earnestness."[31] The seemingly baseless exaggerations, Murau is compelled to explain, function as a basic principle for animating an otherwise repellently boring existence and for making reality comprehensible. "To explain anything properly," he notes, "we have to exaggerate. Only exaggeration can make things clear. Even the risk of being branded as fools ceases to worry us as we get older" (128–129; 65).

Just as Murau's descriptive hyperbole functions as a characteristic of the literary grotesque, so too does Gambetti's laughter act, as it were, as a second-order carnivalesque practice to ensure that the narrator maintains his self-consciousness about his formulations. Much more than using "[Gambetti's] loud, unhindered, and unrestrained laughter" (610; 305 [translation amended, DB]) as a laugh-track, Bernhard writes into his novel a system of carnivalesque checks and balances insofar as Gambetti's laughter marks points of relativization "such as with the toppling of the king at Carnival."[32] Even in the final pages of the novel before Murau reflects upon his conversation with Gambetti "by the open grave" (645; 321), Gambetti's carnival laughter at Murau's self-description as "the greatest artist I knew in the field of exaggeration" (611; 307) infects his teacher in his moment of earnestness: "that afternoon on the Pincio we both laughed more than ever before" (611; 307). Inherent in this laughter, which is both oppositional and relativizing, is an underlying figure of carnivalesque inversion.

---

31 Stevens, "Schimpfen als künstlerischer Selbstentwurf: Karneval und Hermeneutik in Thomas Bernhards 'Auslöschung,'" 85.
32 Betz, *Polyphone Räume und karnevalisiertes Erbe*, 68.

Repetition and Signification

Along with Gambetti's relativizing presence and laughter, Bernhard employs in *Extinction* as in his other works a technique of repetition, both lexical and syntactic, that lends an episodic structure to the narrative. To establish a poetology of repetition, one must first understand the poetic function it serves within Bernhard's writing and prove "that more is hiding behind the seemingly one-dimensional 'repetition étude'."[33] The recurrence of lexical and syntactic structures throughout *Extinction* – and in Bernhard's writing more generally – has garnered significant attention from scholars of all theoretical stripes, particularly as regards its role in shaping textual form.[34] While these aspects of repetition will also be discussed, what is of primary concern here is how repetition functions semiotically. As a manifestation of a carnivalesque practice, how does repetition in *Extinction* affect signification? To what extent does repetition as a semiotic practice involve a gesture of satiric inversion? Before we turn to these two guiding questions explicitly, a look at the extent of repetition in Bernhard's *Extinction* is apropos.

A careful reader may discern four levels of repetition in Bernhard's text. The first of these – and the most seldom treated – is best understood as a metaphoric repetition of ordering systems and concepts and thus as a kind of doubling. To the reviled Wolfsegg, for example, Murau opposes "my beloved Rome" (111; 56). Rome is the positive double of Murau's family's estate and constitutes a separate order; the ambivalence the narrator expresses towards Vienna in the closing pages of *Woodcutters* is nowhere to be found here. In large part this manner of repetition consists in rehearsing strict binary divisions and dichotomous orders; Murau usually associates himself with one while opposing the other. The lower village thus contrasts with the Wolfsegg estate, the gardeners oppose the hunters, and Murau's Uncle Georg counteracts the derision with which he views his parents and siblings. Indeed, one critic notes that this kind of repetition, exemplified

---

[33] Hans Höller, "Rekonstruktion des Romans im Spektrum der Zeitungsrezensionen," in *Antiautobiografie: Zur Thomas Bernhards "Auslöschung,"* ed. Hans Höller and Irene Heidelberger-Leonard (Frankfurt am Main: Suhrkamp, 1995), 56.

[34] A complete listing of secondary literature that treats repetition in the work of Thomas Bernhard would be too extensive to enumerate here. The following two sources, however, engage with the topic critically and contain helpful bibliographies for further reference. Oliver Jahraus, *Die Wiederholung als werkkonstitutives Prinzip im Œuvre Thomas Bernhards* (Frankfurt am Main: P. Lang, 1991); Eva Marquardt, "Wortwörtlich: Formen der Wiederholung im Werk Thomas Bernhards," in *Dasselbe noch einmal: Die Ästhetik der Wiederholung*, ed. Carola Hilmes and Dietrich Mathy (Opladen: Westdeutscher Verlag, 1998), 229–243.

by the relationship between Murau and Uncle Georg and the mirroring of that relationship between Murau and Gambetti, "sets up a parallel genealogy to rival the Wolfsegg line and provides a replacement tradition of authority whose function is to *legitimize Murau's very telling* of an alternative history to that represented by the continuity of Wolfsegg."[35] This alternate oppositional order of which Murau is a part exists as a microcosmic offshoot in which the stuffy hierarchical order of Wolfsegg has no validity or jurisdiction. In emulating his uncle and mentor, the narrator rejects his parents' tradition of living "by the laws laid down for them by their predecessors [...], whereas Uncle Georg lived solely by his own laws, which he himself had made. And these self-made laws he was forever overturning" (46; 23). The model Murau chooses to adopt is one in which fixed hierarchical order is perpetually subject to inversion, revision, and renewal. It is through this kind of repetition that the novel erects a doubling pattern of discourse and counter-discourse and marks Murau as both (reluctantly) of the hegemonic order and an agent of change and renewal within it.

A second mode of repetition is the recurrence of various discursive topics within the text. As these relate more strictly to large-scale plot structures and to novelistic form rather than more microscopic issues of semiosis, let us treat this issue of repetition briefly. (It also occurs with less frequency in *Extinction* than it does in *Woodcutters*, where, for example, the narrator repeats his account of his run-in with the Auersbergers several times over the course of the text.) In *Extinction*, topical repetition or the repetition of narrative tropes may be seen more often as part of the shifting markers of narrative layers and narrated time – such as the recurrent references to Gambetti or the narrative flashbacks to Murau's early life at Wolfsegg. Murau's repeated disquisitions on the nature of photography and his observations of the three photographs of his family in the first section of *Extinction* are exemplary of this type of repetition, just as the multiple thematizations of the Children's Villa and Murau's future plans as the sole heir to Wolfsegg do in the second section. Formally, such repetition delays and defers narrative teleology, effectively lending the text a recursive form.

Bernhard's signature stylistic feature, however, lies arguably in his syntactic and lexical repetitions. In the former, entire grammatical structures recur, generally in discrete passages and episodes, and signal a discursive impasse or narrative stagnation. Whether such repetition of syntax marks significant formal ruptures or signposts depends not solely on the quantitative value of it, but also on the qualitative aspects of its construction. Certainly the aforementioned *inquit*

---

35 Long, *The Novels of Thomas Bernhard*, 182.

formulations count among this kind of repetition. Repeated over the course of the entire novel,[36] their grammatical and formal functions remain constant, although the formulas are lexically varied through verb tense and occasionally through modifiers.

Yet other passages more limited in the scope of their textual distribution also present Bernhard's penchant for syntactical repetition. Two thematically contrasting sections, for instance, act as a narrative panegyric and a narrative tirade. In the first case, Murau sits like his counterpart in *Woodcutters* musing in a chair, hidden away in his chambers in Wolfsegg, praising his student Gambetti. "What would my life in Rome be like without Gambetti, I thought," (512; 258) Murau writes, triggering an otherwise narratively unprompted chain of twenty-one consecutive relative clauses that ends as abruptly as it began: "Gambetti [...], who confronts me daily with new ideas and new questions [...]. Gambetti the anarchist, who under my guidance has become a true anarchist [...]. Gambetti, the greatest doubter I have ever known, who far outdoes me in his doubting [...]" (512–513; 258). The exhaustive enumeration of Gambetti's qualities underscores his importance for the plot and for the subjective self-understanding of the narrator, but the repetition of his name as in the *inquit* presents him simultaneously as a vehicle or catalyst for narration and a structuring element of the narrative form.

Shortly after this episode Murau launches his infamous tirade against Goethe, which contains a similar profusion of relative clauses in addition to a spate of derogatory epithets.[37] "Curiously, my thoughts now shifted from Spadolini to Goethe, the German patrician [...]. Goethe, the honest burgher, the collector of insects and aphorisms [...]. Goethe, the petit bourgeois of philosophy, the man on the make [...]. Goethe, the classifier of stones, the stargazer, the philosophical thumbsucker of the Germans [...]" (575; 290). For Murau Goethe is nothing more than "a philistine philosophical truck farmer" (576; 290) whose German parochialism and mediocrity are overshadowed by the towering figures of world literature who transcend national boundaries. To suggest a general meaning of relative clauses and epithets in their semiotic function would be ignore the particularities of their formal usage, but in this passage, the enumerative, descriptive use of the relative clause allows Murau to interrupt narrative flow with a carnivalesque

---

[36] A particularly high concentration of them occurs roughly between pages 103 and 252 (in the English: 52 to 127) and again from 606 to 617 (English: 305 to 310) and 645 to 649 (English: 324 to 325).

[37] And whose resemblance to invective Adrian Stevens analyzes as a modality of the carnivalesque in his article "Schimpfen als künstlerischer Selbstentwurf: Karneval und Hermeneutik in Thomas Bernhards 'Auslöschung.'"

litany of hyperbolic invective, after which he returns immediately to a discussion of what Spadolini had said about his mother.

As an exemplary pillorying of an old master, Murau's tirade on Goethe also reveals a inherently political conception of literature; it is precisely Goethe's petit-bourgeois appeal and hegemonic role in the canon that Murau attacks as the author's primary deficiency. Considered in the light of its historical context, this passage is a reckoning with a complacent Austrian society that whitewashes and blindly embraces (and not necessarily in that order) a politically sullied tradition[38]: a philippic against national literary essentialism. In short, Bernhard here reveals a universalizing, political, and subversive understanding of literature, all trademarks of a traditional view toward satire as political critique.

This emphasis on the satiric subversion of politics through hyperbolic repetition is also reminiscent of Bernhard's countless disparaging references to Austrian politics in other works novelistic, autobiographical, and theatrical. As with Bakhtin and the indelibly political aspects of his writing, Bernhard bridges the divide between an older conception of satire and a newer mode of satiric writing. As literary constructions, however, both the Goethe passage and the Gambetti episode are narratively unprompted, analogous in their syntactic organization, and exemplary for the ways Bernhard employs syntactic repetition to suspend the narrative through digression. One may thus conceive of syntactic repetition as a narrative strategy that works against the arrival at a novelistic *telos* and, in this regard, see in it a figure of satiric inversion, a carnivalesque device that subverts novelistic genre conventions.[39]

The last mode of repetition in *Extinction* is lexical in nature. To draw attention to the circulation and recurrence of signifiers throughout Bernhard's text is no new endeavor.[40] Certainly one may refer to words that typify Bernhard's style, such as "naturgemäß [naturally]," "scheußlich [horrible]," "Niedertracht [perfidy]," "lächerlich [ridiculous]," and other archetypal signifiers, as part of a strategy of repetition. Here, however, as in the previous discussion of syntax, I refer to discrete sections wherein certain lexemes recur in unusual abundance. As in *Woodcutters*, these moments in the text often involve both repetition within the narration itself and repetition of signifiers in what is narrated: that is to say, a

---

[38] Compare, for instance, the elevation of Kurt Waldheim to the level of a national cultural figure. In spite of the furor surrounding Waldheim's election to the presidency, Bernhard never commented directly on him or his wartime activity as a member of the *Sturmabteilung*. See Gitta Honegger, *Thomas Bernhard: The Making of an Austrian* (New Haven: Yale University Press, 2001), 270, 281–282.
[39] "The carnival culture has no *telos*." Lachmann, "Bakhtin and Carnival," 135.
[40] Jahraus, *Die Wiederholung als werkkonstitutives Prinzip im Œuvre Thomas Bernhards*.

repetition of words and the reportage of its intradiegetic verbal repetition. In short, Bernhard either employs the word in the story, or Murau or some other character repeats it aloud. Frequently such instances point to a semantic satiation, a breakdown of signification engendered by a carnivalesque tirade on the part of the narrator.

In one characteristic episode, Murau reflects on the stultification he detects in those who finish their schooling and cease developing intellectually. Their sole aim, he complains, is the collection of "diplomas and titles" (79; 40). For several pages Murau repeats these two signifiers, both separately and in combination, nearly two dozen times in an attack on the Germanic concern for status over substance. Analogously, Murau contrasts "so-called idleness" (47; 23 [translation amended, DB]) – his and Uncle Georg's preferred mode of being – to the dangerous idleness his parents perceive in it, employing various permutations and iterations nearly twenty times in two pages.

To be sure, the actual number and frequency of repetitions in these and other passages is of less concern than their semiotic function. The intensity of repetition in Bernhard's writing, pathological or not, effects "a focusing of the signifier and the gradual loss of the signified. The more frequently the very same word is uttered – and this also holds true for inner, mute speaking –, the less it is encountered as a carrier of meaning, the more, however, as a mere accumulation of phonemes. Words thus forfeit their semantic character."[41] From another perspective, the function of repetition on the semantic level suggests a displacement of signification from the level of the signifier to the level of form: "Signification [...] arises through repetition, a structure becomes semantic by being repeated."[42] Repetition, we may conclude synthetically from these ideas, subverts the functioning of the text as a set of narrative signs and lends the formal structure of the text a significatory role. Meaning thus shifts from word to form. In this regard, repetition as a narrative strategy accords with an inversion of novelistic norms of teleological narration. Repetition thus brings about a shift in signification that demonstrates how, in the case of *Extinction*, a novel may use the satiric practice of carnivalesque inversion through hyperbole to undermine and disrupt its own semantic workings and narrate nothing but its own writing; it becomes its own metatext.

---

[41] Scheu, "'Ich schreibe eine ungeheure Schrift': Sprache und Identitätsverlust in Thomas Bernhards 'Auslöschung,'" 65.
[42] Jahraus, *Die Wiederholung als werkkonstitutives Prinzip im Œuvre Thomas Bernhards*, 111.

Infinite Paradise

Bernhard's last novel is certainly not comprised solely of self-reflexive references to its inner composition and semantic organization, however. As Bakhtin defined it in *Rabelais and His World*, the carnivalesque also comprises the social universality of carnival laughter, which aimed at inverting hierarchical orders from within. Countering the highly individuated narrative perspective in *Extinction* is the active participation of the text in a larger literary tradition, which it also recounts in the narrative. The traces of this link to other texts are intertextual in nature, evinced both by Murau's references to other works and to unmentioned borrowings and similarities between *Extinction* and Bernhard's other writings.

Consider, however, that this is a fundamentally different kind of intertextuality than that in Jean Paul, for example, or in Judith Butler and Thomas Meinecke (see the final chapters on *Gender Trouble*, *Tomboy*, and *Music*). Bernhard's references outside the text are frequently superficial, plot-level references: mere name-dropping, rather than structuring elements of his narratives. Whereas Thomas Meinecke will base his stories, even his very poetics, on citational practices, Thomas Bernhard does not employ intertextual strategies of such sophistication because the semiotics of his texts do not depend on them. In *Extinction*, for instance, Jean Paul and Franz Kafka evoke an intellectual tradition in the spirit of inverting an established order; it is the satiric practice of inversion that dominates Bernhard's writings on the semiotic level. What we do see in Bernhard is a nascent thematization of worlds beyond the text and thus germinal strains of a more robust kind of formal intertextuality that point ahead to Elfriede Jelinek's experiments with citational practices and to the hyperbolic presence of intertexts in Butler and Meinecke. In short, we see a shift in the practical composition of the satiric effect.

The question at hand is therefore how, within Bernhard's novel, intertextuality is a carnivalesque, satiric practice of inversion that begins to point beyond the pages of the text to the possibilities of intertextual pollination.[43] As evidence of his open receptivity to external influence, Murau mentions his formative develop-

---

[43] The question of intertextuality as a feature of Bernhard's prose has been studied extensively. Some of the most cogent monographs and articles include Tobias Heyl, *Zeichen und Dinge, Kunst und Natur: Intertextuelle Bezugnahmen in der Prosa Thomas Bernhards* (Frankfurt am Main: P. Lang, 1995); Joachim Hoell, *Der "literarische Realitätenvermittler": Die "Liegenschaften" in Thomas Bernhards Roman Auslöschung* (Berlin: VanBremen, 1995); Manfred Mittermayer, "Von Montaigne zu Jean-Paul Sartre: Vermutungen zur Intertextualität in Bernhards 'Auslöschung,'" in *Thomas Bernhard: Traditionen und Trabanten*, ed. Joachim Hoell and Kai Luehrs-Kaiser (Würzburg: Königshausen & Neumann, 1999), 159–173.

ment through reading works of literature and philosophy, through writing musicological studies, and through sharing ideas with Uncle Georg. He not only illustrates this intellectual curiosity by ordering the six libraries of Wolfsegg opened, thereby turning the dank hermeticism of his family's estate on its head, but he also narrates his own constructedness – and that of the novel – as a product of literature, philosophy, art, and intellectual discourse. In his "choice between two worlds" (46; 23), Murau chooses his uncle's world: "Only an imbecile believes that the world stops where he stops. Uncle Georg not only introduced me to literature and opened it up as an *infinite paradise*, he also opened my eyes to the world of music and the arts generally" (34; 17). In essence, Uncle Georg acts as the diegetic medium for Murau's engagement with the wider world of discourse and its reciprocal influence on him. In fact, the narrator's first reaction to the telegram announcing the death of his parents and family is to consider, "calmly and with a clear head" (7; 3 [translation amended, DB]), the suggested readings he provided his student Gambetti, among them texts by Jean Paul, Kafka, and Thomas Bernhard himself (among others). Critics disagree about the degree to which the mentioning of other texts in Bernhard, in particular the nearly fifty authors and over twenty works in *Extinction*, carries significance for the work as a whole.[44] In considering intertextuality as Kristeva formulated the term, that is, as a form of textual dialogism that emerges from the carnivalesque, however, we can discern two primary ramifications for intertextuality as a carnivalesque, inverting practice of satire in Bernhard's novel.

The first of these is the inversion that occurs insofar as intertextual dialogism establishes a resonance or overlap between practices of writing and reading. For example, Murau, the writer of his own documentary extirpation, presents himself less as a successful writer than as a reader. A "short essay on Bohuslav Martinu" finds itself in the dustbin rather than in print (517; 260), and the manuscript he sends to his revered friend and poet Maria is "sloppily written, I thought. When I'm back in Rome she'll go through it with me and take it to pieces, and then I'll throw it away, like everything else of mine that I've given her to read. I've thrown away more manuscripts than I've kept, I thought" (541; 272). His only other mentioned publication, another short essay on a composer (Leoš Janáček), he finds both poorly placed and riddled with typographical errors in an Italian newspaper, "which is the worst thing that can happen to me" (21; 10).

Contrasted with the solitary, isolated venture of his writing, Murau's reading defines him as the inheritor of a rich intellectual lineage. The breadth of inter-

---

[44] See especially the summary and discussion in Hoell, *Der "literarische Realitätenvermittler,"* 23–26.

texts, an *a priori* condition for Murau's cognition and writing, has become a "hallmark of his consciousness [...]. For the hero in Bernhard is himself mainly a reader. He consists of literature, which he indicates with appropriate references to his praxis of reception. He virtually shimmers in the relativity of these literary voices."⁴⁵ The individuated specificity of the work, therefore, is relativized amid the plurality of literary texts that shape it through their dialogue with it. Amid the controversy surrounding the critical reception of Bernhard's reference to other texts, the initial reading list for Gambetti has been interpreted as an exemplary "equally serious and ridiculing, parodic reflection on reading what has been written."⁴⁶ The difficulty of ascertaining and maintaining terminological coherence around constellations of terms like parody and satire aside, this reflection is simultaneously a carnivalesque inversion. Writing, the narrative suggests, is always an active mode of reading. Bernhard constitutes his characters as constructs of reading while inverting satirically the relationship between writer and reader. He achieves this through the use of intertextuality as a carnivalesque gesture of relativization and ambivalence, by alluding to an inversion in the hierarchical order of activity and passivity with regard to writing and reading.

A second ramification of intertextuality in Bernhard's *Extinction*, the notion of inversion as a carnivalesque satiric practice also involves the festive universality and non-closure engendered by intertextual references. In the textual antinomy established between Murau's Rome and Wolfsegg, which has been read as a closed culture of repression,⁴⁷ the distance between each side is considerable and creates a repeated opposition between extremes. Rome, "*the modern center of the world*" (202; 101), counteracts the closure of provincial Wolfsegg in the same way in which the world of literature, that "*infinite paradise*" (34; 17), offsets the stultifying intellectual stagnation of Wolfsegg and its musty, forbidden libraries. When Murau opens the libraries at his family's estate, so too does intertextual dialogism open the discursive boundaries of the novel and undermine the notion of a closed text. Indeed, Bernhard's novel has been read as containing "a kind of intertextual internal network of his own literary production."⁴⁸ Textual similarities between *Extinction* and Bernhard's 1982 "Montaigne: A Story" ["Montaigne:

---

45 Betz, *Polyphone Räume und karnevalisiertes Erbe*, 18.
46 Ingeborg Hoesterey, "Postmoderner Blick auf österreichische Literatur: Bernhard, Glaser, Handke, Jelinek, Roth," *Modern Austrian Literature* 23, no. 3/4 (1990): 73.
47 Long, *The Novels of Thomas Bernhard*, 164–168.
48 Mittermayer, "Von Montaigne zu Jean-Paul Sartre: Vermutungen zur Intertextualität in Bernhards 'Auslöschung,'" 160.

Eine Erzählung"][49] have been uncovered,[50] and a scholarly work on Bernhard devotes significant attention to the adaptation of his film script "The Italian" ["Der Italiener"] from *Extinction*.[51] Other self-references in *Extinction* abound, from ponderings about voyeuristic observation (325; 164) and thoughts from the wing chair as in *Woodcutters* (512, 513, 571, 587; 258, 286, 296), to references to the "ruining" of Nietzsche in Sils-Maria, memorialized in the (very) short story, "Hotel Waldhaus" (158, 498; 79, 250).[52] This intertextual self-referentiality comes closer to the kind of citational practice found in Jelinek, Butler, and Meinecke, but it is not the prevailing structuring practice of the novel.

What is germane here is that a carnivalesque gesture of inversion and satiric play foregrounds these intertextual relationships. As exemplified in Bakhtin and in Bernhard's *Woodcutters* and *Extinction*, the figure of inversion stems from the cache of universalizing, relativizing carnival forms and acts as a satiric semiotic strategy in suspending, toppling, and renewing epistemological orders, in doubling discourses, in distorting narrative perspective, and in creating an ambivalent haze through a surplus of meaning that alters the significatory possibilities of a text. With intertextuality, another strategy for the satiric practice of carnivalesque inversion in written discourse comes into view. In *Extinction* in particular, intertextual references counter the multiple frames and dense layers of narration that provide formal contours to the novel with an ambivalent openness and lack of closure – an uncertainty regarding the novel's very status as a fixed text. It is this carnivalesque openness that marks *Extinction* not just as part of the "infinite paradise" of literature, but as a marker of referential circularity, of "the impossibility of living outside the infinite text."[53]

---

49 Newly reprinted in Thomas Bernhard, *Goethe schtirbt: Erzählungen* (Frankfurt am Main: Suhrkamp, 2011), 31–48.
50 Long, *The Novels of Thomas Bernhard*, 181.
51 Hans Höller and Irene Heidelberger-Leonard, eds., *Antiautobiografie: Zur Thomas Bernhards "Auslöschung"* (Frankfurt am Main: Suhrkamp, 1995).
52 Thomas Bernhard, *Der Stimmenimitator* (Frankfurt am Main: Suhrkamp, 1978), 45.
53 Roland Barthes, *The Pleasure of the Text*, trans. Richard Miller (New York: Hill and Wang, 1975), 36.

Part Two | **Mythification**

6. Between Theory and Literature: Roland Barthes' *Mythologies* (1957)

If for Roland Barthes language is ineluctable, the escape from the "infinite text" impossible, then even common forms of discourse in popular culture are subject to the same semiological pitfalls as literary and theoretical writing. And perhaps this explains Barthes' turn from literature and history in his first two books to popular trivialities in his third. Roman bangs and sweat, Greta Garbo, Einstein's brain, Billy Graham, *neither/nor* criticism, electoral photography, plastic, the Tour de France, the music hall – for Roland Barthes, each of these constitutes a semiological figure, "*a type of speech*,"[1] by which layers of signification obscure the relationship between signifier and signified. In short, they are myths. In his seminal 1957 work *Mythologies*, Barthes combines the narrative, essayistic writing that would become the hallmark of later works like *S/Z* (1970), *Roland Barthes by Roland Barthes* [*Roland Barthes par Roland Barthes*] (1975), and *Camera Lucida* [*La Chambre clair*] (1980) with a theoretical impulse that examines myth – and his narrative episodes – from a metaperspective. In rethinking myths as a problem of signs, Barthes points to a dynamic whereby the proliferation of connotations through myth occludes a proper historicization of them. Some have taken issue with Barthes' notion of connotation and his understanding of semiotics, chief among them Umberto Eco,[2] while others have discovered in Barthes' ineluctable myths a weakness against irony.[3] The advantage of Barthes' notion of myth, taking these criticisms into account, lies in its blurring of theory and literature, in its decided turn toward popular culture, in the curious form and style of Barthes' essayistic writing.[4] The literarization of theory invites Barthes to employ myths of

---

[1] Roland Barthes, *Mythologies*, trans. Richard Howard and Annette Lavers (New York: Hill and Wang, 2012), 217. In this chapter, references to the *Mythologies* will be cited parenthetically in the text and will refer to this, the complete English translation.
[2] Umberto Eco and Isabella Pezzini, "La sémiologie des Mythologies," *Communications* 36 (1982): 19–42; a cogent if damning look at the putative incoherence of Barthes' semiological argument can be found in Roy Harris, *Saussure and His Interpreters* (Edinburgh: Edinburgh University Press, 2001), 137–144.
[3] Christoph Leitgeb, *Barthes' Mythos im Rahmen konkreter Ironie: Literarische Konstruktionen des Eigenen und des Fremden* (Paderborn: Wilhelm Fink, 2008).
[4] For a thorough evaluation of Barthes' essayistic writings in his late work, see Réda Bensmaïa, *The Barthes Effect: The Essay as Reflective Text* (Minneapolis: University of Minnesota Press, 1987).

his own, particularly myths of theoretical coherence and semiotics. In so doing, Barthes makes use of a practice that is inherently satiric, that unsettles notions of the sign and of signification, and that his readers, among them Elfriede Jelinek, adopt in their own writings, both theoretical and literary.

Here I read Barthes' *Mythologies* against the grain and with an eye for its literary procedures and narrative strategies in order to mark the contours of his own mythic practice and deployment of satire.[5] A comparative assessment of Elfriede Jelinek's "Endless Innocence" ["Die endlose Unschuldigkeit"] (1970) – her reading and adaptation of Barthes' myths – provides an entry point into a deeper analysis of the satiric use of myths in her novels *Lust* (1989) and *The Piano Teacher* [*Die Klavierspielerin*] (1983). The aim with this approach is to demonstrate how deploying satiric myths might erase the boundaries between theoretical and literary modes of writing. In bridging these two cultures by way of popular culture, we see a closer semiotic relation between literature and theory – through the history of satire as a master trope – that allows us to read theoretical writings differently, that is, with greater attention to their literary qualities.

Taking as his starting point "a feeling of impatience with the 'naturalness' which common sense, the press, and the arts continually invoke to dress up a reality which, though the one we live in, is nonetheless quite historical" (XI), Barthes sets out to resolve the social confusion between "Nature and History" and expose "the ideological abuse [he] believed was hidden there" (XI). His solution, in a word, is semiological analysis. By turning to semiology, Barthes broadens the scope of his study to include non-literary phenomena that might better illustrate the epidemic infestation by myth, while simultaneously demonstrating the power of semiology to include all manner of modalities of signification. And yet even in his original preface to the *Mythologies*, Barthes admits, almost incidentally, to a singular issue facing his undertaking; "I don't share the traditional belief," he writes, "that there's a divorce in nature between the objectivity of the scientist and the subjectivity of the writer, as if the former were endowed with a 'freedom' and the latter with a 'vocation,' both of them likely to spirit away or sublimate the true limits of their situation" (XII). Instead, Barthes offers himself as an embodiment of "the contradiction of my time, which can make sarcasm the condition of truth" (XII). This admission, it would seem, proffers the reader a fur-

---

[5] For an examination of the satiric-parodic practices in Barthes' *Mythologies*, see Carlo Brune, *Roland Barthes: Literatursemiologie und literarisches Schreiben* (Würzburg: Königshausen & Neumann, 2003), 99–103.

ther explanation for the intractable difficulty, diagnosed elsewhere,[6] of writing about Barthes; situating himself between the supposed science of scholarship and the alleged impressionism of literature, Barthes lays claim to neither. His oeuvre belongs neither to theory and its set of procedural strictures, nor to literature and its domain of narrative practices. Indeed, the problem with interpolating Barthes' self-described essays would seem to be "our inability to learn a certain mode of *reading* with its concomitant expectations"[7] and, perhaps, our inability to take Barthes at his word. Neither this nor that, Barthes bestows upon himself the mantle of something unnamed and quite different, employing a mythological figure of universal rejection or endorsement (*"neither/nor* criticism") that he will later identify as "a bourgeois figure" (267) of the very myths he attempts to uncover.

It is this claim – and his tongue-in-cheek subversion of his own argument – which prompts me to read Barthes less with an eye for theoretical consistency and didactics than for literary practice and a narrative of semiotics. The following pages will offer close readings of five representative myth essays – "Romans in the Movies," "Garbo's Face," "Einstein's Brain," *"Neither/Nor* Criticism," and "Billy Graham at the Vel' d'Hiv'" – and a narrative study of the concluding essay "Myth Today." The focus of these analyses remains Barthes' narrative strategies, in particular the way mythologization is deployed *in his own text* as a satiric practice. In fact, in a later reflection upon myth in 1971, Barthes admits perspicaciously that the "new mythology" he identified years earlier "has itself become discourse, stock of phrases, catechistic declaration": that is, mythical.[8] As a matter of methodology, I will approach the myth episodes no differently from the concluding essay, choosing instead to read the *Mythologies* as Barthes designates himself: as a hybrid without exclusive pretensions or claims to science (theory) or literature.

---

[6] "It is not easy to write about the work of Roland Barthes. One reason is that Barthes has always in some way accompanied his texts with his own anticipated commentary; consequently, to talk or write about Barthes is necessarily, to some extent, to repeat him, quote him, or betray him. Another reason is that the 'object,' 'method,' and 'ideology' of his work have always been subjected to a perpetual displacement." Bensmaïa, *The Barthes Effect*, xxvi.
[7] Bensmaïa, *The Barthes Effect*, xxxi.
[8] Roland Barthes, "Change the Object Itself: Mythology Today," in *Image – Music – Text*, trans. Stephen Heath (New York: Hill and Wang, 1977), 166.

The Satiric Mythology of Roland Barthes

The visual always attracts the discerning eye of Roland Barthes. In the third essay of his book, Barthes examines two filmic signifiers in Joseph Mankiewicz's 1953 film, *Julius Caesar*: the actors' bangs and their incessant perspiration. In witnessing "the Spectacle's mainspring exposed here: the *sign*" (19), the viewer observes a synecdochal reassembly of Romanness in film. Barthes' narrative gaze is likewise an analytic, almost ekphrastic one, incapable of seeing the whole; bangs, foreheads, eyes, faces, skulls, locks of hair, perspiration, plaits – they all fragment for Barthes the homogeneous unity of the ethnic sign in what becomes a lament of the loss of a believable essentialist physiognomy through a "generality" (19). The exoticism of American faces for French eyes (19–20) suggests in Barthes' reading an underlying episteme that cannot admit of ethnic collage, of visual heterogeneity. This is perhaps the most telling of Barthes' literary procedures in this short essay: synecdoche used against synecdoche. The *a priori* assumption accompanying the use of this literary device states that the part represents the whole: that there is in fact a whole. While arguing against investing fragments with meaning and against interpolating "an illegitimate sign" "between the intellectual sign and the visceral sign" (21) Barthes fragments his representations of visual images into parts. Only a synthetic gaze could allow the hybrid impression of the actors in an historical reenactment to form a coherent impression.

In short, Barthes predicates his reading of Romanness in film upon a myth of his own: that of the "perfect integration" of artifice with "general morphology" (20), a myth of ethnicity as an unfragmented whole, as a sign "deeply rooted, somehow invented on each occasion, presenting an inward and secret face, the signal of a moment and no longer of a concept" (21). An underlying prejudice, this hidden myth of ethnic homogeneity is at variance with the synecdochal basis of Barthes' argument, upon which he builds a narrative of heterogeneity. "[C]onfusing the sign with what is signified" (21), by extension, is duplicitous, and yet Barthes implicitly assumes the naturalness of homogeneous appearance. Indeed, for Barthes, disparate semblance and being are an unwelcome, heavy-handed alienation effect that reveals the artifice of the medium.

This Brechtian reference brings us to an important point of comparison between the writing of Barthes and, as we will soon see, of Elfriede Jelinek. In his interpretations of visual images, Barthes explicitly distorts what Brecht deems a defining point of his epic theater, namely, that the viewer see the sutures and seams of the fragmented sign, scrutinize the conventionally unquestioned signification of reality, and be left desirous of revolution. Brecht's model of theatrical performance with the alienation effect thus incorporates a modernist acknowledgement and representation of the semiotic machinations of the sign along with a desire to manipulate them for social change, which Elfriede Jelinek seems to reproduce in her satiric literary practices. Barthes' relationship to the notion of significatory alienation, by contrast, is more ambivalent here.

While Barthes' thought is indebted to Brechtian theory and terminology, his relationship with the German playwright and theorist is not unproblematic.[9] The primary point of contention lies at the disjunction Barthes identifies between politics and semiology (273–274), despite their constitutive dual role in Brecht's poetics.[10] While Barthes might be thought of as a Brechtian thinker in the way he criticizes myth as "*depoliticized speech*" (255) in which the alienated has become naturalized, he nevertheless laments the missing naturalness between signifier and signified in the iconography of Mankiewicz's film. In showing how certain media – here film, but also literature – cannot escape the gravitational pull of myth and thus of depoliticized speech, Barthes seems to concede defeat and advocate a kind of Brechtian acquiescence ["*Einverständnis*"] (271) to a general complicity with a newly mythologized reality. This is all the more striking because it involves a political capitulation as well as a semiological one. The former should come as no surprise, considering Barthes' shifting interest, from the political engagement of literature to its semiotic workings.[11] That he deconstructs mythical aspects of a film's visual material only to remythify them might be thought of as a satiric inversion. Be that as it may, in his satiric writings Barthes lacks the overtly political edge of Jelinek's language, in spite of his use of popular film to argue against the depoliticized speech of myth. Reading Jelinek, and Meinecke later, effectively transforms our understanding of Barthes' seemingly innocuous trivial myths as deeply political, potentially violent constructs, demonstrating that not only the personal, but also the popular is political.

But does not the filmic medium already mythify what it represents by filtering through a fragmented series of reenactments, representations, and shots the reality Barthes apparently wishes to capture in its wholeness? The choice of medium sets up a straw man for the argumentation while offering the reader an example of the very presentation of myth Barthes wishes to criticize. If the artful suppression of visual heterogeneity amounts to a guiding principle, Barthes winks at his reader by suppressing a view of the heterogeneous whole with a rhetorical device

---

[9] For a thorough study of Barthes' ambivalent relationship to Brechtian thought, see Ellis Shookman, "Barthes's Semiological Myth of Brecht's Epic Theater," *Monatshefte* 81, no. 4 (1989): 466–470.

[10] Barthes' separation of writing from politics also shows a historical shift in a certain understanding of satire; once predicated upon a possible political function, here satire takes on a semiological role.

[11] Shookman, "Barthes's Semiological Myth of Brecht's Epic Theater," 460.

(synecdoche) that fragments the whole – in this case the distinctly un-Roman actors – into constituent signs that accord with a homogeneous code of ethnicity. The dissonance between the narrative and metanarrative dynamics in Barthes' essay can be read as a performative, as a self-effacing satire of Barthes' own claims. The irresolvable nature of this dissonance, furthermore, suggests the fiction of the hidden myth, the fiction of ethnic markers as viable signs of authenticity and their participation in "a degraded spectacle, one which fears the naïve truth as much as the total artifice" (21). Cinema provides for Barthes a convenient medium for exploring the complex dynamic of myths and visual signs, and in his essay entitled "Garbo's Face," he employs it as well.

For Barthes, Greta Garbo's face on the silver screen – which he curiously refers to as "an admirable face-as-object" (73) – animates a narrative of cinematic history as well as a semiological fable. As in most of the short essays in *Mythologies*, the author does not so much venture an analysis of myth in his objects of study, reserving this instead for the final essay. Rather, his musings take on a contemplative, literary tone that invite critical reflection upon the narrator's point of view: that of mythologist or that of unreflective author. Are Barthes' essays illustrative of myth in action? Do they mythify their subjects or expose mythification? In "Garbo's Face," Barthes maintains a myth of the "face-as-object" while narrating an allegorical tale of the unbridgeable gap between signifier and signified.

Having withdrawn to a life of seclusion more than a decade before Barthes wrote the *Mythologies*, Greta Garbo enters the text with an air of nostalgic mystery and awe; hers was a power of eliciting "the greatest perturbation, where people literally lost themselves in the human image [...], when the face constituted a sort of absolute state of the flesh" (73). Barthes limns this bygone cinematic time with mournful brushstrokes, likening Garbo's visage to a monochrome sculpture whose beauty, "both perfect and ephemeral" (73), derives from the purity and fragility of snow. The comparison drawn between the face of "Divine" (74) and unindividuated sexuality on the one hand, and the perfection of nature on the other hand, suggests an originary state for Garbo, a presemiotic condition of union with the sign. Barthes employs superlative after superlative to describe the face of Garbo; her eyes are "not at all expressive" (73), her look "an archetype of the human face" (73–74) whose "superlative state of beauty" (74) show her "descended from a heaven where things are formed and finished with the greatest clarity" (74). Her face had an "intellectual perfection, even more than its plastic one" (74). With his panegyric tone Barthes transfigures his "face-as-object," attributing to it a surplus of connotative meaning. For Barthes, Garbo's face is representative of an extinct age in film and thus a myth of one of two "iconographic ages" (74), hers the black-and-white silent era before the fall, after which the essence of beauty was lost to history.

In attributing to the face of Garbo an air of superlative divinity, however, Barthes also elevates the image through an allegory of non-signification. As "a sort of Platonic Idea of the human creature" (74) in Barthes' tale, Garbo connotes the signified at a moment before specification and individualization and in a sense resists narration. "As a *language*, Garbo's singularity was of a conceptual order" (75 [my emphasis, DB]), he writes, contrasting her unparalleled beauty and representative meaning for film history with the "substantial order" (75) of Audrey Hepburn: "Garbo's face is an Idea, Hepburn's an Event" (75). The final binary opposition contrasts the notion of the unnarratable with narration while underwriting a myth of the immediacy of language and meaning. In this text, Garbo's face symbolizes a time in which the sign and the referent still overlap.

From this perspective, Barthes' essay is surprisingly anti-modern and self-undermining. It expresses nostalgia for a mythical epoch whose ending provided the semiological discordance that enabled such a written, on-screen shrine to Garbo's visage in the first place. That the power of Garbo's face manifests itself through the medium of film, however – and Barthes only ever speaks of these images as photographic stills, not as moving pictures – points to the satiric potential of such a mode of writing. The erstwhile semantic immediacy in Garbo's face was always mediated and thus never real; it has no referent outside the non-linguistic medium that represents it. Barthes thus writes an encomium to Greta Garbo while narratively subverting the conditions for its possibility.

By way of contrast, the entry on "Einstein's Brain," which also treats a topic of contemporaneous interest – Einstein had died in 1955 while Barthes wrote the *Mythologies*, two years prior to their publication in book form – engages directly with the notion of myth. Indeed, Barthes fashions this essay as a form of laboratory report, beginning with a direct statement of hypothesis, then proceeding through a section on history, the methodology of his analysis, and ending with a statement of conclusion that confirms the initial hypothesis. More than its predecessors, this essayistic form strives to attain a certain scientificity in its narrative procedures. Gone is the hagiographic haze around Garbo's visage. Barthes instead grapples with Einstein's brain by shuffling through and organizing popular visual imagery and historical circumstances. Yet as in previous essays, he employs a narrative dichotomy – a binary opposition – to further his argument: between machine and magic, research and discovery, science and fiction, logic and imagination.

As a figure of the then-recent past, Albert Einstein belongs to a well-documented popular culture, which Barthes cites primarily through photographs not reproduced in the text. Einstein's legacy exists for Barthes in the form of visual representations of him: thinking with electrodes attached to his brain, standing before his blackboard, and as a cartoonish arch-discoverer whose genius spontaneously produced that famous equation of special relativity. Outmoded notions of science as a mechanical process of research ceded to the mystical synecdoche by which Einstein's genius was inscribed into the inscrutability of a human brain. The concrete visual signifiers that coded Einstein as a "machine of genius" (101) give way to the abstractness of an internal organ that no one has seen, that cannot divulge its secrets, and "the possession of which two hospitals disputed as if it were some strange machine which could finally be taken apart" (100). That "Einstein's brain is a mythical object" (100) is Barthes' hypothesis, but to prove this claim, the author employs images that ostensibly show Einstein as one side of a mythic equation analogous in form to his historical discovery, $E = mc^2$: "Einstein's brain is a mythical object" (100); "Einstein is matter" (100); "that is the myth of Einstein" (101). Ironically, the abstractness of Einstein's brain brings into relief the concreteness of thought: "the image of a formula for knowledge" (101), the reduction of imagination to logic.

Perhaps most telling about this essay is how Barthes contributes to the mythification of Einstein's brain through his mode of writing. Unable to grasp the concreteness of an organ "which has about it nothing monstrous but its cybernetic complication" (102) and whose creases and folds withhold unextractable, inextricable secrets, Barthes turns to metaphors to capture the brain as a source of both logic and imagination. They include comparisons of Einstein to a superman (in both the science-fiction and Nietzschean senses) and matter opposed to spirit. Einstein's thought bears the stamp of mechanical exercises including the "mechanical production of sausages, the grinding of corn, or the crushing of some mineral: he produced thought continuously, as a mill produces flour" (101). In reintroducing the magical aspect of the myth of Einstein's brain, Barthes turns to decidedly more mystical allusions and metaphors, effectively reinforcing the myth and its contradictory union of machine and magic with the idea that Einstein provided a key to the locked mysteries of the universe (101). The "euphoric security" Einstein provides by way of the reductionist myth of his genius "mythically reconciles man's infinite power over nature with the 'fatality' of a rite which man cannot reject" (102). In essence, Barthes writes, in spite of the myth that surrounds the brain of Einstein, the irony remains that death overtook the towering genius, with his brain and the secrets it contains consigned to a specimen jar. In the concluding portion of the essay, the pseudo-scientific formal organization thus unmasks the precarious edifice of quotidian myths through the satiric deployment of irony in the crumbling of the metaphors; Einstein ultimately fails, and neither machine nor magic rescues him.

The dynamic of neither/nor in fact occupies a prominent place in Barthes' *Mythologies*, originating in his preface where he defines himself as allied with neither scientific objectivity nor literary subjectivity. In his essay "*Neither/Nor*

Criticism" Barthes addresses more directly the rhetorical pandemic allegedly affecting contemporary criticism and its fear of making positivistic claims: its "rejection of a priori judgment" (162). As with "Einstein's Brain," this essay, too, mentions myths specifically – myths of timelessness (162), freedom (162), and classicism (163), upon which critics erect Style – but in this case, the myths in question stem from Barthes' previous engagement with historical conceptions of literature and style in his first published work, *Writing Degree Zero* [*Le Degré zéro de l'écriture*] from 1953.[12]

"*Neither/Nor* Criticism" essentially reads as a mythological continuation of this discourse on Literature and History (replete with emphatic capitalizations), and yet turns the joke back upon Barthes in its repudiation of the term "style." In short, it functions as a critical commentary on Barthes' own work and indirectly lampoons both a manner of criticism that operates, as it were, as a photo negative to Barthes' "not-only, but-also" criticism, and the ambivalence of his either-or constructions (274). Neither/nor criticism – "a mechanism of double exclusion" (161) that Barthes refutes as grounded upon a false notion of a critical perspective free from ideology – rhymes with Barthes' own tendencies in *Writing Degree Zero* to replace this gesture with a double *in*clusion, with a surplus of connotations through not-only-but-also: a proliferation of connotative meaning that, he later writes, easily leads to mythification and participates in "that numerical frenzy which we have already encountered several times" (161).

The narrative strategies that structure this particular essay are those of a certain formal mode of critique, some of which Barthes employs himself while maligning them. Evaluation, refutation, and judgment; imagery of impartial justice and balance; polemic; the assumption of a neutral point of view – all these "play a scale's defamatory game" (162) by which the critic weighs his alternatives to deliver a verdict. In refuting this mode of criticism, however, Barthes exposes the mythological contingence of criticism in general; the myth of an impartial point of view – the myth of a degree zero of criticism – guides the critic's arbitration even as a nonpartisan absence of ideology eludes him. Indeed, at the outset Barthes introduces this notion of doubly exclusive criticism as part of a "profession of faith" (161), a set of religious tenets supported by belief rather than fact.

What is striking about Barthes' elaboration of neither/nor criticism is his adoption of an oppositional narrative perspective that paints it as the preferred mode of his go-to sociological antipode: the petite-bourgeoisie. As Barthes attests in his essay "Billy Graham at the Vel' d'Hiv'," the susceptibility of the

---

[12] Barthes, *Writing Degree Zero*; Roland Barthes, *Le Degré zéro de l'écriture* (Paris: Éditions de Seuil, 1953).

petite-bourgeoisie to hollow religious rhetoric suggests its "mental fragility" (111). In attacking a manner of criticism propagated by this social class, Barthes reveals the ideological stance behind his narrative voice, which relies on absolutes of its own. When Barthes sets up an allegedly false opposition of "heavy, prejudicial, dubious words" – the straw men of ideological discourse – and "light, pure, immaterial words ennobled by some divine right" (162) to criticize neither/nor criticism, the text conceals an implicit series of straw men of its own. Among them are the petite-bourgeoisie, faith, and moralization. In so doing, however, – and this, I argue, is the satiric thrust of this particular essay – Barthes admits his allegiance to a "systematic determination" (162–163) his opponents reject, but he counters their manner of criticism with his own kind. His form of criticism propagates mythification by proclaiming its ideological roots openly and offering through its double inclusion the "euphoric security" (102) of a conscious mythological system.

Barthes' distaste for ideological viewpoints that claim to represent "divine transcendence" (163–164) continues in his discussion of Billy Graham's visit to Paris in the summer of 1955. "Billy Graham at the Vel' d'Hiv'" uses the "splendid piece of anthropological raw material here [...] inherited from certain 'savage' cults" (109) and observed at the evangelizer's visit to the Vélodrome d'Hiver as the basis for a cultural analysis. With reference to Marcel Mauss, Barthes aligns this narrative with a style of anthropological criticism that would later give rise to the first fits of structuralism with Claude Lévi-Strauss. Here, however, the tables are turned. Graham and his followers become the objects of anthropological interest and inquiry, expressed by the regret that "that Papuan witch doctor was not at the Vel' d'Hiv' to describe the ceremony presided over by Dr. Graham under the name of an evangelizing campaign" (109). Indeed, like his intellectual forefather Lévi-Strauss, Barthes delineates the anthropological structure of such a gathering and traces its deviations through Graham's own propagation of his "*Message*" (109).

Unlike structural anthropologists, however, this narrator can barely contain his derision for his subjects, undermining an expectation (and myth?) of scientific impartiality: "If God is really speaking through Dr. Graham's mouth, it must be acknowledged that God is quite stupid: the Message stuns by its platitude, its childishness" (110). A wolf in sheep's clothing, the narrative voice prepares the reader for a structural-anthropological study of religious ceremony, but it delivers an excoriating critique of American evangelism in light of its function in Western society, to which, after all, it belongs. In demonstrating the political essence of Billy Graham's style of evangelism as religious McCarthyism, Barthes exposes the falseness of both the myth of evangelical otherworldliness and the myth of scientific impartiality. The practice of undermining one's own narrative perspective is certainly not new; Jonathan Swift famously employed the practices of demographics to a unique end in his 1729 tract, *A Modest Proposal*. While certainly not in the tradition of Swift, Barthes utilizes a similar dynamic with a very different aim: to deconstruct the workings of one myth with the aid of another. This is a quintessentially satiric gesture.

The elaboration of Barthes' pseudo-scientific three phases of religious rite – "Expectation, Suggestion, Initiation," (109) each catapulted into structural importance with capitalization – begins a series of droll ironies that subvert the earnestness of his essayistic endeavor: "Billy Graham," the narrator continues from the first point, "makes us wait for him" (109). In drawing a comparison between Graham and the hypnotist Le Grand Robert, who came to hold Paris under the sway of expectant impatience, the text denies Graham's proselytizing any greater import than hypnotism in exploiting "the best traditions of such spectacles" (109). Graham's speech is one of self-professed divinity and yet riddled with illogical propositions, childishness, discontinuities, and tautologies. Even his visual self-presentation fails to live up to the expectations of "an outré Americanism" (110) – even if this provides French attendees with some measure of relief.

Indeed, as the narrator progresses through his playful analysis of the media evangelist's spectacle, he begins to allude to a subversion of religious precedent and, in a damning conclusion, instead ascribes to such work a veiled political end. In putting an end to homiletic reliance on rhetorical persuasion, Graham, the narrator argues, turns to suggestion and implements a series of strategies which bear an uncanny resemblance to those of low-brow entertainment: "all these operations belong to the classic material of the music hall hypnotist" (111). Graham's successful performance suggests the downfall of the French petite-bourgeoisie by dint of its susceptibility to such cheap tricks (its "mental fragility"), while his charismatic mission seeks to subvert French atheism through a clandestine attempt to couch a political effort – to stem the tide of advancing Communism, particularly among French intellectuals – in terms of a religious reawakening. "Billy Graham's campaign," the narrator concludes from the narrative standpoint of a "Papuan witch doctor," "has been merely a McCarthyist episode" (112). In turning religion into politics, Barthes must employ another straw man to unseat the myth of the Message of religious revivalism. Having appropriating his own mythology for this purpose, Barthes adds both a narrative, literary quality and a satiric impulse to his theoretical enterprise.

From Romans in film to Billy Graham in Paris, we see in these five essays how Barthes deploys mythification as a constitutive element of his narrative strategies, which often consist in annexing a literary or scientific form – in the end a type of pastiche – or employing particular metaphors or literary tropes to overload the connotative layer of extant myths with a surplus of meaning. The increased stratification of myth serves to undermine the furtive and insidious workings of a kind of speech ubiquitous in modern discourse. And yet in using myth-making as a central practice of his writing, Barthes perpetuates it.[13] His reason and justification for this is surprisingly not at odds with his project of describing the mythologies that pervade the world of everyday objects, perception, and thought. In the long essay that concludes *Mythologies*, entitled "Myth Today," Barthes turns his critical (and literary) gaze upon himself in a self-reflective meta-narrative text that examines the omnipresence of myths and their ineradicable nature. Of a sharply different character than the short texts that precede it, "Myth Today" at once approaches head-on the notion of myth *per se* while laying bare its inner workings and thus the inner workings of Barthes' own texts.

Proceeding from a kind of phenomenological perspective, Barthes ventures an elegantly simple definition of myth as a type of speech [*parole*].[14] Several aspects of this opening are striking. First, the essayist Barthes offers no basis for his definition other than a vaguely mythological conception of etymology as the key to the origins of meaning (in addition to the sum of implied theoretical arguments from the preceding short essays).[15] The character of the text here differs from that of the short essays, however. Here, the writing has subheadings to guide and structure what is undoubtedly a kind of argumentation, but these subheadings raise to the level of structure what is present in the argument as mere hypothesis. Indeed, his own preliminary definition, "*myth is a type of speech*" (217), crystallizes immediately thereafter as a bold-faced (and bald-faced) assertion of truth in its function as the next subheading, as if the hypothesis were proven by mere repetition. Likewise, a solitary footnote, the first in the entire book, concedes the plurality of definitions of myth available, and thus the arbitrary choice for this one, while disguising the essay as scientific in character through its references and annotations. The concession, too, accords with a claim, cited earlier, that Barthes' mode of writing anticipates its reader and its reader's criticism, effectively silencing them by proffering its own refutation of itself.[16]

From the initial proposition, the narrative voice proceeds to whittle the ramifications of such a general pronouncement into a usable concept, and the essay uses Barthes' distinctive mode of writing to do this. That is, rather than proceed-

---

[13] "What must be realized is that the techniques Barthes employs here do not fundamentally differ from those that the 'mythic' discourses he critiques also use." Brune, *Roland Barthes*, 101.
[14] Compare the French edition: Roland Barthes, *Mythologies* (Paris: Éditions du Seuil, 1957), 181.
[15] See Harris' discussion of Barthes' semiological shortcomings in his late reception of Saussure. Harris, *Saussure and His Interpreters*; the German reception of these shortcomings can be found in Leitgeb, *Barthes' Mythos im Rahmen konkreter Ironie*, 156–169.
[16] Bensmaïa, *The Barthes Effect*, xxvi.

ing with negative assertions that distinguish the object of study from what it is not and thereby show its terminological contours, the text continues with metaphors: "[...] myth is a system of communication, [...] a message"; "it is a mode of signification, a form"; "everything can be a myth provided it is conveyed by a discourse" (217). The plurality of connotative layers serves, ironically, to veil the notion of myth in a terminological haze that persists throughout the essay; myth is "*a second-order semiological system*" (223), "metalanguage" (224), "a *value*" (233), "speech *stolen and restored*" (236), "a pure ideographic system" (238), "neither a lie nor a confession: it is an inflexion" (240), "speech justified *in excess*" (240), "a language robbery" (242), and "*depoliticized speech*" (255). In essence, Barthes engages in a mythification of the very notion of myth because his theoretical metalanguage has the same structure as myth itself.

In narrating this ontology, Barthes employs a bounty of metaphors but bases his argument on a conception of semiosis that seems to exist outside the historical development he outlined in *Writing Degree Zero*. Language and myth, he argues in *Mythologies*, function according to certain unassailable rules of signification. What he describes is a dual-layered significatory system "constructed from a semiological chain which existed before it" wherein "a sign [...] in the first system becomes a mere signifier in the second" (223). But insofar as myths, according to Barthes, appropriate concepts in ways that conceal or deny their own significatory history as signs, myths convert the resulting signification "suddenly into an empty, parasitical form" (226). Signs appear as ahistorical readymades. The impoverishment of the sign by myth is a result of its loss of history in this process of parasitic confiscation: "In this sense, we can say that the fundamental character of the mythical concept is to be *appropriated*" (229). This is significant with regard to satiric practices for two reasons.

First, by appropriating an extant sign, myths interrupt and occupy a relationship of meaning to concept in "essentially a relation of *deformation*" (232). The ensuing distortion is a result of parasitic occupation, to employ Barthes' metaphor, and resembles the procedures at work in satiric deployments of meaning. The appropriation of extant semiological relations, for example, necessarily involves a reliance on preexisting intertextual or discursive forms, forms appropriated – or cited, to use a different, more neutral term – and deployed again: "*stolen and restored*. Only, speech which is restored is no longer quite that which was stolen: when it was brought back, it was not put exactly in its place" (236). The displacement of meaning Barthes diagnoses in this procedure of appropriation he equates with a distortion. This very deformation of meaning through citation constitutes a primal gesture of satiric practices in general.

Second, the source of such appropriation must be considered: "[...] in general myth prefers to work with poor, incomplete images, where the meaning is already relieved of its fat, and ready for a signification, such as caricatures, pastiches, symbols, etc." (237). In this litany, Barthes lists forms and formal procedures that rely on preexisting discursive material. But beyond the immediate question of myth and its ontology, such forms and formal procedures are also the historically favored modalities of satire. Were these not sufficient grounds to posit a relation between myth and satire, the language in "Myth Today" makes the comparison more credible and compelling.

Like satire, myth here functions through decidedly negative, anthropomorphic metaphors; it distorts, deforms, robs, parasitizes, corrupts, and empties: "nothing can be safe from myth" (242). Its procedural dangers imperil the proper function of a pure, historicized semiological system. This comparison does not presuppose an equivalence between satire and myth. Rather, Barthes' concept of myth constitutes a form of naturalized satire that has lost its satiric edge, part of the general trend he identifies in the naturalization of culture via myth. In effect, myth-making is a crypto-satiric practice that infiltrates all discourses and texts precisely because it is inextricably part of the process of signification. Perhaps because Barthes introduces this concept under the guise of a theoretical tract on a semiological problem, the notion of any genealogical inheritance from the tradition of satire gets lost in the shuffle. This should come as no surprise because, as we have seen, "Myth Today" itself mythifies the very concept in question, the historical roots of which it locates in a concept of metaphor typical for the nineteenth century. That myth stems from a historical notion of literary writing and functions as a satiric practice thus suggests the merging of the satiric and the literary; the history of satire lies hidden within a history of semiologically developing literature.

Endless Innocence and the Literary Reception of Barthes

To connect Barthes' reflections on myth to a mode of writing coded in a more explicitly literary way does not seem far-fetched, as Barthes himself, writing in the preface to the *Mythologies*, seemed concerned only with "the production of *text*, which did not respect this law of the separation of discourses"[17]: that is, the separation of theory from literature, of science from fiction. For her part, Austrian author Elfriede Jelinek displays this conglomeration of discourses in her reception of Barthes and his *Mythologies* in her essay, "Endless Innocence" ["Die end-

---

[17] Louis Jean Calvet, *Roland Barthes: A Biography* (Bloomington: Indiana University Press, 1995), 147.

lose Unschuldigkeit"], which appeared in an edited volume in 1970.[18] A first public grappling with Barthes' notion of mythologies, Jelinek's essay transfers the historical context of Barthes' text from its discussions of French everyday myths and the bourgeoisie, as well as its explicit engagement with Saussurean semiology and ethnology in the vein of Claude Lévi-Strauss, into the European student movement several decades later. In Jelinek's reading of Barthes, the notion of myths as a semiological system takes on much stronger inflections of media influence (particularly television) and revolutionary Marxism by way of Hans Barth's *The Masses and Myth* [*Masse und Mythos*] (1959), Marshall McLuhan's *Understanding Media* (1964, German translation: 1968), and Otto Gmelin's pamphlet "Ringleaders I or Emancipation and Orgasm" ["Rädelsführer I oder Emanzipation und Orgasmus"] (1968).[19] The claim about Jelinek "that her achievement in *Endless Innocence* is limited to a montage"[20] is substantiated. Along with quotations from these three primary works, Jelinek follows Barthes' turn toward popular culture and interweaves into the fabric of her text references from advertisements and television shows as varied as "The Flintstones," "Lassie," and "I Dream of Jeannie." Like the *Mythologies* with its discursive variation, "Endless Innocence" thus defies a clear attribution of genre or discourse. To read it as a theoretical essay is to subject it to a projection of essayistic coherence it cannot withstand. The thicket of citations; the rapid alternation among often unattributed quotations, television advertising references, and Jelinek's original material; the omission of capitalization and most punctuation – all these do not so much challenge the very grammatical foundations of language in a revolutionary upending of discourse, as some would have it,[21] but they do reveal "a disguised but drastic presentation of her theses, which resist classical systematic thinking in a kind of anti-scientific textual labyrinth, a parody of the essay form and of science."[22] As such, "Endless Innocence," like Barthes' *Mythologies*, engages in a mythification of its material, emptying it of its meaning and, in a gesture of political and ideo-

---

18 Jelinek, "Die endlose Unschuldigkeit," 1970; a separate reprint of the essay along with several other works by Jelinek appeared ten years later in Elfriede Jelinek, *Die endlose Unschuldigkeit: Prosa, Hörspiel, Essay* (Schwifting: Schwiftinger Galerie-Verlag, 1980).
19 For a thorough discussion of Jelinek's sources, see Michael Fischer, *Trivialmythen in Elfriede Jelineks Romanen "Die Liebhaberinnen" und "Die Klavierspielerin"* (St. Ingbert: W. J. Röhrig, 1991), 14–16.
20 Fischer, *Trivialmythen in Elfriede Jelineks Romanen "Die Liebhaberinnen" und "Die Klavierspielerin,"* 15.
21 Maria Elisabeth Brunner, *Die Mythenzertrümmerung der Elfriede Jelinek* (Neuried: Ars Una, 1997), 56–57.
22 Brunner, *Die Mythenzertrümmerung der Elfriede Jelinek*, 37–38.

logical engagement, filling it with new signifying potential. It remains Jelinek's initial point of entry into the semiological enterprise of Roland Barthes and the bridge from it to her later appropriations of Barthes' thought in her novels.

If Barthes was concerned in *Mythologies* with mythological modes of thought among the French bourgeoisie and popular culture, Jelinek turns her attentions to the myths that constitute the media landscape and popular political reality of her time. "The lesson of myth [*mütos*]," she writes, "may be considered a theory of revolution (hans barth)."[23] Later, she links the formation of "trivial myths" with the creation of the revolutionary masses. These constructs enable the formation of a larger social myth that will in turn inspire (or incite) social reformation and revolution; from this perspective, the modifier "trivial" evinces a deep irony. As in Barthes, however, the notion of myth in Jelinek is highly ambiguous. On the one hand, trivial myths by her definition are those "whose main principles are paternalistic content in culture & individual form the central social hinges of power monopolistically institutionalized channels of control in which you are met by the common interests of the ruling powers."[24] The social formation Jelinek diagnoses in her examination of myth links three primary discourses that Barthes leaves largely by the wayside: Lacanian psychoanalysis, contemporary media (television), and sexuality. On the other hand, trivial myths represent the means by which social change through mass media is possible, and popular culture, which is anything but trivial, is the nexus of theory and praxis, as it was for Barthes and will be for Thomas Meinecke.

While Barthes is still beholden to a culture based primarily on print media and film, Jelinek sees with McLuhan the rise of television and advertising and reads them, using the repeated trope of "channels of control," as "the super ego of mass communication."[25] The insertion into the text of countless quotations and references from television culture, tabloid newspapers, and advertising continues the ambiguity of Jelinek's stance towards myth. As examples of myth Jelinek lists "woman and her sexuality,"[26] "the bourgeois myth of the 'peaceful coexistence' of the family in a peaceful untroubled bourgeois universe with a protective 'strict but just' father in the foreground,"[27] "that myth of the bourgeois psychiatrist,"[28] "the myth of the communality of all humanity,"[29] "the myth of humani-

---

23 Jelinek, "Die endlose Unschuldigkeit," 1970, 40.
24 Jelinek, "Die endlose Unschuldigkeit," 1970, 41.
25 Jelinek, "Die endlose Unschuldigkeit," 1970, 42.
26 Jelinek, "Die endlose Unschuldigkeit," 1970, 41.
27 Jelinek, "Die endlose Unschuldigkeit," 1970, 51.
28 Jelinek, "Die endlose Unschuldigkeit," 1970, 56.
29 Jelinek, "Die endlose Unschuldigkeit," 1970, 58.

ty,"[30] and "the myth of the man in the doctor's white coat as an enlightener."[31] If one takes these explicit elaborations of "trivial myths" as structurally important for Jelinek's text, one may read a closer connection between Jelinek's critique of bourgeois sensibility in media and her concern for the psychoanalytic causes of this structuring, particularly as her cultural tradition – the cradle of psychoanalysis itself – is steeped in Freudian lore. In fact, this may point to two primary differences between Barthes' and Jelinek's explications of myth.

First, Jelinek's identification of "the old mystification" as "nature instead of history"[32] points to an implicit critique of Barthes as an outmoded mythologist insofar as he provides the basis for her initial engagement with myth. How does Jelinek, then, conceive of the new mystification? While she avoids a direct definition in "Endless Innocence," she alludes through her argumentation to a naturalization of politics whereby myth robs history of its political dimension: "everything: content image and effect aims then to depoliticize to suspend the determining weight of history."[33] Barthes had alluded to the incommensurability of ideology and poetry (specifically in the *nouveau roman*)[34] at the conclusion of the *Mythologies*,[35] but Jelinek counters his claim by documenting the pervasiveness of depoliticization in all forms of media.

A second difference – and perhaps the hallmark of Jelinek's engagement with myth both in this essay and in her novels *Lust* (1989) and *The Piano Teacher* (1983) – is the combination of the semiological problem of myth with one of psychoanalysis and, by extension, gender. Given that Freudian (and in particular Lacanian) psychoanalysis transformed the study of the unconscious into a linguistic and semiological narrative, Jelinek appropriates mythification as a complex practice of signification that always resonates between the guiding frameworks of psychoanalysis and semiosis. In so doing, however, she redeploys the same narrative figuration as Barthes. That is, she employs myths to uncover myths, in this case particularly the myth of the Father/Phallus, the patriarchal basis for the psychic and social order.

---

30 Jelinek, "Die endlose Unschuldigkeit," 1970, 59.
31 Jelinek, "Die endlose Unschuldigkeit," 1970, 63.
32 Jelinek, "Die endlose Unschuldigkeit," 1970, 59.
33 Jelinek, *Die endlose Unschuldigkeit*, 1980, 74; I cite the reprinted version of the essay (1980) here. The original (1970) appears to have an editorial corruption in "das bestimmte gewichte." Compare Jelinek, "Die endlose Unschuldigkeit," 1970, 59.
34 "(by poetry I understand, in a very general way, the search for the inalienable meaning of things)." Barthes, *Mythologies*, 274.
35 Barthes, *Mythologies*, 274.

Through this mythification Jelinek is able to uncover a dynamic of depoliticized and dehistoricized speech (the oppression of women) in her narratives, but at the cost of perpetuating a myth of psychoanalytic cosmogony. That this practice is inherently satiric we have seen in Barthes' *Mythologies*. This argument proceeds further in the following chapters with an examination of Jelinek's novels *Lust* and *The Piano Teacher*. The former, a problematic attempt to render the obscene in a distinctly feminine vein, contrasts in style with the latter, a more traditional novelistic narrative of Austrian cultural myths superimposed upon one another in a story of subjectivity, domination, and cultural patrimony.

7. Elfriede Jelinek's Mythic *Lust* (1989)

Despite her admission of failure in finding "a feminine language for the obscene"[1] in her 1989 novel *Lust*, Elfriede Jelinek nevertheless reveals through language the malicious patriarchal patina of the Austrian cultural paradigms she references. Her violent narrative representation of reality, reduced to a series of paradigmatic tropes, betrays a critical impulse that has been interpreted as satiric.[2] A not uncontroversial Nobel Prize winner in 2004, Jelinek is in fact heir to a long Austrian tradition of authors and satirists whose focus is their own medium: language. From Hugo von Hofmannsthal's amusingly eloquent language crisis, to the polemic writings of Karl Kraus, the cabaret puns of Helmut Qualtinger, and the experimental poetry of members of the Wiener Gruppe in the 1950s, Jelinek draws upon her forebears and focuses on her homeland through the prism of language.[3] From sports and the patrimony of the Austrian musical tradition to capitalism and marriage, the novel *Lust*, for example, situates its broad range of topoi within structuralist and feminist discourses on gender relations and power dynamics in Luce Irigaray and Michel Foucault – which contextualize the novel within the feminist tradition – while drawing upon Roland Barthes' notion of myth.

Aside from its theoretical and political framework, however, Jelinek's novel also participates in an intertextual dialogue about representations of sexuality and sexual desire, a dialogue far more complicated than one of mere polemics. Ostensibly written in response to Georges Bataille's *Story of the Eye* [*Histoire de l'œil*],[4] *Lust* caused widespread consternation and furor in literary and journalis-

---

[1] Sigrid Löffler, "'Ich mag Männer nicht, aber ich bin sexuell auf sie angewiesen': Gespräch über Pornographie, die Sprache des Obszönen, den Haß und das Altern," *Profil*, March 28, 1989, 83.
[2] Konstanze Fliedl, "'Echt sind nur wir!' Realismus und Satire bei Elfriede Jelinek," in *Elfriede Jelinek*, ed. Kurt Bartsch and Günther A. Höfler (Graz: Droschl, 1991), 57–77; Annette Runte, *Lesarten der Geschlechterdifferenz: Studien zur Literatur der Moderne* (Bielefeld: Aisthesis, 2005), 275–299. Jelinek has also personally described her roots in the Austrian satiric tradition of Karl Kraus and Elias Canetti. See John Pizer, "Modern vs. Postmodern Satire: Karl Kraus and Elfriede Jelinek," *Monatshefte* 86, no. 4 (1994): 500–501.
[3] For a comprehensive survey of Jelinek's influences and the literary traditions in which she participates, see Alexandra Millner, "Schreibtraditionen," in *Jelinek-Handbuch*, ed. Pia Janke (Stuttgart: J. B. Metzler, 2013), 36–40.
[4] Georges Bataille, *Histoire de l'œil* (Paris: Gallimard, 1993); Georges Bataille, *Story of the Eye* (New York: Urizen Books, 1977); Ina Hartwig deconstructs this oft-cited notion, lifted wholesale from Jelinek's own interviews, in her book *Sexuelle Poetik: Proust. Musil. Genet. Jelinek.* (Frankfurt am Main: Fischer Taschenbuch Verlag, 1998), 230–233. Brought to a point: "Reference to Bataille's 'Story of the Eye' – a narrative celebrated by prominent contemporaries like Susan

tic circles upon its release, fueled largely by leaked summaries and interviews with the author before publication and stoked by prejudicial assessment of its uncompromising (and unceasing) sexualized language and the horrific imagery of rape and sexual violence that pervades its 250-odd pages.[5] The lust of its title is of a decidedly unappealing kind, transgressing the boundaries of value norms – particularly "in this Roman Catholic country"[6] – in an exposé of sexuality and gendered agency in an Austrian society devoid of empathy and deeper character psychology.

Perhaps because of Jelinek's lifelong engagement with critical theories, *Lust* has often been read as a continuation of a theoretical project – begun with her publication in 1970 of "Endless Innocence" as a summary grappling with Barthes' *Mythologies* – that seeks to dismantle the fiction of social reality as whole and given and instead reveals the active forces at work in obscuring the subjugation, violence, and lack of agency that lurk beneath reality's surface.[7] For some, Jelinek's narrative representation of society under the sign of patriarchal domination involves a destruction of the second-order semiological system that occludes reality's inherently gendered – and thus political – structure.[8] Challenging this assertion, a more contemporary reading of *Lust* interprets this narrative representation not as destruction *per se*, but as a deconstruction that stops short of eliminating the myths. In her particular brand of narrative, so it is argued, Jelinek merely exposes myths as received constructions of social paradigms, thus under-

---

Sontag and Roland Barthes – is [...] perhaps just intentionally deployed bait in the run-up to publication. This reference raises expectations that are then intentionally, or so one might suppose, disappointed" (247).

5 For a review of the historical context of the publication and reception of *Lust*, see Jutta Schlich, *Phänomenologie der Wahrnehmung von Literatur: Am Beispiel von Elfriede Jelineks "Lust" (1989)* (Tübingen: Max Niemeyer, 1994), 7–13.

6 Elfriede Jelinek, *Lust* (Reinbek bei Hamburg: Rowohlt, 1989), 127; Elfriede Jelinek, *Lust*, trans. Michael Hulse (London: Serpent's Tail, 1992), 106. References to *Lust* in this chapter will appear in the text parenthetically, with dual pages numbers of the German original and the English translation, separated by a semicolon.

7 Günther A. Höfler, "Sexualität und Macht in Elfriede Jelineks Prosa," *Modern Austrian Literature* 23, no. 3/4 (1990): 99–110; Marlies Janz, *Elfriede Jelinek* (Stuttgart: J. B. Metzler, 1995); Beatrice Hanssen, "Elfriede Jelinek's Language of Violence," *New German Critique*, no. 68 (1996): 79–112; Bärbel Lücke, *Elfriede Jelinek: Eine Einführung in das Werk* (Paderborn: Fink, 2008).

8 For representative readings from the perspective of demythification, see Christa Gürtler, "Die Entschleierung der Mythen von Natur und Sexualität," in *Gegen den schönen Schein. Texte zu Elfriede Jelinek*, ed. Christa Gürtler (Frankfurt am Main: Verlag Neue Kritik, 1990), 120–134; Janz, *Elfriede Jelinek*, 111–122; and Françoise Rétif, "Die Lust am Obszönen bei Georges Bataille und Elfriede Jelinek," in *Elfriede Jelinek: Sprache, Geschlecht und Herrschaft*, ed. Françoise Rétif and Johann Sonnleitner (Würzburg: Königshausen & Neumann, 2008), 107–118.

cutting their validity with revelations of their arbitrariness and fictionality.[9] Whatever its disposition towards myth, criticism of *Lust* tends to coalesce around two elements that set up a narrative habitus of opposition: gender dynamics and the violent (and tolerated) oppression of women.

To claim, however, that Jelinek's own stance towards these tropes is one of pure opposition, be it destructive or deconstructive, overlooks the complexity of *Lust* and mistakes the underlying narrative ideology for one of coherent feminist criticism. In spite of its saturation with sexualized violence, *Lust* is not solely a text about the subjugation of women or the impossibility of female desire or feminine pornography. It is about this too, of course, but the revelatory dynamic at work in its pages involves exposing not just the trivial myths by which patriarchal society shapes its reality, but also the myths that enable the possibility of Jelinek's narrative point of view. As such, *Lust* both defuses and disassembles constitutive myths – such as sports, music, and capitalism – while constructing others – like the frigidity of women and their lack of agency. For all the tidy critical assertions that Jelinek's *Lust* shatters patriarchal myths, what we find is the production of new myths from the shards of the old. This reinscription of reality into a mythic system of signs constitutes a primary aspect of Jelinek's satiric effect. Hers is a game of language, manifest in the lyric playfulness of her homophonous words, portmanteaus, minimal pairs, and incessant zeugmata. The tenor of the novel is not that of an activist screed, but rather that of a sober, detached collage: a self-referential arrangement of signifiers and signs that, through language, exposes the historicity of trivial myths while suppressing others. Rather than offering a new theory, Jelinek "specializes in developing a poetics that satisfies the hypothesis that language is always already present."[10] In staging a narrative reality predicated upon paradigmatic notions of language, law, helplessness, pornography, and psychoanalysis, Jelinek demonstrates satire to be both a linguistic-semiotic and an ideological construct.

Although listing myth *production* as one of the primary textual (and satiric) practices in Jelinek's *Lust* contradicts certain conventional readings, two bodies of evidence support this conclusion. Critical examinations of *Lust* that focus on the destruction of myths through narrative have generally associated myth production – "which, in general, denotes the concealment of conditions of domination, primarily by 'naturalizing' them"[11] – not with the second-order semiological system envisioned by Roland Barthes in his *Mythologies*, but with a simple mask-

---

9 See Lücke, *Elfriede Jelinek*, 81–90.
10 Hartwig, *Sexuelle Poetik*, 258–259.
11 Janz, *Elfriede Jelinek*, 121.

ing of reality. Following such a logic, a gesture of exposure whereby the one removes the "snot of naturalness [*natürlichkeitsschleim*]"[12] covering reality is equivalent to myth destruction. In his essay on myths today, however, Barthes points not only to the naturalness of mythic systems, but also to the ahistorical character of myths and the ineluctability of mythification.[13]

The first of these, ahistoricity, cannot be resolved by merely revealing the presence of a mythic structure; the layering of signification must be fully historicized. The second of these is more problematic. What such readings of Jelinek fail to take into account when considering her alleged shattering of myths are the clandestine myths inherent in Jelinek's own ideological position, those necessary for its very function. To operate with myths, essentially signifiers that are signifieds for other signs, is a commonplace, and the avoidance of certain myths will necessarily involve the invocation of others. Few critics of *Lust* have attempted to read Jelinek with respect to the myth production of her own position, be it feminist or anti-establishment, focusing their energies instead on her textual deconstruction of the naturalness of cultural tropes.[14]

As Barthes has suggested, "the best weapon against myth is perhaps to mythify it in its turn, and to produce an *artificial myth*: and this reconstituted myth will in fact be a mythology. Since myth robs language of something, why not rob myth?"[15] In approaching the mythology of Austrian society and countering its

---

12 Jelinek, "Die endlose Unschuldigkeit," 1970, 45.
13 Barthes, *Mythologies*, 245–247. Jelinek appears to conflate the terms mythification and mystification (her preference). For this reason, I use them interchangeably here.
14 Hartwig, *Sexuelle Poetik*. A relatively solitary figure in Jelinek scholarship, Ina Hartwig distinguishes herself from her peers through her overt skepticism of both Jelinek's own assertions about her writing and the received knowledge on *Lust*. Her analysis of the sexual poetics in Jelinek's work, specifically in *Lust*, which she reads as a "poetics of annihilation" (276) thus warrants a closer look. Hartwig's historicization of marriage within the context of Austrian legal history, for example, chronicles a gendered narrative of female conjugal duties established by judicial decisions that both legislate female sexual "willingness for self-sacrifice" (237–242) and punish women disproportionately for adultery. That the power dynamics in Gerti's marriage to Hermann essentially constitute the fabric of the narrative thus results not from any notion of marriage as myth, but from one inscribed openly in Austrian juridical history and the penal code. By Hartwig's estimation, and I would agree, the focus on the imbalance of power in the gender wars – the "war of genitals" she prefers to call it (249) – is misplaced: "It is not 'relations of power and ownership' that Jelinek denounces, as some critics would have it, but rather, if she is denouncing anything, the misuse of theorems, of linguistic realities" (265). Instead, Hartwig argues, Jelinek covertly coopts the semiotic strategies of pornographic, juridical, and psychoanalytic discourses to naturalize her own narrative: to mythify a conception of woman as lacking in identity, subjectivity, and sexual desire.
15 Barthes, *Mythologies*, 246–247.

"snot of naturalness" with artificial myths of her own, Jelinek would seem to beat the insistence and insistent circulation of cultural myths at their own game. The modality of Jelinek's satiric practice in fact comports with this suggestion to counter myth not with a destructive force, but with its own means: to seek, as Barthes advised, a semiological solution to a semiological problem. In *Lust* the issue of mythification is ultimately an issue of language, not ideology.

And Jelinek's mythification is virtuosic. The wordplay, double entendres, citational practices, and emphasis on the sound and organization of language over narrative progression points to a decidedly linguistic project: "an overkill of metaphors [...], a semiotic excess."[16] Nowhere in this surplus of meaning does the text explicitly offer criticism of the myths it exposes or of those it deploys. The horrors of Jelinek's imagery and the absence of empathy on the part of the narrative may be said to invite such criticism from its readership through a reception of the abject. But a linguistic project cuts across the grain of scholarship and poses the question of the ontological nature of such a text.[17] What aim does this disjunction serve? One might recognize in the narrative representation of a reality predicated on the production (and deconstruction) of artificial myths a layering of signifiers that overloads the text with surplus meaning – the distortion so often imputed to satire.

If, for Jelinek, Barthes could be summarized with the formula "the old mystification: nature instead of history,"[18] we will see in the following pages her new dynamic – the new mystification – as a conscious and thus artificial 'naturalizing' of politics instead of history. Perhaps by coincidence this deployment of myth-making as a satiric strategy offers a further solution to an intractable problem Barthes diagnosed in his *Mythologies*: the failing of a "synthesis between ideology and poetry."[19] By combining her poetics of myth-making with a satiric gesture, Jelinek continually reinscribes the semiotics of satire – and thus the semiotics of mythification – into politics and ideology.[20]

---

16 Hartwig, *Sexuelle Poetik*, 262.
17 Hartwig, *Sexuelle Poetik*, 260. "If *Lust* is not meant to be critical of society," Hartwig ponders, "which is to say, if it pursues a noble aim, for which reason the bawdy jokes would have to be tolerated because the ends justify the means, then this text would be – a joke?" The ethical dimensions of making a joke of such earnest material notwithstanding, I would argue that Hartwig alludes to the satiric dimension of *Lust*.
18 Jelinek, "Die endlose Unschuldigkeit," 1970, 59.
19 Barthes, *Mythologies*, 274.
20 For a further discussion of the repoliticization of myth, see Lücke, *Elfriede Jelinek*, 29.

The Lust That Wasn't

Judging by the critical reaction to Elfriede Jelinek's *Lust* upon its publication in 1989, the novel consists of both an onslaught of repellent sexualized imagery and "a condensing of narration that makes reading *Lust* almost as unpalatable as the kind of 'lust' in which the prose trades."[21] On the one hand, "metaphoric overkill" permits a saturation of the text with sexualized double entendres and multiple layers of meaning. On the other hand, this curious language shapes a narrative that refuses to grant more than schematic identities to its archetypal characters – "the Woman," "Father" or "the Direktor," "the child" – essentially rendering them less accessible to readerly empathy or pity. Jelinek's novel reads thus as a kind of anti-fable, recounting through wordplay the attempts of the protagonist Gerti to escape her domineering husband Hermann's insatiable, violent sexual appetite into the ostensible salvation of the young student Michael. The ubiquity of maltreatment, rape, and violence forecloses any possibility of escape, leaving Gerti to commit infanticide. An absence of psychological depth, reflection, and motivation characterizes the text, along with a style that draws upon and cites the inversions (and verses) of Hölderlin's poetry to a degree that has led one critic to dub it a "poem in prose" by pointing to its affinity for lyric rather than epic language.[22] Questions of genre aside, this assessment of Jelinek's text gets to the heart of the matter, which is not the sexual imagery[23]: "[...] the most important aspect of *Lust* is not what is named or denoted in the language of objects [...], but rather its play of signifiers – that is, the 'metalanguage' of connotation, by means of which (in Roland Barthes' terminology) a 'secondary semiological system of sense' is constituted. That which is denoted remains more or less constant, vis-à-vis the play of connotations."[24] While myth-making serves as a framework for the proliferation of connotation, Jelinek achieves this surplus of signification not as a secondary system of sense but as a further, tertiary layer of meaning. Indeed, the "play of signi-

---

21 Janz, *Elfriede Jelinek*, 122.
22 "*Lust* is therefore an unmatchable chain of witty catachreses, metaphors, hyperboles, paranomasies, and plays on words of all sorts." Hans H. Hiebel, "Elfriede Jelinek's Satirical Prose-Poem 'Lust,'" in *Elfriede Jelinek: Framed by Language*, ed. Jorun B. Johns and Katherine Arens (Riverside, CA: Ariadne, 1994), 56.
23 As one critic rather drily puts it: "If one were in fact to quantify [...] the thematic proportions of the text to the point of evaluating its words statistically, it would turn out that at best one quarter of the total number of pages deals directly with sex, linguistically and thematically speaking." Matthias Luserke, "Ästhetik des Obszönen: Elfriede Jelineks 'Lust' als Protokoll einer Mikroskopie des Patriarchats," *Text + Kritik: Zeitschrift für Literatur*, no. 117 (1993): 61.
24 Hiebel, "Elfriede Jelinek's Satirical Prose-Poem 'Lust,'" 56.

fiers" – the polyvalent metaphors, the minimal pairs, the homophonous words, the portmanteaus, and the literary citations – essentially gives the novel form while allowing the surplus of meaning provided by the signifiers to counter the textual myths with new, artificial ones.

In the opening passage of the novel, for example, Jelinek sets up the gendered dynamic of domination and possession, inherited partially as a commonplace from feminist discourses and underscored by a language that resonates between religion and psychoanalysis. Woman's domain is separate, unseen behind the peculiar composite "curtains" that both demarcate her realm and hide her from sight "in her house [*Gehäuse*]" (7; 7), an enclosure of sorts that suggests captivity but also the paradigmatic connection between femininity and beastliness: be it as a "pet [*Haustier*]" (33; 29) or the "animals [*Viecher*]" in the "byre" (146; 120). Marked only by a definite article, which ironically only emphasizes her indefiniteness, the woman of the opening stands in solitary opposition to others capable of possession on a zeugmatic level: possession of "homes [*Eigenheime*]" – a sign of economic status – and "qualities [*Eigenheiten*]" – signs of differentiated identity. Even the poor, Jelinek writes, have faces that distinguish them from the woman without qualities although they, too, prove derivative of the Direktor, pointing in their sleep to their connections to him, a polar point of orientation. In her first intertextual reference, Jelinek links their fealty to him – "their eternal Father" who "dispenses truth as readily as he breathes out air" (7; 7) – to that of the woman via the quasi-religious overtones of a bastardization of Hölderlin.[25] The unnamed man is the condition for the possibility of life, source of breath and truth, unquestioned in his dominion, through Hölderlin the link to a high cultural tradition – and focused solely on possessing this one woman, "this woman. His woman" (7; 7). His is a primordial Adamitic state, still linked with nature, "as unknowing as the trees all around" (7; 7).

Only at the end of this opening passage does the narrator allude to the Direktor's marriage – and adulterous lechery – albeit without making an explicit connection between him and the woman in her enclosure. Indeed, the text draws a veritable curtain between the woman and the man, separating them with the lowly poor and thereby refusing the reader the certainty of their marital union. The closing, which reads as a line from a fairy tale, transfigures what would appear to be a marriage predicated upon domination into a seemingly idyllic relationship of symbiotic interdependence. With no shame before each other, the two "laugh. They have been in the past, are now and ever shall be all things to each other" (7; 7). The combination of present and past verb tenses likewise suggests a

---

[25] For a fuller examination of this reference, see Janz, *Elfriede Jelinek*, 115.

frozen eternity of reliance and contentment, a relationship without a history of turmoil or, incidentally, of the violent rapes and molestations that occur in the ensuing pages.

The strategies Jelinek employs in the opening – the definite articles that evoke archetypal figures without histories, the allusion to power dynamics of relationships, the animalistic metaphors, the minimal pairings with zeugma – all suggest a staging of an ahistorical myth of patriarchy through literature, religion, capitalism, and, if we take the reference to the Father to be suggestive of Freudian or Lacanian discourse, psychoanalysis. The intersection of at least four discourses on this point – the suggestion of feminine difference or alterity – magnifies the intensity of the rhetoric. The superimposition of a male poetic history, a gendered conception of almighty divinity, the maleness of management hierarchy, and the masculine basis for models of the psyche and psychic development affirms the notion of male domination expounded in the opening. It also simultaneously occludes the disparate histories of these discourses. Through this occlusion the novel produces a myth of patriarchy, a sign of unquestioned authority and domination whose signifier, in turn, operates as a sign of these discourses of social formation: a second-order semiological meaning. Patriarchy has a history, but its connotations of power and domination appear timeless as a result of the ahistoricity of the discourses to which it refers.

And yet Jelinek adds a third degree of semiological obfuscation. Couched within a novelistic context, the lyric playfulness of her language brings itself into sharp relief as an end in itself, and the dynamic of language ultimately mythifies the notion of man as well. Reading the first sentence of the passage as an illustration of a linguistic issue, one finds a hidden dynamic based on a semiological platitude. Marked by the definite article as a general case, the woman becomes a signifier, and the signifier "woman" is separated from other signifiers that also possess qualities. Woman, the text suggests, is thus distinguished from other signifiers by difference, an elementary principle of semiotic theories since Saussure. The arbitrariness of this difference, an ahistorical principle of semiotic thought in its own right, illuminates the patriarchal discourses – language, religion, capitalism, and psychoanalysis – as predicated upon a mere idiosyncrasy of language.[26] If all that separates woman from man is the whimsy of language, then man too is always syntagmatically dependent on woman, an explanation that accounts for the conclusion of the opening, that they "have been in the past, are now and ever shall be all things to each other" (7; 7). The myths Jelinek cites in the incipit

---

[26] One might contrast the ways in which these discourses are problematized in Roland Barthes' *Mythologies* and treated in Georges Bataille's *Story of the Eye*.

thus exhibit a peculiar tension between the rhetoric of their foundation – one of gendered hierarchy – and that of the governing myth (language) – one of interdependence.

From this perspective, *Lust* operates differently on the narrative and mythic levels. While propounding a story of violent subjection and abjection, the novel erects a gendered hierarchy within the framework of language, wherein hierarchies yield to syntagmatic substitution and arbitrariness. Given the irruptions of wordplay and metaphor in the novel – the "semiotic excess" from before – the suspicion that the novel is reduced to a joke in the absence of social criticism is not far off the mark. Proceeding from that suspicion, the surplus of metaphor and wordplay in Jelinek's text proffers the reader not a joke, but linguistic playfulness as a counterbalance to the violent hierarchies of the plot. Minimal pairs like *Eigenheim* [home] and *Eigenheit* [quality] and other homophonies amount to more than stylistic cleverness. Their omnipresence in the text serves to underscore the gossamer qualities and contingencies of language upon which the myth of patriarchy is based. By the same token, Jelinek, in revealing the perilously constructed cardhouse of masculinist myths, must employ one of her own: that of language as a system of arbitrary differences for conveying meaning. The narrative level of the text thus engages in a mythologization of cultural patrimony-as-patriarchy, while the mythic level of the text – the metanarrative – deconstructs the edifice of hierarchies in the story through performative games of language.[27]

The violence and gender imbalance of the narrative level is likewise premised upon a myth of female frigidity and male potency. Despite differing treatments of this topic in Jelinek's other works, "the desexualization of 'the Woman' in *Lust* lacks a – narrated – prior history. Her desexualization is, as it were, the a priori, the precondition for the indefatigably repeated appropriation of the Woman by the Man [...]."[28] Whether this *a priori* condition for the subjugation of Gerti by Hermann points to a pervasive misogyny in Jelinek's thought is immaterial (though compelling). Its deployment within the mythic structure of the novel again demonstrates the intersection of the foundational myths – the overlap of capitalist desexualization of women with psychoanalytic postulates of feminine frigidity, for example – while simultaneously unmasking their veiled contingency and thereby deconstructing them as falsely ahistorical absolutes.

---

[27] They are performative insofar as they demonstrate the contingencies of language through consonantal shifts, vowel shifts, minimal pairs, suffix substitution, homophony, and portmanteau blending.
[28] Hartwig, *Sexuelle Poetik*, 250.

That Jelinek mobilizes myths of her own counters the claims of critics who argue that reading her work amounts "to practicing the destruction of myths,"[29] "the *deconstruction* of myths,"[30] or even "the shattering of myths."[31] In his own estimation, however, Barthes had warned that "the very effort one makes in order to escape [myth's] stranglehold becomes in its turn the prey of myth: myth can always, as a last resort, signify the resistance which is brought to bear against it"[32] and thus guarantee its recurrence; "nothing can be safe from myth,"[33] even attempts to dispel it. But to turn it upon itself, to mythify myth, is the "best weapon" against it.[34] Jelinek's redeployment of myth through language thus activates a new semiological layer of meaning, a new series of condensations and displacements that counteract the substrate of masculinist myths and with which the reader and critic must contend. "This is why Jelinek's 'linguistic destructions,' wordplay, jokes, puns, and neologisms are not just negative shattering of language, which is to say, destruction. They are [...] already 'différance in operation' [...]."[35] From this perspective one might argue that Jelinek's writing deploys its critical potential in the use of myth "when it exposes the metalanguage that informs the sexually explicit, licentious, and scandalous rhetoric it parades, to the point where philosophical and cultural traditions – whether it be the institutions of the church and family, Vienna's venerable music culture, or Germany's philosophy of 'Geist' – turn out to be the very accomplices of pornography."[36] It is precisely from this gesture of using myth to expose the fallacious and insidious underbelly of cultural discourses – and their link with one another – that Jelinek's *Lust* derives its satiric impulse, and by which satire as a purely semiotic practice (unwittingly) regains its critical drive.

---

29 Janz, *Elfriede Jelinek*, 113.
30 Lücke, *Elfriede Jelinek*, 29.
31 Brunner, *Die Mythenzertrümmerung der Elfriede Jelinek*.
32 Barthes, *Mythologies*, 246.
33 Barthes, *Mythologies*, 242.
34 Barthes, *Mythologies*, 246.
35 Lücke, *Elfriede Jelinek*, 30.
36 Hanssen, "Elfriede Jelinek's Language of Violence," 97.

Repetition

With the unsettling of fixed connotations through the innuendo of its metaphors,[37] the novel brings together disparate discursive strands in individual signifiers whose multiple meanings are superimposed as palimpsests in the story. This satiric intersection of discourses appears most visibly in these multivalent signifiers Jelinek repeats throughout her text: the word *Bach* [stream, or the composer's name], for instance, which appears in various forms twenty-four times.[38] Its narrative significance derives from the fact that it is a topographical marker of landscape, a reference to a patriarchal musical tradition, a part of the idiom *den Bach runter gehen* [to go down the tubes, to go up shit creek], a metaphor for urination and the abject,[39] but also for nature, and of course the infamous site where Gerti dumps the corpse of her murdered, nameless child. From the outset, the novel codes *Bach* as feminine, in spite of its linguistic gender; Gerti functions for her son "as a babbling brook" (12; 11 [translation amended, DB]) that courses below, "to be heard somewhere far beneath him, in the depths" (12; 11). The metaphor both suggests maternal support and adumbrates the infanticide in the concluding pages as the brook carries away his body: "The Mother meanwhile keeps loving the child more and more and down the tubes, this child" (158; 130 [translation amended, DB]).

But Jelinek also denotes with *Bach* a literal stream flowing close to Gerti's home (60, 74; 51, 63), its current hampered by the winter frost (61; 51) and polluted by the toxins dumped into it by her husband's factory (66, 69, 99, 133, 168, 173; 56, 59, 83, 110, 138, 142). Upon these topographical meanings Jelinek projects a further metaphoric layer, one reminiscent of the Prater scene in *The Piano Teacher*, in which a stream of urine combines with sexual voyeurism and pleasure. Here, too, this same stream connotes a stream of urine, vomit, or semen, a meaning that evokes the abjection by which the subject constitutes itself and from which, in *Lust*, men repeatedly derive pleasure (101, 192, 210, 222, 236; 85, 157, 171, 180, 192). By the same token, Jelinek contrasts this imagery of abjection with a myth of unsullied nature (187, 223; 152, 181) that nevertheless carries off social and sexual

---

37 Hartwig makes a solid case for considering the "pansexualism" in the novel as a problem of language. See especially *Sexuelle Poetik*, 259–270.
38 Jelinek, *Lust*, 1989, 12, 60, 61, 66, 69, 74, 99, 101, 133, 152, 158, 168, 173, 186, 187, 192, 210, 214, 222, 223, 227, 236, 238, 255; Jelinek, *Lust*, 1992, 11, 51, 56, 59, 63, 83, 85, 110, 124, 130, 138, 142, 152, 157, 171, 174, 180, 181, 184, 192, 194, 207.
39 For an extensive study of how abjection functions as a means of constituting the subject, see Julia Kristeva, *Powers of Horror: An Essay on Abjection*, trans. Leon S. Roudiez (New York: Columbia University Press, 1982).

effluent (152, 214, 227; 124, 174, 184–185). In this haze of multivalent connotations, Jelinek ultimately combines strands of naturalness, feminine identity, cultural patrimony, abjection, and purifying flow, which resonate with the idiom 'to go up shit creek' (238; 194).

With the final appearance of *Bach*, Gerti exercises her agency in a decisive move: returning her murdered child to the maternal, purifying waters of nature that will carry away evidence of her crime and, through the abjection of this corpse, help her assert her subjectivity. "Now the woman is at the stream [*Bach*], and the next moment her son sinks in, contented. Perfect peace is beckoning" (255; 207). The tenor of the description is one of religious ritual, of ceremonial sacrifice: a return to nature in which the child himself is complicit as he sinks contentedly into the stream. "The mother carries the child," Jelinek writes, alluding both to Gerti's disposal of her son's lifeless body and, with the generality of the definite article, to pregnancy and the relation of mother to child, "and then, when she grows tired, drags him along behind her" (255; 207). Reunited with her natural sign, the stream, the mother then witnesses her dead son expunged from memory as he returns to his origin, undifferentiated from nature. To read *Lust* as a narrative of discursive intersections in multivalent signifiers is not to argue that these signs – in this case *Bach* – ultimately resolve their disparate connotations. On the contrary, Jelinek denies the reader this final resolution, thus maintaining the governing myth of significatory arbitrariness with which she began. It is in this unresolved connotative dissonance that Jelinek's satiric potential comes to the fore, for it is here that the satiric practice of layered mythification exposes the underlying mythic discord of the narrative. By orienting a reading of this novel around the repetition of *Bach*, for instance, one can see the satiric drive that results from the superimposition of mythic discourses via the arbitrariness of the sign (and thus the signifier).

Lust can also be interpreted with respect to its repetition of other signifiers aside from *Bach*, of course; one might consider other natural imagery *Berge* [mountains] or even the primary signifiers *Vater* [father], *Mutter* [mother], and *Kind* [child]. What such readings of *Lust* ultimately bring to light is a novelistic structure organized less according to teleological narrative (in its oft-maligned absence of plot: "a soap opera – like all of Jelinek's 'stories'"[40]) than by what one might term, with Julia Kristeva, the semiotic elements of its language: the eruptions of sound and non-representational aspects of the text that disrupt the story and thereby provide formal signposts and markers. If *Lust* is read as a chronicle of the crystallization of female subjectivity out of a paradigm of male domination,

---

[40] Janz, *Elfriede Jelinek*, 112.

for example, this structuring semiotic element comes to the fore in the repetition of words and sounds associated with feminine identity. For the protagonist of the novel, the ultimate signifier marking her agency is her name: the signifier that denotes her exclusively, in contrast to the generality of "the Woman."

Pursuing this kind of reading – tracing the (rare) use of the protagonist's proper name, for example – reveals a hidden relation between the narrative and metanarrative levels, insofar as the metanarrative is the story of Gerti's formation of identity. The (statistically significant) proliferation of "Gerti" in three chapters of the fifteen total suggests a narrative centered around three general scenes of Gerti's self-assertion. Their commonalities ultimately point to a tale of identity formation through semiotic differentiation. In other words, Gerti's narrative path to agency mirrors a semiotic dynamic in the metanarrative by which the signifier is accorded meaning through difference. Within the context of *Lust*, this assertion of narrative difference is necessarily one of violence and gendered opposition, the cutting of ties of spousal and sexual possession.

In light of the incipit, examined extensively above, it is no surprise that the novel names Gerti for the first time after more than fifty pages and, significantly, after her husband Hermann (56 and 18, respectively; 47 and 17 in the English). Of the fifteen chapters of the book, three name Gerti fifteen times or more while the other twelve chapters restrict themselves to but four or fewer mentions of her proper name.[41] This strikingly disproportionate distribution of "Gerti" in the text lends the more saturated textual passages a particular significance. Given that the proper name is a marker of difference by which a signifier corresponds to a unique referent, the three chapters in question mark a breakdown of the dynamic of ownership by which Gerti remains an undifferentiated object of her husband's possession and sexual desire. A closer examination of these passages in chapters eight, thirteen, and fifteen reveals an alignment of this metanarrative of semiotic differentiation with a narrative of increasing female agency under a patriarchal regime (of signs), but one with a satiric inversion.

The first two of these chapters involve Gerti's escape and escapades with Michael, the young student whose momentary interest in Gerti amounts to nothing more than the amusement of an easy conquest. With one of the few moments in which the third-person narrator apostrophizes the reader directly, the eighth chapter begins: "In all seriousness I call upon you: air and lust [*Luft und Lust*] for one and all!" (105; 88). Through her admonition, the narrator announces the beginning of a process of differentiation, advocating for everyone (and thus for

---

[41] By my count, "Gerti" appears in chapter eight 21 times, in chapter thirteen 30 times, and fifteen times in chapter fifteen.

Gerti, too) with the subtlety of a minimal pair the space of individuation and a desire of her own. The narrator's challenge sets in motion a proliferation of the female protagonist's proper name and, with it, the first evidence of Gerti's own reflections, combined with Jelinek's typical wordplay: "That is to say, even the plainest of women can make a man feel at home [*heimelig*] before paying him back [*heimzahlt*] with secrecies [*Heimlichkeiten*] and devotion [*Anhänglichkeit*]. This young man who has entered her life might be the great intellectual? Now everything will be different from how it was planned. We'll make a new plan on the spot. Our heads will swell good and proper" (106–107; 89 [translation amended, DB]). Besides its striking allusions to *Heimat* [homeland] and *Heim* [home] through similarly sounding signifiers like *heimelig*, *Heimlichkeiten*, and *heimzahlt* that mark a range of negative and positive connotations, this excerpt points to Gerti's individuated life ("her life") and the dynamic of differentiation through her conscious choice for Michael and her own development of a new plan for herself. The passive planning ("Now everything will be different from how it was planned"), which divests Gerti of agency, yields to the act of mapping out a new plan and to the image of self-inflation, as if Gerti's ego is enlarged through such an act. What follows is Gerti's first use of language, and at fever pitch: "Come on, she yells to Michael. As if she were demanding money of a shopkeeper who hates us customers" (107; 89). The scream, as the bloating before it, magnifies and intensifies the hitherto meek presence of Gerti in the text while, in its sexual call to him, seizing the desire accorded to her by the narrator.

Spurred on by this desire, Gerti engages consensually with Michael in a series of sex acts that nevertheless fail to release her from the mythic domination of man's possession. Notwithstanding two appearances of the genitive that reveal Gerti as the possessor rather than the possessed – "Gerti's jolly husband" (109; 91) and "Gerti's husband" (118; 98) – the language of Jelinek's novel still binds her character to imagery of inanimate function and property. She is the automobile the man must maintain: "a major service every few thousand miles" (113; 95). He awakens in Gerti "who wants to experience and attend to the highest heights" (116; 96 [translation amended, DB]) a sexual desire of her own: "desire has drawn Gerti out of herself, has struck a spark from her little pocket lighter, but where's this draught come from that's made the flame burn higher?" (118; 98). With the explosion of these flames of lust, Michael activates a growing sexual dependency as the "hero, who will provide shade on hot days and warm her on cold" (118; 98), reinstalling himself as a powerful male aggressor and possessor, the progenitor of her desire. The imbalance of deeper feelings (120; 100) leads the text to tamp down on Gerti's emergent subjectivity. "This young man," Jelinek writes, "created and conquered the white and awe-inspiring mountains of flesh before him. Like the evening sun, he has touched that face with red. He has taken a lease on the woman, and as far as she's concerned he can now grope under her dress whenever he likes" (124; 102 [translation amended, DB]). The text reinscribes the male as the dominant force through a series of metaphors that establish him as a godlike figure, a creator of natural beauty, who retains the right of sexual possession. As the chapter closes, the narrator warns the reader of the impending doom of Gerti's nascent dependency in mistaking "the old as the new" (124; 103): "And our declining star teaches us nothing at all" (124; 103). As Michael regains the upper hand over Gerti's pangs of desire, so too does Gerti's proper name disappear. Compared with 21 citations in chapter eight, the next four chapters average three mentions each of "Gerti." Only when the protagonist again strays from her oppressive husband in chapter thirteen – only when the signifier asserts its difference – does the proper name reappear in great number.

There an intoxicated Gerti pursues Michael and his friends on the ski slopes. The narrative situation has changed; the physical, verbal, and sexual abuse to which she is subjected do not accord with her sexual desire. What the reader witnesses here is the individuation of Gerti as a discrete object, a toy used for fun and derision, "a butt of ridicule like her entire sex [sic]" (197; 161). Jelinek inverts the connotation of the proper name as a sign of agency and employs it in this chapter as a marker of extreme objectification, an appellation of a woman "[t]ested so wrathfully in the school of life" (199; 162). In fact, in only one third of its appearances does Gerti's name appear as the subject of an active-voice sentence and in these cases with minimally active verbs: "Gerti and Michael slip" (196; 159), "Behind these mountains, Gerti has collapsed" (197; 160), "Gerti can follow everything very clearly" (200; 163), "Gerti has to prise her mouth open" (203; 165), "Gerti takes a lengthy break in a pub on the way" (208; 169), "Gerti sits silent" (209; 169), "Gerti gets up and sends her purse flying on the floor" (212; 172). Her name functions otherwise exclusively as an object of action and abuse.

As Michael and his friends molest Gerti in the snow, tearing at her person, her drunken desire for Michael, "a fine fire" (203; 165), is gradually extinguished by violent maltreatment and Michael's alcohol-induced erectile dysfunction. Reflecting upon the failure of her desire, Gerti finally realizes the limits of her own subjectivity: "Her mind is rioting in her head, banging at the walls of the skull it is contained in, that is to say: it goes to the limit" (207; 168). Only within her mind does she maintain agency, albeit violent agency. The myth of the arbitrary sign exposes the illusion of subjectivity through its expression in arbitrary language. In a satiric gesture Jelinek unravels the patriarchal myths of her text while superimposing upon them a myth of language that reveals its own inherent violence.

The final chapter marks the culmination both of Gerti's attempts to assert her own agency, and of the signifier's endeavors to establish its viability through difference. Narratively, the passage depicts four stations in her despair: her fruitless hammering at Michael's door to be rescued from her pursuing husband, Hermann's rape of her in front of Michael, the couple's return home, and her son's murder. For the first time, the female protagonist maintains her name while being assaulted. Once dragged back to the Direktor's car, however, she, along with her name, loses all grammatical agency, becoming as she was on the ski slopes the mere object, albeit personalized, of sexual violence. "This woman," the narrator laments, "never will [*darf*] she properly feel at home on this earth" (236; 192). This lamentation certainly also may be understood more generally as a protest of women's rootlessness within patriarchy and language. Her status subject to the permission of an unnamed order, "this woman" maintains a perpetually unstable existence, especially in language, which Jelinek illustrates in this chapter in particular.

The precariousness by which the signifier maintains its separateness, by which language maintains difference, is expressed in the explosion of homophonous word pairs that litter the chapter: *verfugt* [grouted] vs. *verfügt* [disposed] (235; cf. 191), "Es beginnt, leise zu schneien [Snow begins to fall softly]" vs. "Es beginnt, leise zu schreien [A faint screaming begins]" (235; 191), *Strömung* [stream] vs. *Stimmung* [sentiment] (236; cf. 192), *stampft* [stamps] vs. *strampelt* [kicks] (237; 193), *Losung* [scat] vs. *Lösung* [solution] (239; cf. 194), *Scharen* [throngs] vs. *schartigen* [thonged] (241; 196), *schauen* [gape] vs. *erschauern* [shudder] (241; 196), *strampelnd* [thrashing] vs. *stammelnd* [stammering] (242; 197), *züngelt* [licks] vs. *Zunge* [tongue] (244; 198), *Posten* [posts] vs. *Postern* [posterns] (245; 199), *Auftauchen* [presentation] vs. *Auftauen* [thawing] (247; 201), *Schaft* [shaft] vs. *schafft* [makes] (247; cf. 201), *Herde* [hearth] vs. *Herren* [lordsandmasters] (248; 201), *leitende* [managerial] vs. *liebende* [loving] (250; 203), *erneuert* [renewed] vs. *erneut* [again] (251; 203–204), *schwillt* [swelling] vs. *schwingt* [arising] (252; 205), *Betterln* [little beds] vs. *betteln* [begging] (253; 206), and *welk* [flaccid] vs. *Welt* [world] (254; 206). The focus on near homophony suggests an emphasis on the materiality of the signifier,[42] its physical properties as a series of phonemes, and its dependence upon difference for meaning. With the extreme sonic similarity of these words, Jelinek points to a perilously upheld difference in signs, which in turn signifies the inherent fragility of the linguistic system and mythic models based upon it. If the dictum at the chapter's opening is indeed correct that "people are never at a loss for words [*Sprache*], nor is there any more than words concealed in them" (235; 191), then the text ultimately constitutes humankind through language; self-referentially, it establishes the characters in

---

[42] See Bataille, *Story of the Eye*; Bataille, *Histoire de l'œil*.

the novel as phantoms of language and thus as false objects of empathy. As Gerti's name fades from the text after she has been brought back under the dominion of her husband, she is nevertheless still able to act. The final infanticide amounts to just as liberating a deed of identity formation as it is a horrifying perpetuation of the patriarchal violence perpetrated against Gerti.

Having predicated *Lust* upon a myth of language, Jelinek reveals the fallacy of myths governed by an arbitrary system of signs. *Lust* can thus mobilize mythification as a satiric practice by causing an overload of meaning in irresolvable discourses and connotations; mythification short-circuits the narrative thrust of the novel. And because this superfluous layer of myth causes a semiotic breakdown in the various substrata of masculinist myths in the text, *Lust* also demonstrates both how critical potential may be ascribed to satire and how politics – by 'robbing' inherently political myths of their function – may be reinscribed into mythology.

8. Viennese Paradigms in Elfriede Jelinek's *The Piano Teacher* (1983)

While the archetypal protagonists in *Lust* traverse the topography of the Austrian countryside, Jelinek takes a different tack in her relationship with the capital. The narrator of her 1983 novel, *The Piano Teacher*, evokes an image of Vienna petrified in the omnipresence of its historical past.[1] This novelistic enterprise is contoured and textured by references to the constitutive myths of old Vienna: psychoanalysis, hysteria, art music, modernist literature, cultural patrimony, political conservatism, sports, and the violence of a recent war. These strains of disparate discourses saturate the text in the form of allusions, passing references, brief citations, and longer structural quotations, intertwining, intersecting, and overlapping throughout. In its incessant repetition of these myths, Jelinek's novel operates analogously to the later *Lust*, laying the groundwork for the author's use of myth as a satiric practice in novelistic writing.

Perhaps most striking about Jelinek's *The Piano Teacher* is the wealth of interwoven discourses that recall the ponderous historical freight of the city in which the novel takes place. *The Piano Teacher* is a novel of Viennese mythologies, each of which guides and influences the narration by providing fodder for its narrative and its peculiarly visual-spatial narrative perspective. These myths likewise anchor the text within a particular field of literary history and literary tradition. Jelinek's references to psychoanalysis, for example, come as no surprise in a text that takes place in the cradle of Freudian analysis. But they are not, as we shall see, solely expository references to a place and its history. Instead, they invoke a discipline and its discourse, from Charcot to Freud to Lacan, and embed them within the narrative structure of the text. As such, Jelinek acts as a discursive heir to her modernist Viennese forebears whose contemporaneous writings placed them in intimate contact with the beginnings of psychoanalysis (Arthur Schnitzler and Frank Wedekind, in particular, come to mind).

Within the governing psychoanalytic myth of the constitution of the human psyche resides a second myth, a constellation of categories of psychological disturbances and irregularities that emerges from Jelinek's novelistic case study of her protagonist Erika Kohut: hysteria, neurosis, and psychosis. The first of these

---

1 "Only the things that have proven their worth will continue to do so in this city." Elfriede Jelinek, *Die Klavierspielerin* (Reinbek bei Hamburg: Rowohlt, 1983), 15; Elfriede Jelinek, *The Piano Teacher*, trans. Joachim Neugroschel (London: Serpent's Tail, 1999), 12. References to *The Piano Teacher* in this chapter will appear in the text parenthetically, with dual pages numbers of the German original and the English translation, separated by a semicolon.

in particular traces its history through Freud to nineteenth-century Paris. Its origin in the pathology of the mind are the nearly inescapable walls of Jean-Martin Charcot's hospital, the Salpêtrière. Like the mythification of psychoanalysis itself, *The Piano Teacher* feminizes hysteria, thus allying itself with an implicit history not only of mental illness, pathologization, and hospitalization, but also of genderedness and conceptualizations of the feminine body. In a particularly notorious scene, Erika – both "a younger hanger-on [*Anhängsel*; also appendage, DB]" (34; 31) of her mother and a quasi-spousal caretaker "until death do them part" (34; 31) – reenacts the split in her psyche (daughter and husband) by cutting her genitals with a razor (90; 86). In such passages, Jelinek's novel evokes the visual and theatrical documentation of hysteria that Charcot undertook and that influenced Freud's elaboration of his theories. Interpreted from this perspective, the novel's complex narrative perspective can be read as a chronicling of hysteria as well as a visual, literary adaptation of Charcot's photographic enterprise of pathological documentation: in short, as a narrativization of the history and invention of hysteria through its (visual) representation.[2]

At the intersection of this visual mode of narration and the different strains of psychoanalytic history appears a trope of voyeurism and scopophilia. What constitutes the visual character of the narrative voice in Jelinek's novel likewise projects itself into the varied stagings of surveillance and observation, both pleasurable and clandestine. An episteme of knowing through seeing suffuses the text, linking this technique of marking spatial relations and boundaries, identities, and narrative perspectives to a more implicit narrative of the gaze as such. Drawing upon the shifting visual-spatial character of the narrator's point of view, this paradigm sets up a dynamic between text and reader in which the latter becomes an involuntary participant in the action. Reading resembles viewing insofar as the reader, following the narrator's example, figures as a voyeur whose gaze surveys and penetrates the narrative. From this perspective, narration, especially in the visual register the narrator employs, involves learning how to become a voyeur. In conjunction with psychoanalysis, voyeuristic tropes will figure prominently at a key turning point in the novel, indicting the reader by dint of his complicit observation of the action.[3] The text thus suggests that reading, to put it pointedly, amounts to pathological behavior.

---

[2] For a reading of *The Piano Teacher* as a novel of hysteria, see Michèle Pommé, *Ingeborg Bachmann, Elfriede Jelinek: Intertextuelle Schreibstrategien in "Malina", "Das Buch Franza", "Die Klavierspielerin" und "Die Wand"* (St. Ingbert: Röhrig Universitätsverlag, 2009).
[3] That Austrian film director Michael Haneke adapts this particular scene to chilling (and parallel) effect in his film *La pianiste* (2001), based on Jelinek's novel, merely underscores the central

No less pathological, however, is the myth of music. For Vienna as the veritable capital of classical musicianship, just as much as for *The Piano Teacher*, music functions as an ostinato that signifies, at least superficially, both the age of Mozart and Beethoven as well as the trials and tribulations of musical achievement. It is an *idée fixe* that saturates the discursive framework of the text. By no means is it solely Erika's means of employment, nor the foundation of her relationship with her student, Walter Klemmer. Rather, Jelinek invokes a myth of music as an "untearable net of directions, directives, precise commandments" (193; 190). She thus ascribes to music the determinant, phallic qualities we see in the patriarchal linguistic system she cites, and intimates a deeper set of problems with signification that the text explores subtly and in parallel with music, namely: to what extent can music and language produce meaning? How does signification function? That Jelinek's novel casually equates music with language invokes yet another myth we encountered in Barthes' *Mythologies* and *Lust*: that of the arbitrary linguistic sign.

To the extent that Jelinek draws an analogy between language and a non-representational system like music, we might read music's inherent lack of referentiality as a threat to the representational nature of language. By all but equating a myth of music with that of language, Jelinek undermines the conception of language as a fixed, determinate system of signification divorced from subjective perception. Indeed, without a system for producing absolute meaning, the text would seem to fall apart into its constituent units – words – and reveal itself as an artificial construct. Put differently, the undermining of a myth of language as a signifying system presupposes and anticipates the failure of a myth of literature as a medium of invariable meaning.

Ultimately, then, the master myth of *The Piano Teacher* is that of literature itself. Sutured together from its constitutive myths and intertexts, Jelinek's novel is a patchwork of parasitized discourses, from Barthes and the nineteenth century to tropes of homecomings and of the novel itself. This is the unmistakable mark of satire. Like the invention of hysteria through photography and performance, satire also invents itself through the medium of its transmission; it may thus be understood as a pathological practice. From this perspective, satire comprises a set of highly performative strategies that parasitize and theatricalize discourses and types of speech. The analogous function of hysteria and satire

---

role of visuality and the filmic gaze as a mythology of violent, gendered voyeurism. For the classic reading of the genderedness of the filmic/voyeuristic gaze, see Laura Mulvey, "Visual Pleasure and Narrative Cinema," *Screen* 16, no. 3 (1975): 6–18.

sheds an interesting light upon their situation within the field of concepts. To what degree may we speak of both within the same breath? How might we understand satire as a pathology? To address these questions, one must first explore the discourses in Elfriede Jelinek's *The Piano Teacher* as well as the ramifications of their juxtaposition and intersection.

Parasitized Discourses and Viennese Tropes

Perhaps the most recognizable myth in Jelinek's novel, psychoanalysis appears repeatedly in various guises and from various schools: from Freud's clinical couch to Jung's expansion of his ideas to the feminine, from Heinz Kohut's focus on self psychology and development of the self to Lacan's appropriation of psychodynamics in his fusion of psychoanalysis and linguistics. That the tropes of Freudian psychoanalysis, to name one example, undergird the text is undeniable, and certainly Freud's reciprocal relationship with literature and narration echoes here as well. The narrator reports with what one might describe as a sterile tone, interested less in providing an impartial third-person narrative than in issuing an on-going analysis. Rather than attempt to contour and crystallize the characters narratologically, the text treats them instead as psychoanalytical case studies, an aggregation of symptoms and psychic ruptures. Erika and Walter are not psychologized *per se*, but pathologized: she as a hysteric,[4] he as a violent man not in control of his drives.[5] Erika becomes a cipher for the Electra complex, for hysteria, for neuroses and psychoses related to her covert sexual appetite, self-mutilation, sadomasochism, and voyeuristic behavior – in short, for the diagnoses found in treatises on psychologically deviant female patients in Vienna (and in Charcot's photographic record a generation prior). She is, in the punning words of one critic, "the discursive product of 'hyst-Erika'."[6]

That Erika's surname resonates with that of Viennese-born psychoanalyst and psychotheorist Heinz Kohut is an indication of the level of discursive interweaving that occurs in Jelinek's novel. Founder and proponent of the school of self psychology, Heinz Kohut casts an intertextual shadow on the text by way of his notion of the healthy formation of one's tripartite self, derived as it was in

---

4 "Her hobby is cutting her own body" (90; 86).
5 "No amorous couples are unnerved by Herr Klemmer, for he has come here not to gawk, but to commit brutalities without being seen. His unused drives are turning malevolent, all because of that woman" (255; 250).
6 Pommé, *Ingeborg Bachmann, Elfriede Jelinek*, 181.

opposition to Freud, through relationships.[7] Erika, for her part as a citation of this discourse rather than a literary character *per se*, provides an implicit critique of her namesake's theories of empathy and the treatment of personality disorders. Furthermore, her antagonistic relationships with her mother and with Walter – not to mention her position as a proxy for her absent father, hospitalized in the Viennese asylum Steinhof, a milieu familiar to us in the writings of Thomas Bernhard[8] – moors and mires Erika further in the discourses of hysteria, neurosis, and psychosis.

With what some might diagnose as an Electra complex,[9] or to use Freudian terminology a "feminine Oedipal attitude," Erika finds herself in the singular position of having replaced her father entirely. She is his representative: "Her father promptly left, passing the torch to his daughter" (7; 3). This metaphoric substitution causes a doubling of her character as both familial breadwinner and subjugated underling, husband and daughter in one: "the married couple: Erika and Mother" (263; 258),[10] theoretical object and subject of forbidden sexual desire, wielder of the Phallus as "torch," and "property" of the mother (9; 5). Maternal resentment – in both directions – lingers since neither woman may sexually consummate her relationship with the mentally unstable father figure: the mother because of the absence and impotence of her husband as well as the incest taboo on her relationship with her daughter; Erika because of her mother's effective obliteration of her father through his admission to the asylum, in addition to the incest taboo on her relationship with her mother. The citation of this constellation of Freudian-Jungian libidinal desire becomes explicit only once when the psychosexual tension lurking within this theoretical construct erupts to the horror of both parties involved. In her final "love attack" (236; 232), Erika seeks a clear view of her mother's genitals, a compound signifier of male sexual desire, phallogocentric lack, linguistic void, and source of birth: "She is

---

7 For elaborations of these theories, see Heinz Kohut, *The Analysis of the Self: A Systematic Approach to the Psychoanalytic Treatment of Narcissistic Personality Disorders*. (New York: International Universities Press, 1971); Heinz Kohut, *The Restoration of the Self* (Chicago: The University of Chicago Press, 2009).
8 Perhaps the most prominent example would be Bernhard's short novel *Wittgenstein's Nephew*, in which the protagonist, a patient in Steinhof's medical wing, relates his friendship with Paul Wittgenstein, nephew of the famous philosopher and a patient in its psychiatric ward. Bernhard, *Wittgensteins Neffe*.
9 Repeated mention of her spousal relationship with her mother in light of her father's "abdication" culminates in Erika's incestuous "love attack" (236–239; 231–235).
10 Allyson Fiddler, *Rewriting Reality: An Introduction to Elfriede Jelinek* (Oxford: Berg, 1994), 130.

flesh of this flesh!" (237; 233). Like the opening and closing scenes, it too is a journey home to the source and origin of existence, *Muttermund* [cervix, but also "Mother's mouth"] (237; cf. 233), which Lacanian discourse, for example, equates with lack.

Further manifestations of this myth of psychoanalysis are the displacements and shifts, both subtle and jarring, in the narrative perspective. The gaze of Jelinek's unnamed narrator, the "invisible spectator" (216; 213), circulates about the action, at times unified with the voyeuristic gazes of Erika or Walter, becoming the mouthpiece of their thoughts, and parroting their points of view: "Almost unintentionally, she peers out from the *prison* of her aging body" (82; 78 [my emphasis, DB]). The prevalence of reported speech facilitates this blurring of boundaries between third-person and first-person narration, further compromising the notion of a unified narrative perspective and, with it, of a unified subject. With this oscillation in perspective, which mimics the alternation of the sterile gaze of the analyst with that of the patient, the text demonstrates the porous nature of inside and outside, of subject and object, despite its best efforts to provide strict boundaries for the unconscious; "[t]he outside and the inside should not be confused," the narrator notes, "each belongs in its place" (99; 95). By traversing the boundaries between detached third-person narration and an empathetic mode, between reportage and confession, the invisible "I" in Jelinek's novel encompasses an entire spectrum of identities, ranging from an external observer chronicling the narrative to a more diffuse, fluid, disembodied voice capable of melding with each character. The question remains: who is speaking? Uncertainty – whether the narrating voice is a single entity or a conglomeration of varied narrative perspectives lodged within a single narrative authority – arises in part because of the myth of the fragmented self in psychoanalytic discourse.

While this myth reveals a reception not only of Freud, Jung, and Kohut, but also of Lacan, this lattermost theorist appears primarily within the framework of linguistic applications of his mirror stage. Questions of self-identity and subjectivity plague Erika Kohut and are acted out within the narrative: for example, in the conflicting references to Erika as both daughter and husband to her mother. Yet these concerns are of a piece with the ability of language to signify. As a construct of language herself, Erika is subject to the failure of the myth of literature (through Jelinek's analogy of literature and music) to create coherent, consistent meaning. The artificial construction of meaning through layered myths – myths of myths, as in both Barthes and Jelinek's *Lust* – is a constitutive satiric practice in *The Piano Teacher* as well, unmasking the mythology of the novel. In producing meaning through artificial signs, the text reconstructs one myth in particular: that of hysteria.

The Construction of Hysteria as Myth

Defined by the frigid sterility of language that chronicles her thoughts and repressed emotions, Erika Kohut reenacts through her masochism, outbursts, and sexual habitus the narratives of hysteria played out not only in the analyses of Sigmund Freud and Josef Breuer, but also in the theatrical spectacles and spectacular theatrics of Jean-Martin Charcot's patients a generation earlier.[11] For Freud and Breuer, the early cases of hysteria in Anna O., Dora, and Nora came to determine the very methodology of psychoanalysis through the development of the "talking cure," thus linking hysteria inextricably with language and speech. Yet hysteria also continually plagued Freud's attempts to form a coherent conception of the female psyche and, in his wake, has become a central antagonist of both femininity and the theoretical considerations of feminism.[12] Concomitantly, it signifies the tenebrous neurotic and psychotic disturbances for which psychoanalysis came into being. It is, to quote a colleague of Charcot's, "A Proteus who presents himself in a thousand guises and cannot be grasped in any of them."[13] Hysteria is, as it were, a cipher for psychoanalysis as much as it is for the slippery conceptualizations of feminine identity: "It was the symptom, to put it crudely, *of being a woman*. And everyone still knows it."[14] Formulated more pointedly, as a product of mimesis propagated by photography, hysteria crystallizes as a myth, a second-order system of signification that pathologizes womankind and echoes the claims of sexual frigidity projected onto the female subject.

By photographing and thus documenting and preserving the hysterical paroxysms of his female patients, Charcot (one of Freud's teachers, incidentally) created a visual model for hysterical outbursts and behavior.[15] Charcot himself did not so much archive images of hysteria for posterity as he provided the conditions for the possibility of its invention and pathologization. After Charcot, hysteria is thus nothing more than a performance of a pathology, a product of a medial intervention – in short, posing for the camera. The hysteric woman, in her appropria-

---

[11] See especially Georges Didi-Huberman, *Invention of Hysteria: Charcot and the Photographic Iconography of the Salpêtrière* (Cambridge, Mass.: MIT Press, 2003).
[12] Maria Ramas, "Freud's Dora, Dora's Hysteria," in *In Dora's Case: Freud-Hysteria-Feminism*, ed. Charles Bernheimer and Claire Kahane (New York: Columbia University Press, 1985), 150.
[13] Pierre Briquet, *Traité clinique et thérapeutique de l'hystérie* (1859), quoted in Didi-Huberman, *Invention of Hysteria*, 25.
[14] Didi-Huberman, *Invention of Hysteria*, 68.
[15] The countless photographs in his book amount to a kind of photographic archive of the many faces of hysteria. Didi-Huberman, *Invention of Hysteria*.

tion and proliferation of pathological symptoms, "is thus (also) an actress."[16] Through performance, the hysterical female body and its shifting symptoms and signifiers defy attempts to read them and impose upon them a diagnosable meaning. In the pathological sickness imposed by a masculine order, the hysterical female body thus remains a locus of feminine meaning hermetically sealed off, illegible and opaque to the therapeutic, ostensibly rehabilitative male gaze.

Both the imitative aspect of hysterical performance[17] and resistance to signification appear in Jelinek's novel. Unlike Charcot's *hystérie traumatique*, however, the hysteria one might recognize in Erika Kohut derives less from histrionics and a desire to escape the sanitarium than, to speak with Freud, libidinal and psychic disturbances that manifest themselves variously in her acts of self-mutilation, numbness, emotional and sexual frigidity, and voyeurism. Evidence of psychological perturbations and nervous disorders proliferate in the text, which might be read as an analytical case study of hysteria (not a legitimate diagnosis).[18] These physical and psychic symptoms – Erika's pathological behavior, that is – go hand in hand with her repeated wishes for self-annihilation and the reassurance of her bodily existence. This paradoxical juxtaposition of construction and destruction of identity restages the ambivalence of hysteria itself, for it "brings the body to bear and destroys or injures it at the same time."[19] It is precisely this incommensurable union of self-affirmation and self-destruction that Jelinek's novel recounts. One might even speak with Klemmer in apostrophizing Erika by declaring, "I have a feeling that you despise your body and that you only value art, Professor Kohut" (69; 65). In this regard, Erika is merely a literary placeholder for a series of hysterical behaviors and symptoms, which are themselves fictional performances.

This paradox goes a step further, however. In his history of hysterical spectacle, Georges Didi-Huberman demonstrates how, in a vicious cycle of visual attention and escapism, so-called hysteric women engage in imitative theatrics for the camera[20]; this clever performative strategy both excludes and exalts the hysteric woman as an object of medical curiosity. On the one hand, hysterics were subject to permanent incarceration and experimentation, yet on the other hand, they are the privileged objects of scrutiny and study, a locus of cryptic meaning and the

---

16 Lena Lindhoff, *Einführung in die feministische Literaturtheorie* (Stuttgart: Metzler, 2003), 144.
17 "Mimesis is the hysterical symptom par excellence. Hysteria is considered to be 'a whole art,' the art and manner of 'theatricalism,' as is always said in psychiatry, and which no theatricality is strong enough to equal in its swaggers." Didi-Huberman, *Invention of Hysteria*, 164.
18 Fiddler, *Rewriting Reality*, 148.
19 Lindhoff, *Einführung in die feministische Literaturtheorie*, 142.
20 See, in particular, chapters two, three, and four of Didi-Huberman, *Invention of Hysteria*.

site of surplus signification. Charcot's hysterical women thus both perpetuate hysteria and expose it as a fiction.

Similarly, Jelinek's narrative underscores the falsehood of hysteria and hysterical performance as myths. The fictionality and literariness of the novel draws attention to the construction of hysteria through its chronicling of Erika's pathological symptoms and its revelation, in the rape scene, of their artificiality. The visual pathologization of symptoms and litany of neuroses and psychoses in Jelinek's text likewise imitate the historical paradigms that preceded them. In this "involuntary parody," the paradox of the suffering hysteric erupts in "an inability to fit into the female role, which is simultaneously an over-fulfillment of this role. [...] It makes visible the artificiality, the violence, the pathology of female role assignment, which the patriarchal system seeks to conceal behind the semblance of nature."[21] Much as the hysteric parasitizes a slew of medical symptoms and expectations, so too does Erika imitate and recycle the psychoanalytic cases that lay the foundation for the novel, thereby perpetuating a fiction. In founding a myth of the hysterical woman, she simultaneously unmasks it as mere theatrics. In the imitation and redeployment of discourses, the figure of the myth can be read as a figure of satire: a dark double that parasitically feeds from its host discourse, both separate and dependant, comprised of like material but constituted and structured differently.

But how does the visual element of hysterical theatrics – that most important of its historical facets since Charcot – play itself out within *The Piano Teacher*? To what extent does this myth of hysteria as a visual construction affect the structure of the novel itself, and what ramifications does it have for other myths? And because the historical trace of hysteria may indeed parallel the trace of satire in unusual ways: what is the relation between satire and hysteria? To address these questions, let us turn to a related narrative element: the shifts in and spatiality of the narrative perspectives. With its sharp focus on visuality, sight, and voyeurism, the text continually suggests an implicit spatial frame of reference for the action through its use of particular signifiers, its references to limited vantage points, and the reiteration of the verbs like "see," "look," "watch," and "observe."

In the novel's opening passage, for instance, the reader already witnesses the subtle shifts back and forth in the spatial position of the narrative voice. Initially, only slight shifts in diction hint at deviations from the vantage point of Erika's entrance. The narrator initially positions herself grammatically as an external observer, but the daughter, whom the text marks explicitly as a late thirtysome-

---

21 Lindhoff, *Einführung in die feministische Literaturtheorie*, 143.

thing, nevertheless registers as "the baby" and "the child" (7; 3) whose motives "to escape her mother" (7; 3) the narrator insinuates in concert with Erika's mother. The narrator thus parasitically appropriates the diction of each character's perspective, temporarily aligning herself with a particular vantage point.

And yet the view to the action glides almost unnoticeably away from the mother's position to that of the outside observer again in discussing the absence of the father after Erika's birth. Characteristic of the external narrator's position is a reliance on poetic language: literary metaphors in particular; "like a whirlwind" and "like a swarm of autumn leaves" (7) characterize not only the manner of Erika's sudden entrance, but also signify a particular narrative register and a subtle strategy for differentiating between the perspectives of the erstwhile external narrator and those of the novel's figures. Employing poetic language essentially serves not only the indexical function by which the text announces its literary character, but also the semiotic function of attributing utterances to the narrator. What complicates this strategy, however, are the instances in which this semiotic index coincides with an alignment of Erika's, the mother's, or Walter's perspective, that is, when the narrative perspective comprises a superimposition of multiple semiotic strategies.

Only after Erika's abrupt entrance into the apartment while attempting to escape notice does the perspective shift starkly yet again. It is then that the mother, briefly allied with the narrator, receives the appellation "Mama" (7; 3), reversing the perspectival alliance brought to bear with "the child." Standing before her daughter's door, the mother "confronts her. She puts Erika against the wall, under interrogation—inquisitor and executioner in one" (7; 3), a first instance of Jelinek's beloved zeugma, which she uses to such great effect in *Lust*. In relating the mother's questions why Erika has come home so late (7; 3), the narrator relativizes her omniscient position and remarks on Erika's mockery of her last student.

What follows is a drastic shift to the first and second person, which strips away the ostensible impartiality of indirect discourse: "You must think," the mother accuses, "I won't find out where you've been, Erika" (7; 3). The alternation from one narrative perspective to the other here is immediate, prepared perhaps only by the prior indirect quotation. All indexical signs of citation are absent here, superimposing the narrative perspective of the narrator and the mother; for all intents and purposes, literary and grammatical, they effectively become one. By turns the narrative voice allies itself with the mother through its infantilizing diction ("the child" for an adult) and shifts back imperceptibly to Erika's vantage point. Indirect speech, metaphorical language, the immediacy of the present tense, and the shifts in diction all mark the narrative perspective and code its volatility.

Beyond the narrative voice, seeing and sight – particularly in clandestine observation and in voyeuristic undertakings – play a constitutive role in organizing the relations of subject and object in Jelinek's novel. That spatial relations arise between the subject and object of the gaze is a logical consequence of the language employed to describe seeing. Indeed, in a link to the psychoanalytic myth of maternal influence Jelinek cites throughout her novel, Erika's mother and grandmother, the "female brigade" (37; 33), provide a model to Erika of voyeuristic surveillance and pleasure as well as its force, as they observe the neighbors from on high, "armed with binoculars" (39; 36). This specular medium amounts to a weapon in their hands, ensuring that their countryside neighbors listen obediently while Erika plays the piano from within their fortified retreat.

Erika's own visual undertakings are decidedly different, however, and are almost exclusively voyeuristic. Rather than derive sexual pleasure from her voyeurism, she aims to negate her body through seeing: "All Erika wants to do is watch. Here, in this booth, she becomes nothing" (55; 51). Reduced to a point perspective of pure gaze, Erika loses her humanity: she is "a compact tool in human form" (55; 51). Even the narrative perspective is that of purely ekphrastic description as its gaze floats over the pornographic theater and renders it visible. The reader, unlike Erika "the unrevealing viewer" (112; 108), need not enter follow her inside but can watch at a safe remove the tabooed passivity of Erika's scopophilia: "But Erika doesn't want to act, she only wants to look. She simply wants to sit there and look. Look hard. Erika, watching but not touching. Erika feels nothing" (56; 52). The text suggests a parity of Erika's voyeuristic visit to the pornographic theater with the reader's observation. In drawing the analogy, the novel forces the reader into a similar mode of passive spectatorship, which is repeated time and again. In her secret self-mutilation, her visit to the pornographic theater, her voyeuristic twilight walk to the Prater to observe the Turkish man and Austrian woman engage in sexual intercourse from behind bushes (143; 141), and the sadomasochistic sexual desires she describes in her letter to Walter, we witness a recurrence of scopophilic pleasure that entangles the reader in a web of voyeuristic activity. Erika's mode of being is one of controlled and controlling observation and voyeurism: "She has to keep looking" (58; 54).

Put differently, scopophilia is a dominant semiotic strategy in Jelinek's text, defining the narrative structure and narrative perspective, if not the experience of reading. The text fetishizes and sexualizes the *act* of clinical observation, never the observed image. Only gradually through this strategy of superimposing the reader's gaze onto Erika's does the novel ultimately position the reader as an unwitting voyeur of Erika's ostensibly hysterical sexual perversions. Readers are trained through Erika's own encounters, which are mediated by her own gaze and instruments of seeing (her binoculars, the glass behind which she watches the female dancers at the theater).

When the reader finally appears explicitly in the text as "the invisible spectator" (216; 213) peering over Klemmer's shoulder, the narrative perspective begins to replace Erika as subject of the gaze with the reader, effectively splitting the superimposition of perspective. Only during the notorious rape scene in the concluding passages of the novel does the horror of this transition become apparent. Exposed as a voyeur to a rape, the reader stands alone as master of the gaze, absorbing the full visual terror of the sexual assault and the ethical consequences of his position as reader. In other words, the text exposes narration as a continued exercise in voyeuristic pleasure and, conversely, of scopophilic terrorism.

This very rape scene functions as a semiotic turning point in Jelinek's novel, for it is here that the narrative exposes the game of perspectival cat-and-mouse for what it was: a myth of seeing, of clinically objective visuality. But this narrative strategy breaks down the wall between the narrative and metanarrative levels, between diegetic and non-diegetic perspectives, between text and reader. The artificiality of narration reveals itself both through the now obviously voyeuristic perspective imputed to the reader, as well as through the patchwork of myths that saturate the novel. Erika is at once the object of the reader's gaze and nothing more than a residue of mythological material, "[a] topic for humor magazines" (268; 263). Walter, too, is no more complex; "Klemmer," the text notes self-referentially, "is material for a whole novel" (268; 263). Thereafter, Klemmer is known as "K.," as if the novel were suggesting a parity between him and the mysterious protagonist from Kafka's unfinished novel *The Castle [Das Schloß]*. Not unlike *Lust*, the narrator has removed herself from the action and receded to a mostly neutral point of view, reducing the objects of her gaze to archetypal figures, "the woman" or "the daughter," "the man," and "Mother" (268–270; 263–265). As the violence escalates, the reader inhabits the narrator's omniscient perspective and shares her gaze, penetrating even the barriers keeping Erika's mother from witnessing the damage wreaked upon her "private one-person zoo" (272; 267) while cross-cutting into the apartment's foyer to view the "work of destruction" (273; 268) as Klemmer forces himself upon Erika.

If this shift in perspective is uncomfortable for the reader, it is a reflection of the breakdown in the charade of hysterical theatrics, the collapse of Erika's pretended pathological status. Finally, it is a matter of language and hermeneutics: "Erika tearfully protests that this isn't what she wanted, she wanted something different. Well then you'll have to express yourself more carefully next time, the man replies. Kicking her, he demonstrates the simple equation: I am I" (275; 270). Both in Erika's earlier letter that delineated what she in fact wanted and in general, the novel suggests, violence erupts – and violent metaphors proliferate –

from an imprecise use of language. Erika as a woman, so the implication goes, cannot control the contingencies of language multiplied through citation, zeugma, and metaphor.

In losing control of language, Erika loses control of her tenuous identity. In fact, immediately following the rape, Erika herself is erased from the text. Sentence after sentence begins with "he": "He advises her not to tell anyone. For her own good. He apologizes for his behavior. He explains his behavior by saying he just couldn't help it. Things like that happen to a guy. He makes some vague promise to Erika, who remains lying on the floor. I have to go now: The man demands forgiveness in his way" (278; 273). For the rest of the chapter and not until the following one, Erika no longer appears in the text as the subject of the action. She has vanished, effaced by language and the rape's "work of destruction." She is no longer the subject of the narrative gaze, but rather the object of its sinister violence and violent oppression through language. From his own voyeuristic perspective, the reader has participated, if unwittingly, in Erika's rape and linguistic subjugation.

A Myth of Music: Connotation out of Control

Aside from hysteria and the visuality of the narrative perspective, music constitutes a master trope in Jelinek's novel. Erika's musical milieu mirrors the myth of music and musicality that pervades the novel. References to Viennese musical culture along with citations of Schubert song cycles and, arguably, literary adaptations of musical forms not only anchor the novel in a discourse linked inextricably to the novel's setting, but also supply a network of myths that the text deploys satirically. By citing a particular paradigm of music, Jelinek incorporates a system of non-representational signification, one lacking in denotation but infinite in its connotative potential. This incorporation of a myth of music reciprocally affects and deconstructs a myth of the linguistic sign in which the link between signifier and signified – between sound and meaning – persists. Music, the text suggests in its close alliance of music with literature, evokes for language deeper questions about the production of meaning, comprehension, and understanding: questions that Jelinek's novel addresses with other myths as well.

Music, however, also signifies an alternate order through its notation, one that corresponds roughly to a Cartesian coordinate system, a cage of bar lines. For Erika, musical notation, like music itself, provides not meaning, but a system of law and order, similar to that which a myth of psychoanalytic pathology enjoins upon her through the figure of the mother: "Erika has been harnessed in this notation system since earliest childhood. Those five lines have been controlling her ever since she first began to think. She musn't think of anything but those five black lines. This grid system, together with her mother, has hamstrung her in an untearable net of directions, directives, precise commandments, like a rosy ham on a butcher's hook" (193; 190). Here, the order of the logos is a domineering framework that structures Erika's thought through its prescriptions and requirements, but not through semantic meaning; music as an alternate order of patriarchy supplants language.

This myth comes to signify the substitute semiotic order into which Erika has developed, one which hampers her mastery of the linguistic sign. "[H]arnessed" in music, which provides "new laws" (153; 151), Erika forsook language; instead, the text suggests, music replaces language as a means of signification for her. As a non-representational system, however, music lacks referentiality, which further exacerbates the crisis of meaning exhibited throughout the narrative. In *The Piano Teacher* the myth of music refers to a structuring principle, "[t]his grid system," that configures difference through repetition and contrast, and gives a semblance of signification through order.

Repetitions of *Bach* and its diminutive *Bächlein* abound, with connotations similar to those found in Jelinek's later novel, *Lust*. As a literary trope, these reoccurrences of *Bach* both demonstrate the ambiguity of connotation and the signifier, reflected in Erika's imputed inability to be precise, and they link the myth of music through connotative association to other discourses. With *Bach* we thus witness discursive points of intersection. *Bächlein* as simultaneously a diminutive of the name Bach and a rivulet, to name one example, connotes both the destructive feminine and the maternal in its link of Erika's mother's musical enthusiasm (29; 26) with the abject – urine, that "the soft trickling and rustling" (150; 148 [translation amended, DB]) – and the blood of self-mutilation with menstrual blood (47; 43–44). In this latter example the text alludes to Schubert's *Winterreise*, but one might also read "Just keep following my tears, and the brook [*Bächlein*] will take you in" (47; 44) more generally within the context of the recurrent scene of Erika's self-mutilation: as a cipher for her introduction into the semiotic system of music (rather than language). To follow her existential despair is to gain entrance to Bach himself, to be embraced by music as a proxy for language.

Elsewhere, the connotative plurality of *Bach* is no less present. During a private performance of Bach's second concerto for two keyboard instruments, Erika performs for the first time under the direct observation of Klemmer, stoking his nascent lust as he watches her "from behind" (66; 62 [translation amended, DB]). "Bach rushes [*rauscht*] by earnestly," (66; 62) the text declares, superimposing a metonymous reference to the concerto onto the *Rauschen*, the white noise, of nature. Either the composer or the brook (or both?) "swirls into the presto movement" (66; 62), a semantic overburdening through metaphor. Jelinek combines natural imagery to underscore the notion of *Bach* as stream while setting the sentence in the context of a performance of a Bach concerto. As Klemmer ponders the inexorable procession of sounds, the *Bach*, be it the sound or the stream, "has come to rest. His [or its] run is finished" (70; 66). Music, the myth suggests, is both flow and noise, movement and interference, progression and the absence of referentiality; only the active agency of a listener (or reader) may supply it with meaning. This pluralizing of potential meanings results from the mythification of music as a signifying system without the capacity for discrete referentiality, as a superego without an ego, issuing commandments into the ether. In the central satiric gesture of Jelinek's novel, the tension from the contradictions among these mythic systems – music, language, psychoanalysis – causes them to break down, thus pointing to a problem with the coherence of meaning and signification: to connotation gone wild.

Jelinek addresses and critiques this myth of music as a prison-house of thought and the myth of language as a prison-house of the psyche by playing them off each other and other myths: by using mythification as a satiric practice. The scene of Erika's self-mutilation illustrates this dynamic by reenacting the Lacanian mirror stage, exposing the incommensurability of signification with subject formation. Consider first Klemmer's admonition to his piano teacher that she despises her body (69; 65) and Erika's insistence upon denying her sexual drives through the power of will. The latter, in her experience, always triumphs over the "assets of the flesh" (169; 167). "Erika," the narrator declares in this vein, "would gladly cross the border to her own murder" (110; 107). But her physical and sexual self-denial unto death is doomed to fail because the body–mind dichotomy is a mythic one. On the one hand, Erika's physical self is an object foreign to her own gaze and knowledge, "dreadfully alien to her" (91; 87), its secrets resistant to her attempts to unlock and expose them through acts of self-mutilation: "Never has her body—even in her standard pose, legs apart in front of the shaving mirror—revealed its silent secrets, even to its owner!" (111–112; 108). On the other hand – the self-denial and repudiation of the body evident in her "hobby" notwithstanding – the gesture of slicing open one's skin is predicated upon the persistent presence of one's physical self. Denying the body through self-mutilation only preserves it, makes it painfully present. What ultimately results from this play of self-mutilation and, later, from Erika's sadomasochistic instructions to Walter is, ironically, the reinforcement of her fragile, diffuse sense of self rather than its sublimation. In other words, her denial of her physicality reinforces its existence, thus subverting her will.

The split Erika effects upon her body, however, is already one the myth of psychoanalysis had inscribed into her psyche. If Erika's acts of self-mutilation are read as an attempt to become a subject, one might grasp this performance of subjectivity in the razor scene as a reenactment of the Lacanian mirror stage. In Jelinek's case study of a pathologized woman, the unconscious desires enter the conscious realm through language, and so too must the proverbial psychic split be written on the body. The gaze into the mirror thus literalizes and critiques Lacan and his theory of formation of the subject. Indeed, in his essay on the mirror stage, Lacan argues that psychoanalysis act as a counterbalance to existentialism because of the "subjective impasses" it causes and which he lists: "a freedom that is never so authentically affirmed as when it is within the walls of a prison; a demand for commitment that expresses the inability of pure consciousness to overcome any situation; a voyeuristic-sadistic idealization of sexual relationships; a personality that achieves self-realization only in suicide; and a consciousness of the other than can only be satisfied by Hegelian murder."[22] Given the significant overlap between these "impasses" and Erika's own symptoms, her exercises in self-mutilation are best understood as a latent commentary on Lacan's theory. To effect the split between the self and its image is to foreclose the integrity of the body, to pathologize the self.

In the scene of reenactment, Erika stands before her shaving mirror while sterilely observing the separation of her wounds and the birth of anthropomorphized flaps of skin, once united, which are unable to identify their own image: "In the mirror, the two halves also look at themselves, laterally inverted, so that neither knows which half it is" (91; 87). Erika's performance of this Lacanian act effects the split in self-recognition of "her own body" (91; 87), but only alienates her further from it. The wholeness of the previously fused halves of her wounds which had "shared joy [*Freud*] and sorrow for many years" (91; 87) is now cleaved through by a gesture that renders her forever ambiguous. Here, too, Jelinek's pun on Freud revels in the ambiguity of the signifier and thus the multiplication of meaning. The ambivalence of Erika's hobby in separating joy from sorrow with the incision reflects the ambivalence of psychoanalysis in constructing the condition for its own possibility: the wounded psyche. By performing Lacan, Jelinek satirizes a myth of psychoanalysis in which the mirror stage signifies both proper psychological development and irreversible linguistic disruption and self-mutilation.

What effect then, ultimately, do these various myths have when acting in concert? Given that *The Piano Teacher* superimposes various myths – secondary

---

[22] Jacques Lacan, "The Mirror Stage as Formative of the 'I' Function, as Revealed in Psychoanalytic Experience," in *Écrits: A Selection*, trans. Bruce Fink (New York: W. W. Norton, 2002), 8.

semiological systems – the satiric dynamic in Jelinek's text consists in disrupting the coherence of naturalized meaning in these myths by playing them off one another. In appropriating and juxtaposing disparate discourses, Jelinek parasitizes a trove of Viennese myths and allows their residual meanings to shift, change, and dissolve in their stratification. In the case of *The Piano Teacher*, this mythification draws considerably from citational and intertextual procedures. As in *Lust* the resulting discursive intersections produce surprising juxtapositions of high and low culture. The Faustian moment of deliverance – "Just let this moment linger [*verweilen*], it's so good" (46; 43) – as a marker of Erika's incestuous encounter with her cousin's penis; a snippet of Schubert to comment upon her self-mutilation; Schiller's *Wallenstein* as a rejoinder following an assignation in a school bathroom (186; cf. 183); an invocation of Goethe's "The Sorceror's Apprentice" to justify a rape (278; cf. 274) – all of these color the cited discourses in a strongly negative, violent light. What this strategy of debunking myths brings about, however, is not so much a trivialization of art or an exaltation of violence or pathologized sexuality. Rather, these references call attention to the artificiality of myths. The revelation of the potential violence in language and the farce of hysteria, for example, also amount to a reinscription of ideology into literature. Jelinek's novel, the thrust of its satire goes, is inherently political and thus a "playful, postmodern foregrounding of the theoretical within the fictional."[23]

At this intersection point of literature and theory (and politics), Erika is the locus of the satiric deployment of these myths; she is the means for criticizing the very myths that combine to form and shape her. The critique of signification, the reenactment of the mirror stage, and the collapse of her pathologized hysteria through an insidious rape all lay bare literature as comprised of what it is itself: artificiality, a fiction predicated on perilously constructed semiological systems. What one might conclude from Jelinek's mythification in *The Piano Teacher* (and in Barthes and *Lust*) is a shift away from the hyperbolic transgressions of Thomas Bernhard towards a more overtly self-referential mode of self-presentation. The satiric text for Jelinek proclaims its discursive paradigms (in this case, its myths), and yet it also theorizes them implicitly by way of their intricate linkages and its subtle criticism of them. From this perspective Jelinek's satire bears little resemblance to the carefully directed parodic excesses and polemic diatribes that preceded it. Instead, she redeploys semiotic strategies in place since Jean Paul, carrying the satiric procedure of mythification to its extreme in the fine literary

---

[23] Fiddler, *Rewriting Reality*, 127.

traditions of an Austrian focus on language. The satiric elements in Jelinek appropriate the narrative strategies of literature and literary theory, becoming a kind of parasitic chameleon. In this shift, we witness the dawn of satire's disappearance against the backdrop of a literature that had already contained elements of its own satire.

Part Three | **Citation**

9. From Stage to Page: Judith Butler and *Gender Trouble* (1990)

In 1999, in a review of four books by Judith Butler that was rancorously titled "The Professor of Parody," Martha Nussbaum excoriates her subject, marking Butler now as derivative, now as politically ineffectual. With charges leveled alternately at Butler's "hip quietism"[1] and her challenging writing style, Nussbaum argues that Butler's flights of theoretical fancy constitute a retreat from the realities of political engagement. They point instead to an "absence of a normative dimension"[2] that could anchor Butler's thought in concrete reality, and to a "neglect of the material side of life."[3] Butler, she writes, embraces "a type of verbal and symbolic politics that makes only the flimsiest of connections with the real situation of real women."[4] Her theory, in short, is faulted for being theory, not practice – or for perpetuating this dubious distinction. Aimed at Butler's notion of parodic performance, the crux of Nussbaum's criticism maintains that Butler's pessimistic non-activism turns back the clock on political feminism by precluding any actual subversion of the hierarchical (Foucauldian) power structures upon which society, politics, and culture are predicated. The advances of parodic performance are too few, too insignificant, and too divorced from social and political reality to have any bearing on social change, Nussbaum counters, and the ostensible incoherence of Butler's theories exacerbate this deficiency, driving them deeper into social and political irrelevance.[5] What instigates Nussbaum's diagnosis and ultimate condemnation of Butler's theories is a problem of language: of shifting politics and feminism from the stage to the page.

Yet Butler's modality of political feminism is as much at issue as her mode of writing. Nussbaum's criticism that Butler's style is "dense with allusions to other theorists, drawn from a wide range of different theoretical traditions"[6] does not elevate Butler in Nussbaum's estimation. In identifying a network of theoretical

---

[1] Martha C. Nussbaum, "The Professor of Parody: The Hip Defeatism of Judith Butler," *New Republic* 220, no. 8 (February 22, 1999): 45.
[2] Nussbaum, "The Professor of Parody," 42.
[3] Nussbaum, "The Professor of Parody," 43.
[4] Nussbaum, "The Professor of Parody," 38.
[5] Contrast this with the fact that in 2010 Butler won and, to the surprise of those assembled, turned down the Berlin Christopher Street Day Prize for Civil Courage. For a description of the controversy, see Annette Kögel, Jörn Hasselmann, and Ferda Ataman, "Heftige Diskussionen nach Kritik an CSD," *Der Tagesspiegel Online*, June 20, 2010, http://www.tagesspiegel.de/berlin/stadtleben/butler-auftritt-heftige-diskussionen-nach-kritik-an-csd-/1864540.html.
[6] Nussbaum, "The Professor of Parody," 38.

forebears that includes Michel Foucault, Sigmund Freud, Louis Althusser, Monique Wittig, Gayle Rubin, Jacques Lacan, J. L. Austin, and Saul Kripke, Nussbaum zeroes in on what she perceives as theoretical incoherence, a failure to "assume the responsibility of advancing a definite interpretation among the contested ones."[7] Indeed, "[t]hese figures do not all agree with one another, to say the least; so an initial problem in reading Butler is that one is bewildered to find her arguments buttressed by appeal to so many contradictory concepts and doctrines, usually without any account of how the apparent contradictions will be resolved."[8] Judging from the criticisms of Butler's theoretical coherence and efficacy, one may conclude that Nussbaum reads Butler as a feminist gone astray, a theoretician who resists any easy or productive collusion between theory and practice, and an academic who couches her ideas in obfuscatory language formulated to conceal their derivative lack of originality: a professor of parody, or so the title goes. Despite the occasionally venomous invective in her review, Nussbaum unwittingly provides a productive opening for examining this particular habitus of reading. Such varied citational practices attest to a literary vein in Butler, beholden to an intertextual mode of writing incompatible with certain conceptions of the academic establishment. To expose how Butler's writing fails to dovetail with extant modes of scholarship, as Nussbaum attempts, is a less fruitful approach than reading Butler as a rhetor.

Within this framework, Judith Butler thus is an author of texts to be read for their deployment of narrative strategies and citational procedures. The efficacy of her political feminism and the coherence of her theories are not at issue here; insofar as these aspects are debated more adequately in other forums, Butler's ideas will occupy me to the extent that they constitute themselves as products of intertextual discourse and via intertextual practices. The notion of parodic performance, however, that marks the rhetorical culmination of her second publication, *Gender Trouble* (1990), plays a central role in Butler's earlier work and may serve as an exemplary construct derived from intertextual engagement. The construction of this theory through citational practices and the resulting semiotics of parody point to the relation between such practices and the legacy of satire in twentieth-century discourse. As a nexus of intertextual practices, *Gender Trouble* – a title that is already an altered quotation[9] – serves as the first case study

---

7 Nussbaum, "The Professor of Parody," 38.
8 Nussbaum, "The Professor of Parody," 38.
9 Butler notes that her title derives from the 1974 John Waters film with Divine, entitled *Female Trouble*, which she claims shows gender as "a kind of persistent impersonation that passes for the real." Whether the same characterization pertains to her own book's title and the nature of

for examining the legacy of satire in the practice of citation. In the course of the following pages, three close readings will attempt to bring to light the filiation of citational practices in Butler's study. From the relation of her notion of gender identity constructed through parodic performances, to her reading of Foucault's study of hermaphrodites, to the final discussion of performance and the link between parody and politics, I read Butler's writing from the perspective of its narrative construction. Her conception of performance is of particular interest here. Indeed, the theoretical formulation of performance forms the basis of the semiotic and intertextual enterprise in Thomas Meinecke's novels *Tomboy* (1998) and *Music* [*Musik*] (2004), both of which thematize Butler and employ textual practices found in *Gender Trouble*.

Gender and Its Discontents

Finding passages in *Gender Trouble* reliant upon citational strategies poses no difficulty; certain types of citation are of course constitutive practices of academic argumentation, and Butler's text certainly directs itself toward a scholarly readership. But her use of citation extends beyond the usual engagement with the academy and its rhetorical conventions. Here I am more interested in Nussbaum's accusation, which accused Butler of drawing upon and failing to acknowledge the complexities of the various theoretical foundations in her argument. This particular mode of citation belongs less to the arsenal of academic procedures than to a narrative use of intertexts without regard for the coherence of their respective content. Butler employs citational practices, in other words, as much for their own sake as for rhetorical flourish and a search for a textual identity. In the preface to the second edition of *Gender Trouble*, Butler admits her debt to "'French Theory'" but defends the "syncretic vein" by which she reads these various schools as an "intellectual promiscuity" that marks it as American (x). The cross-pollination of diverse discourses through their juxtaposition, this textual promiscuity recalls the same narrative practice employed throughout Jean Paul's oeuvre and in the works of Thomas Bernhard and Elfriede Jelinek, a practice that deeply affects the semiotic workings of a text. She thus adopts a literary strategy with a history in satiric fictional writing. Two representative passages from *Gender Trouble* chart this syncretic generation of concepts from occa-

---

the theoretical text itself is an interesting question in and of itself. *Gender Trouble: Feminism and the Subversion of Identity* (New York: Routledge, 1999), xxviii. In this chapter, all subsequent references to *Gender Trouble* will be made parenthetically in the text.

sionally disparate theoretical foundations. They show how Butler's use of citation structures the recursive academic narrative of her text and, through its unconventionality constitutes a parodic assertion of textual identity. In a manner of infinite regression, Butler deploys performative techniques to buttress her argument about performance.

This most famous of Butler's books does not, however, consist solely in a sustained argument about performance. With her seminal text, Butler delivered a critique of the doxa of political feminism from within its establishment, reconsidered its terminology, and recounted a history of gender epistemology through language. When she criticizes Butler's shift away from political activism, Nussbaum misreads the thrust of the text; as a theoretical document, *Gender Trouble* – and a subsequent volume intended to clarify her position with regard to reality and materiality, *Bodies That Matter*[10] – radically rethinks the framework of language deployed in political feminism. Words and signification, Butler argues, have a common history in theories that perpetuate binary gender models and thus oppression. *Gender Trouble* thus does not argue for the transfer of subversive efforts away from political reality but gives enormous weight to the invisible power relations concealed in everyday nomenclature.

As a narrative text, however, *Gender Trouble* employs conventional first-person narration as a kind of *Entwicklungsroman* [novel of development] that traces the history of gender through its interactions with other protagonists. Among the heroes are Michel Foucault, Sigmund Freud, Jacques Lacan, Claude Lévi-Strauss, Julia Kristeva, Monique Wittig, and many others: precisely the litany of disparate theorists whose heterogeneity Nussbaum had faulted and Butler had championed. It is here that citations come into play. If Butler's narrative recounts the coming-of-age of gender, and thereby its deconstruction, then its encounters with these theorists and related concepts like phallogocentrism and compulsory heterosexuality form interlocking episodes of terminological contouring and development. In charting her own identity as an American theorist through her "intellectual promiscuity," Butler sketches a parallel, equally promiscuous process of formation for the term gender.

The parallelism stems from an analogous adoption of different theoretical frameworks in crafting a representative identity. This throwback to heterogeneous historical schools of thought and styles and their reactivation in a genealogical narrative of gender might be termed a pastiche, to speak with Fredric Jameson. Yet this pastiche belies the seminal distinction Jameson had made between pastiche

---

[10] Judith Butler, *Bodies That Matter: On the Discursive Limits of "Sex"* (New York: Routledge, 1993).

and parody in the essay that preceded *Postmodernism, or The Cultural Logic of Late Capitalism* (1991). The arbitrariness and "cannibalization" of styles that Jameson diagnoses in pastiche contrast with the "satiric impulse" he reads in parody:

> Pastiche is, like parody, the imitation of a peculiar mask, speech in a dead language: but it is a neutral practice of such mimicry, without any of parody's ulterior motives, amputated of the satiric impulse, devoid of laughter and of any conviction that alongside the abnormal tongue you have momentarily borrowed, some healthy linguistic normality still exists. Pastiche is thus blank parody, a statue with blind eyeballs.[11]

But the claim that pastiche as "blank parody" resists any critical or ideological use of old styles or forms amounts to a pipe dream. No citational procedure that transfers a sign from one context to another does so without carrying with it the intertextual palimpsest of its former meaning. Indeed, it is through such intertextual citations that meanings proliferate and are superimposed. Jameson reads the supposed arbitrariness of such citations as a sign of unconscious influence rather than a conscious choice for heterogeneity: or, to put it differently, as a sign that marks (the end of) a historical epoch rather than as an index of intertextual significance.[12] His definition of pastiche thus neglects to account for the critical gesture inherent in the very use of extant forms and styles, and the fact that such forms and styles themselves signify.

Around the same time as Jameson's nascent thoughts on postmodernism develop, Gérard Genette, in his study of hypertextuality, conceives of pastiche as a related counterpart to parody, not as an evacuation of its critical potential. The former consists of the iteration of a formula – namely, a genre – while the latter performs a transformation of a discrete quantity – a text.[13] For Genette, the variance between the two terms lies not in their designation of distinct historical periods, but rather in the two ways they operate on texts and create intertextual interdependence: through imitation (pastiche) and transformation (parody). Pastiche and parody thus both maintain their capacity to alter meanings; any generic imitation or textual transformation will necessarily involve a degree of distortion or alteration. Parody's laugh, which in Jameson pastiche had silenced, resounds again in Genette as the effect of a ludic intertextual operation. In opting to call

---

[11] Given the context of Jameson's use of the term satire, the meaning of satiric impulse more closely aligns with a mocking or critical gesture. In effect the shift from parody to pastiche involves the ostensibly uncritical reuse of old forms. Jameson, "Postmodernism, or The Cultural Logic of Late Capitalism," 65.
[12] To define the postmodern period as lacking in style – thus necessitating a recycling of older styles – is, moreover, a fallacious claim.
[13] See Genette, *Palimpsests*, 78–85.

Butler's *Gender Trouble* a pastiche in Genette's sense, I wish to draw attention to the critical energy she maintains in imitating a literary genre (the novel of development) in a theoretical work. Such a reading of Butler further illuminates the relation between theoretical and literary modes of writing by demonstrating the narrative impulses and procedures that construct theories and arguments.[14]

Citation and Narrative

To her very first chapter Butler prepends three terms and five quotations. From the beginning, and before she has written more than a few words of paratext, she establishes the aims of her enterprise: first, to differentiate gender from the bookended words sex and desire; second, to engage with the genealogical roots of the project. Sandwiched somewhat awkwardly between sex and desire, the word gender can be seen as related to its neighboring signifiers and yet tenuously independent of them: a sign struggling to differentiate itself while maintaining an anchor in a discourse of sexuality and power. The single sentences that follow, one apiece culled from Simone de Beauvoir, Julia Kristeva, Luce Irigaray, Michel Foucault, and Monique Wittig, function less as mottos than as a common precipitant for what follows – a catalyst providing the initial impulse to the text. In the first chapter of her book, Butler introduces Beauvoir, Irigaray, Foucault, and Wittig, each of whose conceptions of gender mark off the terrain of Butler's narrative.

Her grouping of these disparate theorists reveals a narrative cosmogony of gender that begins with a kind of biblical *fiat lux* moment. Foucault, who comes to be an omnipresent protagonist and the progenitor of the book, provides the juridical framework that enables the construction of gender through discursive institutions and systems of power. Seizing upon this birth of gender from discourse, Beauvoir cleaves woman from the side of man as his Other, though she implies, in Butler's reading, the continuing presence of feminine agency and volition in this last prelapsarian idyll. The moment of the fall in this crypto-allegory comes when Irigaray "argues that women constitute a paradox, if not a contradiction, within the discourse of identity itself. [...] Within a language pervasively masculinist, a phallogocentric language, women constitute the unrepresentable" (14). Cast out of representable discourse, woman becomes a "point of linguistic absence, the impossibility of a grammatically denoted substance," an impossible subject (15).

In citing Irigaray's understanding of women, Butler points to the moment when women lose agency and subject status. The "masculine signifying econ-

---

14 Compare, for example, the expository writing of Hélène Cixous.

omy" (17) denies women both voice and identity in its reign of terror. "Instead of a self-limiting linguistic gesture that grants alterity or difference to women," Butler writes, "phallogocentrism offers a name to eclipse the feminine and take its place" (18). This effacement of women by dint of their unrepresentability in discourse leads us to the central issue at stake in defining gender; any attempt to differentiate gender necessarily involves the deployment of a medium that precludes it: (masculinist) language. Butler's critique of the political feminist movement in fact revolves around its use of language in a "colonizing gesture" that "uncritically mimics the strategy of the oppressor instead of offering a different set of terms" (19). Despite attempts to circumvent language, women according to Irigaray are doomed to apply to the problems of feminism a masculinist discursive framework because no other exists.[15]

In this reading of Butler's Genesis of gender, Monique Wittig provides salvation after the fall. By unsettling the binary division of gender – that is, the male/female, masculine/feminine dichotomy – Wittig hopes to implode the entire category and effect a "disruption and displacement of heterosexual hegemony" (25). This act of subversion within compulsory heterosexuality would both reorder discourse from within, thus working with the constraints of language that govern it, and create an entirely new framework for thinking gender. The rub for Butler is twofold. First, this requires feminism to take leave of universalizing terms like "women" and "the feminine," and second, feminism must redefine and reorient itself within a new linguistic framework that rejects binaries. Charting the course of such a radical shift, which Butler endeavors to do in the ensuing pages of *Gender Trouble*, requires careful rhetorical footwork in navigating the perils of having pulled the terminological rug out from under political feminism.

Indeed, Nussbaum's critique of Butler appears to stem largely from her displeasure with a new theorization of feminism under the sign of linguistic subversion and, concomitantly, from personal philosophical differences regarding the locus of power in discourse. As Butler's foil, Nussbaum more or less explicitly rejects the Foucauldian view that locates power in language, putting her faith instead in the concrete power of activist, political, and juridical institutions – which Butler considers already inherently shaped by masculinist language. For Butler – and by extension for Wittig – the political issues at stake are physical manifestations of a deeper epistemological problem caused by the "masculine signifying economy." Nussbaum concerns herself primarily with remedying the

---

15 Indeed, Lacanian psychoanalysis carries on the masculine framework established by Freud, just as Derridian Deconstruction foregrounds the notion of logocentrism (to which Irigaray adds gender).

concrete ills of gender inequality while accusing Butler of a solipsistic brand of feminism unconcerned with "the material suffering of women who are hungry, illiterate, violated, beaten."[16] Butler, by contrast, alerts her fellow feminists to the degree their efforts perpetuate inequality through an unreflective use of language and offers a solution for overcoming this challenge, ultimately shifting the emphasis of political feminism from rectifying external symptoms of oppression to attacking what she perceives to be their causes.[17] The contrast between their views thus points to a rift within the feminist movement stemming from Butler's and her predecessors' focus on language and signification.

To return to the opening passage of *Gender Trouble*, we note that the invocation of Monique Wittig does in fact direct Butler's narrative decisively toward the problem of gendered language. This use of citation in the incipit provides a narrative context for the claims that follow (she alludes to her own notion of performance only on page thirty-three). In this reading, gender is a product of ordered fiction, its development a genesis story from Foucault to Wittig as announced by the mottos (in spite of the curious omission of Kristeva from the narrative dynamic). In tracing the transformation of gender from Foucault through Beauvoir and Irigaray to Wittig, *Gender Trouble* is comprised of both a history and a story. The personal anecdotes from the prefaces, including Butler's narration of a family history of gender trouble that subjected her "to strong and scarring condemnation" (xix), establish a dynamic in which the theorist manifests herself in the narration and narrative perspective of the text, even as she initially suppresses the first-person pronoun.[18]

The short, ordered mottos; the first-person narrative voice that does not assert so much as chronicle the past; the use of citation as an element of narrative structure rather than as an academic means of support; the inclusion of Kristeva among the mottos and her omission from the opening; and the signature rhetorical questions – all appear here first and set up a suspenseful narrative genealogy for Butler's protagonist: gender. If in describing the genesis of gender Butler deploys a largely fragmented French tradition of discourse analysis and feminism, she nevertheless weaves these disparate threads into a coherent narrative

---

[16] Nussbaum, "The Professor of Parody," 44.

[17] Butler addresses the material aspects of her argument more directly in her follow-up to *Gender Trouble*: *Bodies That Matter*.

[18] The first chapter of *Gender Trouble* has a mere three instances wherein the narrating voice uses the first-person pronoun in its various permutations (7, 17, 19). The chapters that follow, however, abound in them. The brief ten-page conclusion, for example, has eight instances of it. At the outset, Butler permits the past to speak through the "I" of her sources, allowing her own narrative subjectivity to take shape over the course of the text.

by modeling the narrative structure on that of a quasi-biblical cosmogony of gender. Cited theorists serve as theoretical source material and narrative signposts through the text. Butler's rhetorical questions, which are clustered primarily in the midpoints of her chapters[19] rather than at the ends as Nussbaum claims,[20] often introduce smaller textual sections, thereby impelling her narrative forward. The trajectory of Butler's story, furthermore, does not march teleologically through history, as the placement of Beauvoir shows. Without chronological genealogy as the ordering principle of the narrative, citation fills the void to give coherence to the narrative by imbricating theories.

With Wittig, however, Butler reaches an apparent impasse. How might one continue to theorize gender after toppling binary conceptions of it? What is left? The answer, it seems, lies with and beyond Foucault. His short introduction to the diaries of Herculine Barbin, a hermaphrodite, illustrate in Butler how the assertion of any gender identity is merely "a regulatory fiction" (32). If indeed institutions – among them language, law, and other instantiations of power – regulate the very possibility of gender, then gender becomes a contingency that must accord with regulatory practice to be intelligible. Any reading of it ultimately relies on this illusion of intelligibility contrived by a hermeneutic enterprise, through an interpretation that mistakes expressive signs as emanations of an identity. But Butler concludes that these expressive signs themselves mask an underlying nothingness, a process of smoke and mirrors: "There is no gender identity behind the expressions of gender; that identity is performatively constituted by the very 'expressions' that are said to be its results" (33). This switch of identity and expression – that is, that the latter engenders the former, rather than vice-versa – relieves gender of its terminological freight and opens it up as a space for signifying practices that are inherently citational. Throughout her exposition, Butler not only traces the narrative of gender from its place in the history of sexuality (and *The History of Sexuality*) to its deconstruction as a commonplace. She also writes a metanarrative that reveals gender as a citational aftereffect, that "brings into relief the utterly constructed status of the so-called heterosexual original," which is "nothing other than a parody of the idea of the natural and the original" (41). The very narrative device with which Butler structures her text is that which performance deploys for signification; citations amount to "imitations which effectively displace the meaning of the original" (176).

---

[19] In the passage under discussion, pages three to thirty-three, all rhetorical questions occur between pages seven and twenty-five.
[20] Nussbaum, "The Professor of Parody," 38.

As a form of imitation, citation in Butler functions not only as a means of drawing from and participating in related academic discourses. It also acts as a constitutive means of structuring her narrative and provides the condition for the possibility of identity through performance. If Wittig undermines the conventions of gender binarism with her theory, Butler's solution for conceiving of gender after its deconstruction involves the very strategy she uses to align her textual identity with the French theoretical tradition: citation. Drawing upon disparate source material, these citational practices orchestrate performances of gender into coherent readings of culturally accepted commonplace identities or – and this anticipates Butler's deferred discussion of performance and its potentialities – subversive transgressions that challenge notions of gender binarism. Citation thus remains the constitutive element of both performance and Butler's narrative of gender.

Citation and Performance

With the instantiation of performance as the key to gender identity, Butler inaugurates a theory that serves as the logical development in a story beginning with Foucault and ending with Wittig, thereby tracing a narrative account of gender from its formation within institutions of discourse to its questioning as a construct of heterosexual hegemony. If we continue our reading of *Gender Trouble* as a narrative text, however, we find that Butler's tale of gender formation interrupts itself at this point. "Gender," she concludes, "is the repeated stylization of the body, a set of repeated acts within a highly rigid regulatory frame that congeal over time to produce the appearance of substance, of a natural sort of being" (43–44). This initial definition of gender as the product of performance shifts the focus from the agent of formed identity to the acts of identity formation. The move from doer to deed, from subject to performance, however, occasions a long digression through the history of psychoanalysis in a second, parallel narrative – the history of the subject.

Traversing the field from Freud to Lacan and finally to Kristeva, who brings her back to the subversion of identity through performance, Butler demonstrates the inherent gender binary in the formation of the subject in order to expose the historical contingency of gender and to unsettle notions of naturalness, to wipe away the "snot of naturalness" to borrow Jelinek's colorful term. In spite of Butler's avowed distaste for the masculinist bent of Freud's and Lacan's theories of psychic development, in psychoanalysis her narrative of gender formation encounters a school of thought that emphasizes the contingencies of development and the "acquisition of gender identity" (74) rather than its ontological predetermination. Citing psychoanalytic theories, particularly Lacan's ideas of the Symbolic and the Phallus, allows her to undermine their narratives of the formation of the subject and show instead that "all gender ontology is reducible to the play of appearances" (60) and thus not subject to gendered absolutes. If such is the case, or so the story goes, gender exists only on the plane of the play of contingent signifiers and signifieds. Gender, in other words, has no referent.

At issue in Butler's narrative are the ramifications of problems of referentiality and signification. Hers is an epistemological shift away from real absolutes toward illusory constructions, toward exposing the contingencies of discourse taken as given. While not the first to articulate such problems – here her debt is owed to Deconstruction, among others – Butler sees in the arbitrariness of signifiers the potential for a subversive assertion of gender identity, contingent though it may be, to challenge the masculine-heterosexual signifying economy. To do this merely requires challenging the "tacit collective agreement to perform, produce, and sustain discrete and polar genders as cultural fictions" (178) and as such the blind assumption of fixed meanings and identities. Wittig's exclusionary construction of an alternative lesbian identity Butler rejects because it would instantiate compulsory heterosexuality through its dependence on the act of exclusion. "The more insidious and effective strategy it seems," she writes, "is a thoroughgoing appropriation and redeployment of the categories of identity themselves, not merely to contest 'sex,' but to articulate the convergence of multiple sexual discourses at the site of 'identity' in order to render that category, in whatever form, permanently problematic" (163). In other words, Butler wishes to cause gender trouble.

For her theory of performance to be practical, the performative citational acts through which gender is constituted must have a signifying medium. The site of many theoretical inscriptions, the body – located at the intersection of discourses of naturalness and artificiality, interiority and exteriority, and prediscursive and constructed identities – acts as such a vehicle for gender. To invoke the body as the medium for performative representations of gender, Butler first challenges a conception of the body as given and whole. Rather, she argues, it offers a preferred canvas for citational performative practices precisely because its visible signifying surface, the skin, constitutes a liminal mediating boundary between interior and exterior. In other words, the body has the unique capacity to perform gender due to its constant state of significatory flux, its own lack of fixed meaning.

As before, Foucault inaugurates the narrative through citation. His discussion of the body as the "surface and scene of a cultural inscription" (165) sets the stage for examinations of the concepts of transgression and abjection in Mary Douglas and Julia Kristeva. In this passage, Butler reveals the degree to which Foucauldian critique underpins her own narrative; his understanding of discursive power relations and sexuality laid the groundwork for initial questions about the stability of gender categories, while his theorization of the body as "the inscribed surface of [historical] events" (165)[21] allows Butler to redeploy the body as the medium for a legible gender identity. This manner of citation not only reveals the contingency of Butler's theory – not Foucault's complex theories *per se*, but short, decontextualized quotations from them are valid *a priori*. It also demonstrates the degree to which Foucault is worshipfully invoked as a muse who effects a proliferation of citations. Derived from Nietzsche, his notion of the body as a site of cultural inscription (166) makes possible a discussion (and rejection) of Mary Douglas' claims regarding transgression and ordered (binary) cultural meaning. Kristeva, likewise, explores, as a result of Foucault's understanding of the body, the reassertion of corporeal boundaries (and thus subjectivity) through the process of abjection. Foucault sets in motion the narrative dynamic by virtue of his mostly unquestioned citational authority. As a protagonist in the narrative of gender identity, he acts as a corrective, guiding force throughout *Gender Trouble*. He unleashes the story at its cosmogonical outset by pointing out "that juridical systems of power *produce* the subjects they subsequently come to represent" (4) and reins it in at its close with his notion of cultural inscription on the body, literally inscribing himself into the text. Through Foucault, the narrative becomes coherent; his is the epistemological framework through which the text is read and according to which all other intertexts are organized and evaluated.

With Foucault, the final elaboration of the theory of performance brings about a peculiar intersection between the narrative and metanarrative levels of the text. Through Foucault, Douglas, and Kristeva, and on the basis of theoretical constructs from poststructuralism, feminism, and psychoanalysis, Butler concludes that gender results from the play of superficial corporeal signs that beguile the interpreter with the illusion of depth and naturalness. "That the gendered body is performative suggests that it has no ontological status apart from the various acts which constitute its reality" (173), she writes. The acts that constitute its reality, however – and the acts that constitute Butler's narrative – are themselves citations. Essentially, the theory of performance reveals itself as a narrative fiction as much as it does a viable theoretical model. As a kind of novel of gender formation, *Gender Trouble* uses novelistic procedures of narrative development – literary exposition, formal pastiche, narrative teleology, suspenseful deferral, and the progressive formation of identity – that lend it its literary qualities.[22] By the same

---

[21] Michel Foucault, "Nietzsche, Genealogy, History," quoted in Butler, *Gender Trouble*, 165.

[22] This may be contrasted with the role of literature in Foucault as a medium in which history inscribes its epistemes. Cf. Michel Foucault, *The Archaeology of Knowledge*, trans. A. M. Sheridan Smith (New York: Harper & Row, 1972).

token, Butler's text derives its scholarly flavor from its rigorous relation to and citation of theoretical precedent. This analogical character, however, subverts the text's professed aim to recount the historicity of discursive constructs by claiming, in effect, that it was always so or it was never otherwise. With citation, Butler's diachronicity of gender becomes a synchronicity of eternal imitation, the perpetual practice of parodic citation, and by extension a satiric effect. "[J]ust as the psychoanalytic notion of gender identification is constituted by a fantasy of a fantasy," Butler writes by analogy to another theoretical model that posits no history of psychic development, "[...] so gender parody reveals that the original identity after which gender fashions itself is an imitation without an origin" (175). All signification, the text suggests, is merely citational and imitative, inverting the dominant epistemological model for meaning-making while revealing the underlying myths upon which its commonplaces are founded. In other words, all signification is inherently satiric in its jarring dissonance with the intuitive assumptions of human cognition. Signs are nothing but performative fabrications.

The perpetual recontextualization of citations through performance disrupts any fixity or continuity of meaning that might result from the "stylized repetition of acts" (179) that constitute contingent signs, such as gender identity. As Butler's narrative of gender attests, for example, the palimpsests of theoretical precedents remain, their meanings reactivated through citation. Indeed, just as the specter of Foucault looms large throughout *Gender Trouble*, so too does it hold sway in Butler's conclusion. In insisting upon the difference between expression and performance and seizing upon the latter, Butler notes that "[i]f gender attributes and acts, the various ways in which a body shows or produces its cultural signification, are performative, then there is no preexisting identity by which an act or attribute might be measured; there would be no true or false, real or distorted acts of gender, and the postulation of a true gender identity would be revealed as a regulatory fiction" (180). To conclude that gender is a regulatory fiction merely confirms the assumption Butler had made with the help of Foucault pages earlier in the text.[23] Like the *Entwicklungsroman*, which traces the development of nascent qualities in its protagonist, so too does Butler's narrative contain a degree of stagnant circularity that uncovers its conclusions in its opening, in spite of narrative progression.

---

[23] To a certain extent, Foucault makes this argument in Butler's initial invocation of him, though a more explicit discussion of regulatory fictions occurs later during Butler's discussion of Herculine Barbin. See Butler, *Gender Trouble*, 4, 32.

10. Performing Theory in Literature: Thomas Meinecke's *Tomboy* (1998)

In his novels *Tomboy* and *Music*,[1] Thomas Meinecke further narrativizes Butler's theory of the performativity of gender identity, a central concern of much of Meinecke's novelistic work. In these novels he cites Butler in a way that illustrates and complicates her theories, while assuming a parodic posture that extends Butler's concerns almost *ad absurdum*. Riffs on gender trouble and *Gender Trouble* expose a poetological program that conflates theory with literature, as well as a literary performative gesture that unveils the intertextual contingencies and borrowings inherent in a literary-theoretical text. Like *Gender Trouble*, Meinecke's work implicitly questions its own originality, but does so with citational practices that attempt to go beyond the medium of the written word. Indeed, in his five Lectures on Poetics at the University of Frankfurt in 2012, Meinecke elaborated his poetic method by quoting exclusively from secondary literature and reviews of his work and spinning records that he had mentioned in his prose.[2] This citational *bricolage* in the form of "inventories, quotational puzzles, and apparent readymades"[3] has been a constitutive element of his writing since his first published literary texts, *Beating around the Bush* [*Mit der Kirche ums Dorf*] and *Wood* [*Holz*].[4]

Tomboy, however, marks a turning point away from narrative conventions into a more experimental vein that adopts these "procedures of recording, citing, and enumerating"[5] not only as the central narrative strategy, but also as the crux of the narrative itself. Like his literary forebear Hubert Fichte, Thomas Meinecke replaces description in his work with "procedures of listing and of taking inventory, of copying, note-taking, and rewriting. His writing is constituted by absorb-

---

[1] Thomas Meinecke, *Tomboy* (Frankfurt am Main: Suhrkamp, 1998); Thomas Meinecke, *Tomboy*, trans. Daniel Bowles (Las Vegas: AmazonCrossing, 2011); Thomas Meinecke, *Musik* (Frankfurt am Main: Suhrkamp, 2004).

[2] Thorsten Gräbe, "Thomas Meineckes Poetikvorlesung: Ausdenken ist verboten," *Frankfurter Allgemeine Zeitung*, February 9, 2012, sec. Feuilleton, http://www.faz.net/aktuell/feuilleton/buecher/autoren/thomas-meineckes-poetikvorlesung-ausdenken-ist-verboten-11642364.html. To compare the published version of these lectures, see Meinecke, *Ich als Text*.

[3] Hubert Winkels, "Lob der Kybernetik: Thomas Meineckes Popprogramme und Prosaminiaturen," in *Einschnitte: zur Literatur der 80er Jahre* (Köln: Kiepenheuer & Witsch, 1988), 206.

[4] Thomas Meinecke, *Mit der Kirche ums Dorf: Kurzgeschichten* (Frankfurt am Main: Suhrkamp, 1986); Thomas Meinecke, *Holz: Erzählung* (Köln: Kiepenheuer & Witsch, 1988).

[5] Eckhard Schumacher, *Gerade Eben Jetzt: Schreibweisen der Gegenwart* (Frankfurt am Main: Suhrkamp, 2003), 190.

ing and working with preexisting material."[6] Here, in *Tomboy*, intertextual borrowing and citation come into sharp relief as the most conspicuous elements of Meinecke's prose and, originally, involve textual citations of multiple media, including music, record jackets, liner notes, interviews, and so forth.

In addressing Meinecke's transmedial intertextual practices, much of the critical scholarship adopts the author's own musical terminology, comparing his writing process to the sampling and mixing procedures of a DJ (Meinecke is a DJ and musician as well, long the front man for the band F. S. K.). Despite the occasion reflection on the disparity between citation and sample,[7] most critics of Meinecke have not addressed the aptness of adopting this nomenclature for literary studies. Notions of sampling, mixing, remixing, and sound – transferred to literature – further bedevil and obfuscate the preexisting involutions of intertextuality, citation, repetition, and signifying within literary terminology.[8] These metaphors for intertextuality and citation charge readers with the task of differentiating new terms from old, of cleaving and demarcating arbitrary discursive boundaries to justify a terminological substitution. Because of this disparity and the focus on satire as a mode of writing, the terms sampling, mixing, or remixing do not figure into my argument to refer to intertextual borrowings or citations within Meinecke's works.

Nonetheless, the performative character of Meinecke's self-presentation in hundreds of newspaper interviews,[9] and the attempts in his novels to combine

---

6 Schumacher, *Gerade Eben Jetzt*, 184.

7 Florence Feiereisen, "Identitäten im Remix: Literarisches Sampling im Fadenkreuz von Postmoderne und Postkolonialismus," in *Literatur der Jahrtausendwende: Themen, Schreibverfahren und Buchmarkt um 2000*, ed. Evi Zemanek and Susanne Krones (Bielefeld: Transcript, 2008), 289. See also her more recent monograph, *Der Text als Soundtrack, der Autor als DJ: postmoderne und postkoloniale Samples bei Thomas Meinecke* (Würzburg: Königshausen & Neumann, 2011).

8 Moritz Baßler identifies one significant problem in employing musical terminology to refer to literary procedures: "In attempting to reconstruct the DJ-poetology of [Meinecke and Rainald Goetz], the question has yet to be answered regarding what criteria determine the sequence of material in spinning records or in the novel. What is the 'associative rule' (83 [*Rave*])? Goetz poses this question, but his hypothetical answers don't provide any further help for literature. Quantifiable musical criteria like speed (for example: beats per minute) are hardly transferable to prose, and even more importantly: the decisive objectifying factor of successful 'DJ culture' – the unmitigated reaction of a dancing audience, the feedback of the physical sensation evoked – doesn't apply to the novelist." *Der deutsche Pop-Roman: Die neuen Archivisten* (München: C. H. Beck, 2002), 146.

9 Of the numerous interviews, I cite four representative cases: Ulrich Rüdenauer and Thomas Meinecke, "'Der Reiz des Rhizomatischen': Ein Gespräch mit Thomas Meinecke über Schreiben unter dem Vorzeichen von Techno, die Faszination für bestimmte Orte und hellblaues Frottee," *Sprache im technischen Zeitalter* 40, no. 161 (2002): 106–17; Jan Wenzel and Thomas Meinecke, "Vielleicht

disparate media, superficial or not, point to a media-historical development in the citational strategies of satire that cannot be ignored. In employing intertextual practices that structure his narratives – and that uniquely consider music and nonliterary media part of the "infinite text" – Meinecke's works point to a transmedial aspect of satiric practices we have not yet seen. Even in Elfriede Jelinek and Thomas Bernhard, where references to musical works abound, such references are of a different kind, serving as mythic paradigms in the case of Jelinek, or as elements of an inverted epistemology in the case of Bernhard. In contrast, Meinecke predicates his use of satiric citational practices on no extant conventions; quotations and borrowings are legion and play a formal role in Meinecke's texts, as they do in Jean Paul's, for example, but Meinecke's work, especially from *Tomboy* to his more recent novels, actively attempts to flout the boundaries of the written text. Put differently, these transmedial citational practices give the lie to a rootedness of satire in a fixed written medium and point to an elision between the written and the spoken word, to the flexibility of significatory potential in performance (a fact Karl Kraus already knew in combining his writing with stage performances and lectures). That satiric practices may transcend not just genres, but forms and media as well, underscores the importance of conceiving of satire as a semiotic construct rather than a purely literary one. Meinecke exploits these transmedial channels of semiosis to cite and borrow forms, practices, and content from literature, theory, and music.

As an archive of contemporary discourse on gender, *Tomboy*, by way of example, with its "practice of citing without quotation marks," may be read as a multimedial pastiche of the form of theory.[10] For better understanding the legacy of satiric discourse within postwar intertextual practices, this knotty terminological differentiation between parody and pastiche plays a crucial role, both in systematically analyzing the ways citation and intertextuality function within Meinecke's texts, and in historicizing such practices within theoretical and literary discourses. If *Tomboy* thus aesthetically stages the theories and intertexts it refers to, then its characters embody and illustrate theoretical concerns as "pure discursive events," establishing an ironic distance between literature and theory.[11] In

---

kann man ja immer wieder dasselbe Buch schreiben: Thomas Meinecke spricht mit Jan Wenzel über Hedy Lamarr, Paul Gilroy, Kodwo Eshun, Hubert Fichte und den Atlantik," *Edit*, no. 26 (2001): 60–65; Eckhard Schumacher and Thomas Meinecke, "Pop, Literatur. Ein Interview mit Thomas Meinecke," *Kritische Ausgabe* 5 (2000): 19–20; Daniel Lenz and Eric Pütz, "'Ich bin so ein Pop-Sommer-1982-Typ': Ein Gespräch mit Thomas Meinecke," *Neue Zürcher Zeitung*, August 23, 1999.
10 Baßler, *Der deutsche Pop-Roman*, 135, 140.
11 Axel Dunker, "'Alle tanzen, doch niemand kennt die Platten': Pastiche, Sampling und Intertextualität in Thomas Meineckes Roman 'Tomboy,'" *Weimarer Beiträge* 52, no. 1 (2006): 106.

other words, Meinecke's novel may be read as an aesthetic literarization of theory that ironizes theory through its performance of it, in effect closing the gap between literary and theoretical writing by approaching the same problem from a different angle.[12] It is through the intertextual web of association in *Tomboy* that Meinecke "dissolves the discourse of depth, the subtext, in favor of context, essentialism in favor of discursive superficiality."[13] In this chapter, I examine the satiric practice of citation through Meinecke's trademark intertextuality. It is this ironic distance between Meinecke and Butler through pastiche – and through the link between the satiric effect and pastiche – that the "permeability between theory and narrative, between philosophy and aesthetics, which has been the basic theorem of poststructuralism since the late work of Roland Barthes," comes into focus as well.[14] Through the satiric effect of citation, postwar fiction and theoretical writings find common semiotic ground.

Tomboy

In adopting Judith Butler's critique of gender binaries from *Gender Trouble*, Thomas Meinecke refashions the theoretical context of gender theory and embeds it into a literary framework. The merit of this shift from a scholarly study of gender to a literary rendering of its premises in *Tomboy* lies in the transfer of emphasis from feminism, politics, and sociology – from textual externalities – to an aesthetic form that self-reflexively engages with the very system at the heart of feminist, political, and sociological signification: language. Within the boundaries of this new redeployment of theory in fiction, Meinecke's novel explores the limited means of language to designate a fully synthetic gendered condition comprising elements of these binary oppositional terms – much less a new gender (or genders) on par with, but beyond the polar dyad male–female. On the one hand, the model of hybridized synthesis fails to explode the binary because it always bears the scars of its two sutured components – male and female – thereby surreptitiously buttressing a duality it should overcome; it can never completely sublate its constituent parts. On the other hand, the emergence of a tertiary gender or of multiple genders defies the current capacity of language to integrate a plural gender continuum into extant biological, sexual, and queer discourses.

---

12 Dunker, "'Alle tanzen, doch niemand kennt die Platten'," 110.
13 Dunker, "'Alle tanzen, doch niemand kennt die Platten'," 115.
14 Dunker, "'Alle tanzen, doch niemand kennt die Platten'," 110.

Given the curious combination of a narrative mode of writing with theoretical discourse, the reader may do well to interpret Meinecke's novel as a supplement that supersedes the original by virtue of its own performance. Its imitation of Butler narrativizes theories and ideas and reflects in its complex form, shifting narrative perspective, and exposed lines of reference the thorny *Geschichte* (in the historical and narrative senses) of gender politics and identity. Several of Butler's own writing strategies – the substitution of a conclusive proclamation by a series of complex unanswered questions, her challenging academic prose – reappear in Meinecke's text in a way that suggests both a serious approbation of Butler's mode of writing when used for critical reflections, and a rebuke of its density when referring to matters so real as the manner by which gender shapes identity. The earnestness of Meinecke's narrative exploration of gender identity and theory implies that any parodic or satiric imitation of Butler is nevertheless all in good fun, but one cannot help but note the jarring juxtaposition of literariness with academic inquiry. The novel opens with an invocation of queerness, its first word, "Rosarot [pink],"[15] describing the gleam of nearby rock quarries in the setting sun, which is immediately countered by a theoretical query: "Had the artificial encroachment into nature become an element of so-called natural beauty?" (7; 1). Already Meinecke has set the stage for the ensuing thought experiments by conjuring a metaphor of queerness alongside a fundamental debate within Butler's critique of feminism: the possibilities for the naturalness or artificiality of discourse.

Questions of the artifice of nature and the naturalness of artifice – the "electric pink" of the glowing rocks (7; 1) – are rudely interrupted by banality: a run in the protagonist Vivian's stocking. Here the text turns abruptly away from the stilted opening and the attraction of nature and interrogates further. The Barthesian understanding of pantyhose as text, as something to be read and untangled – as fabric, tissue, woven discourse, "an artificial amplification of nature" (7; 1) – occasions a series of overwrought questions that set the tone for the novel; the rhetorical questions, academic jargon, and theoretical concerns in *Tomboy* attest to the primacy of the critically interrogative mode of thought here and in *Gender Trouble*. In Meinecke's novel, however, these conventionally academic strategies are employed in questions of quotidian existence, a turn to popular culture that had begun in Barthes and grown fully fledged in Jelinek.

---

15 Meinecke, *Tomboy*, 1998, 7; Meinecke, *Tomboy*, 2011, 1. References to *Tomboy* in this chapter will appear in the text parenthetically, with dual pages numbers of the German original and the English translation, separated by a semicolon.

10. Performing Theory in Literature: Thomas Meinecke's *Tomboy* (1998)

From an incessant questioning of the implications of media, material, and pop culture emerges a narrative economy that revels in the tangential. Recursion replaces teleology, circulation replaces narrative succession, rhetoric replaces reportage. The interrogations here are thus not only the reported thoughts of the narrator and the figures in the novel. They also constitute formal breaks that uncover and reflect upon the conditions and process of signification. Such a narrative economy uses a poetological currency derived not from a novelistic mode of writing, but instead from theoretical tracts, philosophical analyses, and academic considerations that resist narration in favor of description and hermeneutics, without a teleological drive towards totalizing synthesis: a poetics of the rhizome, to speak with Deleuze and Guattari.

The inquisitive gesture that elevates the banality of a run in a stocking to the level of Barthesian text also points to four primary theoretical concerns in the narrative. The first of these is the leveling of epistemological hierarchies that otherwise label only certain cultural domains and objects as permissible fields of serious inquiry for the production of knowledge. In emancipating all objects of study from the strictures of this regulatory framework, Meinecke's novel translates the reception of scientific theorems and ideas from the lecture hall to the bedroom; the narrative economy moves always from the abstract to the concrete. When Vivian considers the consequences of cyborg theorist Donna Haraway's interpretation of the sciences as a mode of social narration and signification, for example, she poses a provocative question that has meaning for her and her group of friends: "what, then, was heralded by Angela's impressive cock? To what extent were the natural sciences a continuation of politics by other means? Could the objects of the natural sciences in turn act performatively? Was Vivian's vulva a material-semiotic node of production? Frauke's breasts nothing but the mandatory outcome of an exclusively discursive construction?" (57–58; 51). That Vivian turns her critical gaze directly to the erogenous "body islands" so prevalent in her friendly discussions smacks of an indifference to tone. To what extent may we read this passage as a pastiche of questions posed in cultural and gender studies? As a serious inquiry that seeks to break the taboos and boundaries separating critical academic reflection from quotidian concerns? Or as merely a series of legitimate questions about the signifying potential of one's body?

Given the second theoretical concern in Meinecke's novel – the body's potential for signification – this passage can and must be read as both simultaneously: as a pastiche that performatively subverts the normative use of scholarly language and fuses hitherto separate realms of study through its transgressive play. It is an imitation and repetition of scientific language and discourse, which, in the context of the novel, nevertheless poses valid questions. For Meinecke's text (and its characters), the body is a site of semiotic inscription whose conditions of signification are the focus of academic curiosity and exploration. As part of the textual fabric of the novel, Butler's theory of gender and identity crystallizes within the narrative as a cited point of reference, but the circle of women, men, and gender-neutral characters in the novel embodies *in concreto* the questions, difficulties, snags, and indeterminacy of normative gender dynamics that Butler takes such pains to theorize abstractly. Mapping this abstraction onto specific cases in point, the final sentence of the book illustrates in its succinctness the fluid identity politics embraced by the novel's characters and elaborated by its theoretical reflections. To ask "[w]hat will we wear?" (271; 240) displaces the locus of signification: from the body itself as a site of inscriptions to the changeable layers of clothing, signs themselves, that aid in our performance of gender and identity. For Vivian and her entourage, the question of what to wear is tantamount to wondering: who and what shall I be today? Clothes make the man [sic], a proverb to be taken literally, gains currency as a rule of gender politics and the implicit theory of signification in Meinecke's novel.

A corollary concern of the signification of the body, the question of the naturalness of identity and inherent meaning serves as a third point of refraction for the theoretical undercurrents in *Tomboy*. Mimetic performance through attire or gesture, as Butler describes so carefully (and as Meinecke articulates through his novel), exposes the artificiality of all fixed meanings through imitation and repetition; these evoke the illusion of fixed meaning and show the shifting semiosis of the signifier. From citations of seemingly archetypal models, performances create the illusion of referents and reinsert them as cultural artifacts into the pool of available sources. This feedback loop upholds the illusion of an intact sign through what amounts to rhetorical persuasion and, thereafter, through convention. In effect, imitation and repetition demonstrate the diachronicity of the sign through the satiric practice of citation, which always alters meaning.

What is striking about this dynamic in *Tomboy* is how the explicit textual discussions of performance reveal this process of significatory trickery while concomitantly participating in it. By dint of its medium – text, fiction, book – the dissemination of this theory engenders an extended moment of self-referential excess by uncovering its own artificiality and that of all fixed meanings. In other words, the novel carries the theory to its ultimate extreme by wrapping it in its own cloak of fictionality. Couched in these terms, *Tomboy* raises the question of where one draws the boundary between the presumption of real truth in a theoretical vein and the explicit denial of real truth within a fictional mode of writing. If language is the medium of signification and thus performance, how might one distinguish between performance and reality? For Butler, reality is performance, and Meinecke's novel echoes this assumption. The importation of a theoretical framework with a certain claim to (performative) facticity nevertheless belies any discrete boundary between fact and fiction, between theory and literature. The suture point between the two is that of artificiality through performance, the illusion of naturalness through language.

Highlighting language and its fiction, in turn, is a fourth theoretical paradigm elaborated continually in Meinecke's novel. While Butler's concern in *Gender Trouble* and subsequent studies has been the production of meaning and identity through performance, Meinecke's text – again by virtue of its medium – poses the question of semantic comprehension and interpretation. *Tomboy* expands upon a conventional notion of reading that limits it to a visual or aural intake of printed signs. Reading in Meinecke instead provides both the means to receive the imitative, signifying performance as well as the tool for drawing discursive archetypes into a performance. Put differently, reading is a multipronged process involving complex conceptions of textuality, hermeneutics, and intertextuality. As such, it is advisable to avoid terminological confusion by employing these terms separately, depending on which type of reading Meinecke invokes.

Of foremost importance in examining this imitation are Meinecke's expanded conception of textuality and notion of intertextuality. The former offers an understanding of text by which ordinary non-linguistic signs are also subject to a hermeneutic gaze; the world becomes text. Thus Vivian's run, to name one example, fixes the interpretive eye of its beholder, becoming a sign waiting to be read and understood. While reading, hermeneutics, and understanding – vast subjects in their own regard – are crucial to the overall process of signification of which Butler describes a part, *Tomboy* does not focus on the theoretical intricacies of these terms. Emerging from a historical period to some extent inured to the novelty of poststructuralist analysis, it instead narratively explicates a contemporary theory of textuality and intertextuality. By chronicling the investigative impulses of academic research in Vivian's thesis on Otto Weininger, Korinna's study of erogenous zones, and Frauke's dissertation on Jesus' foreskin, Meinecke transforms the process of academic inquiry into narrative form, but he also demonstrates through this narrative the cross-pollination of concepts and ideas that results from the juxtaposition and interweaving of these women's projects. In other words, the novel engenders a dynamic of intertextuality within its pages by relating these three feminist projects (and their authors and authors' identities) through an understanding of "text" propagated by poststructuralism and expanded by gender studies. Disparate theses and identities thus unite under the aegis of a common epistemology. What constitutes this epistemology is, in a word, intertextuality.

Intertwined with academic discourse on originality, this concept, involving textual interchange, cross-pollination, and citation, reinscribes itself into the model of performance that Butler identifies as the underlying mechanism responsible for the borrowings and citational aspect of signification. The ramifications of this symbiosis between intertextual performance and signification are wide-ranging. For one, the modalities of intertextuality, imitative borrowings and citation, gain currency not only as deictic references to influence, but also as the very modes by which meaning becomes possible. Given that Butlerian performance always involves an invocation of normative paradigms – an invocation understood here as always satiric – intertextuality functions as an *a priori* for this process of signification. Without paradigmatic models to cite, there can be no performance, as Butler denies the notion of originary or inherent meaning. Only by redeploying extant modalities of meaning in new contexts and for new purposes can a new meaning arise. Intertextuality thus epistemologically underwrites all processes of signification based upon performance.

In *Tomboy*, this intertextual *a priori* also sets loose a whirlwind of theoretical complexities in the narrative. While the diegesis openly displays the circulation of intertextual happenings through overt references, the novel itself reveals its intertextual foundations on the formal level as well. Citations, both attributed and unattributed, imbue the text with a patchwork character, highlighted particularly by the episodic narrative, which is visually divided into 239 short sections, some bearing relation to the preceding ones, others leaping from the blank space between paragraphs to other narrative strands. Meinecke employs this formal technique in all of his subsequent novels as well. The episodic division pulls the reader's attentions from teleological narrative progression and offers him instead a series of short anecdotes, at times almost aphoristic in character, which redirect interpretive emphasis to the discovery of interrelations, interlockings, and interweavings: in short, to the intertextual content of the work. While short formal divisions facilitate the anecdotal and aphoristic narrative, which in turn makes possible the physical divisions of the text, neither the form nor the content of the novel is responsible for its overall shape. What guarantees this reciprocal interdependence of form and content – what serves as the condition for its possibility – is the citational modality of their fragmentation, Meinecke's primary textual procedure.

In the uninterrupted flow of quotations, one particularly politically problematic feature of the narrative remains prominent, however. Citation, an invocation or appropriation of words, thoughts, ideas, or processes of signification, repeatedly displaces the ability of the speaking subject to say "I" with any authority. Deictic by its very nature, citation points away from the speaker (or the text) in an economy of permanent deferral and external reference; the third-person supplants and supersedes the first-person. That Meinecke foregrounds this procedure ultimately covertly undermines the development of identity within the novel when the appellations of protagonists – Vivian in particular: "the philologist"

(149; 140), "the student [*Studentin*]" (9, 43, 60, 75, 180; 3, 37, 54, 68), "the master's candidate [*Magistrandin*]" (10, 42, 49, 81, 147, 158; 4, 36, 42, 74, 138–139, 149), "the collegian [*Studierende*]" (9, 32, 161; 3, 25, 151), "the twenty-four-year-old" (31, 68, 157; 24, 61, 148), "the soldier's daughter" (24, 110, 152, 173; 18, 103, 143, 164) – continually generalize and relativize by dint of their metonymy. The particularity of identity yields to the generality of categorizations, general classifications, and monikers. This denial of subjectivity through the eternal displacement of the "I" reveals itself less as a new literary technique than as a citation: of standard theoretical discourse.

One might argue that first-person narrative – or rather narrative in any of its permutations as fictional discourse – is anathema to theory's implicit claims to truth; to couch theorizations in terms of fictions and anecdotes is to limit their sphere of influence by grounding them in narrative specificities that disavow possible claims to universality. To be sure, theory utilizes narrative modes of writing, but the epistemology of fiction – in which empiricism exists for its own sake, not for extrapolation onto a generalized, catholic truth – has no place in a theory that subscribes to impartial scientificity. A key passage illustrates the ways in which both the narrative of *Tomboy* and the metanarrative of its semiotic procedures crib this strategy of generalization from theoretical nonfiction, substituting politics for identity and subsuming the individual into the collective: "The deconstruction of identity," Meinecke writes, "does not exactly mean the deconstruction of politics, Judith Butler says, but presents precisely those terms by which identity is articulated as political" (237; 227). While affirming an affinity for Judith Butler, Hans Mühlenkamm's citation nevertheless reveals the nettlesome prospect of appropriating Butler's theory of performance wholesale. Proposing a retreat from blanket terms like woman and an embrace of more individualist concepts arising through performance, Butler relocates politics from a binary movement of "us vs. them" to pluralistic, individual challenges to the hegemonic order. And yet, Hans notes, clandestinely counter to his idolized theoretician, "I may have a broken relationship with power, but I'm talking about the same power that first permits me to say I" (237; 227). By virtue of his slippery grasp on power, Hans is bound to a political movement that ostensibly champions individual notions of identity and allows him to assert his subjectivity – at the expense of his independence from the political collective: "[I]dentity formation," he remarks, "only functions by way of the dirtiest procedures of exclusion" (238; 227).

Yet even sublimation of the self in the political collective does not obviate the need for new ways of thinking about language and identity. No amount of willfully serpentine linguistic twisting suffices to eliminate the pairedness of linguistic terms for gender. Bridging the gap between a binary conception of gender and an analogous understanding of gender plurality or continuum is an intractable, if not impossible, linguistic conundrum, and Meinecke certainly does not overcome this hurdle. Indeed, despite Meinecke's playful games with gender designations in *Tomboy* – Frauke Stöver's betrothed, Angela, ostensibly a transgender woman, is a prime example – the deficiencies of language appear ineradicable. Stöver's partner, for instance, always oscillates between "Angela" and "Angelo" without ever resolving into a third, differently gendered alternative. Meinecke's epithets like "Frauke's fiancée" (65; 56) attempt to circumvent this problem, but gender, biological or otherwise, nevertheless inscribes itself within the terms. In German particularly, no neutral, grammatically ungendered personal designation is tenable.[16] Circumlocutory linguistic tactics notwithstanding, gender in *Tomboy* remains theoretically emancipated, albeit permanently subject to practical, semantic polarization. The text toes but never crosses the threshold to complete gender freedom, much less freedom from gender. How might one overcome dual biological and sexual gender determinations in language and in discourse? To what extent does this duplicitous linguistic paradigm inhibit or prohibit supersession by an emancipated conception of gender? Given Butler's (and Meinecke's) proposal for gender pluralism, *Tomboy* illuminates an irresolvable conflict within the semiotics of language: a recalcitrant terminological dualism that infects and influences signification, versus the putatively unlimited possibility of signification in language. Language, it would seem, falters.

Meinecke offers an alternative, however. In a central episode, surprising as much for its brevity as for its abruptness, the text displays its linguistic deficits while pointing beyond its pages to a semiotic system in which linguistic binaries no longer hold sway: the space of non-linguistic performance. This discursive space lies beyond the horizon of accurate representation. A mimetic adaptation of it by language distorts the inherent ambiguities in a manner analogous to sketching a three-dimensional geometric shape in two-dimensional space. Details are lost, contours are eliminated, entire facets vanish, and the reduction necessarily strips layers of meaning and significance from the original. In this episode, the reader sees, through his intertextual adaptation of Butler's stylistic idiosyncrasies

---

16 Certainly the German language is capable of employing a grammatically neutral, neuter term to refer to persons, but aside from neuter nominalized adjectives, which read awkwardly, the options, excluding diminutives, are limited to biologically genderless nouns (*Opfer* [victim], *Mitglied* [member], etc.). Such neutral options, moreover, might be considered semantically inappropriate and, in light of Butler's critique of discrete gender categories, may suspend the binary, but only at the cost of replacing it with a triad. A continuum of gender designations seems to lie beyond the immediate scope of German, since it is a language with discretely gendered nouns.

and her formal strategy of rhetorical questioning, Meinecke alludes to a space where fixed binary identities – and gender roles – are suspended.

The passage in question occurs towards the end of the novel during an outing to the Judenwald, part of the larger Odenwald, near Altneudorf in Baden-Württemberg. *Tomboy*'s protagonist, Vivian Atkinson, and the now very pregnant Korinna Kohn venture into the hills in a portion of the Odenwald at a site whose discursive over-determination sets the stage for a climactic performance of gender and doubling. Its very name a syntagma of binary opposites, Altneudorf is likewise a proxy for Tel Aviv; the title of Theodor Herzl's novel *Altneuland*, the Hebrew translation of which lent the city its name, conjures forth a series of other interrelations. The narrator's litany of associations with this location – "Altneudorf. Tel Aviv. Altneuland. Theodor Herzl. Daniel Boyarin too. West of the village the Steinach River, the slopes, the Judenwald, the Jews' Woods" (214; 204) – marks what is colloquially called the Judenwald as the point of intersection among various discourses relevant to the narrative, among them binary opposites, Zionism, relations between Judaism and femininity, relations between Judaism and sexuality, Jewishness and Germanness, gender, and identity. As a combinatory term itself and with its panoply of discursive strata, the Judenwald further encodes natural landscape as an archive of conflicted history, much as the stone quarry had lent it significance as a record of conflict between humanity and nature, between artifice and naturalness. Put differently, the Judenwald and Altneudorf themselves embody an intertextual understanding of place and, as placeholders for multiple discourses, bear a multilayered signification that must be confronted.

Indeed, it is with the reductionist semantics of gender that Vivian's and Korinna's assignation in the woods of the Judenwald attempts to do battle. Presumably in her third trimester, the pregnant Korinna, bisexual, removes a dildo from her backpack and, with insouciant self-evidence, straps it on to penetrate a confused Vivian, "heterosexual by compulsion" (215; 205), all while discussing Judith Butler, the paradox of the lesbian phallus, and the discursive possibilities it harbors. Meinecke captures the moment of penetration with a flurry of Butlerian interrogatives that underscore the ambiguity of the moment. Dubiously inherited oppositional signs of masculinity and femininity – penetration versus reception, penis versus vagina, phallus versus void, athletic versus cosmetically made-up, "the svelte, unfertilized body [*Leib*]" versus "the breasts of the pregnant woman" (216; 206) – momentarily lose their meaning, along with gender, in sex. In this tangled, polysemous performative act, the text intimates, lies the possibility of emancipating gender, not in the narration of it. By adopting Butler's technique of posing ambivalent, unanswerable rhetorical questions, too, Meinecke claims for literature a crucial theoretical strategy for overcoming the limitations of narrative description.

On the one hand, language proves incapable in this instance of representing the semiotic complexities of sexual experience except through narrative. The complex sexual dynamic between Vivian and Korinna resists the application of simple, binary labels like heterosexual, homosexual, or even lesbian. On the other hand, the text employs signs that reinforce the gender binary through doubling, thereby failing to depict the sexual performance accurately or adequately. "The she-man. The she-male. The phallic woman. The lesbian phallus" (215; 205) – with this string of hybridized terms, Meinecke begins the passage, repeating terms composed of binary opposites. Yet this strategy is surprisingly effective precisely because of its repetitive insistence upon composite signifiers that are inherently ambiguous, and productively so. While the combinations do not collapse into separate terms – and the binary thus remains intact – each names a referent without a clear gender identity. A phallic woman is neither entirely female, nor entirely male, and thus subverts and transgresses boundaries established by commonplace gender discourse. It is paradoxical, yet signifies. This combinatory gender-bending nomenclature bears a morphological relation to the epithets Meinecke employs in reference to Vivian and Korinna, fashioned as they are from either male-female substantives or stereotypical opposites: "magistrate's daughter [*Richterstochter*]," "soldier's daughter [*Soldatentochter*]," "tennis player [*Tennisspielerin*]," "American-German woman [*amerikanische Deutsche*]" (215; 205). In this way, a resonance emerges between the problematic designations drawn from theoretical gender discourse and the appellations of the protagonists. Like the theories of gender they debate, the protagonists figure as conglomerations of oppositions, discrepancies, contradictions, and paradoxes. Any discrete gender identity projected upon them is continually complicated, if not rejected, by the text.

It is significant that the dialogue between Korinna and Vivian ceases as the passage progresses. As words fail to grasp the sexual dynamic between the two protagonists, both narratively and theoretically, first-person action cedes to pure third-person description of the performative sexual act. The battle against gender binarism "on the level of symbolic and corporeal morphogenesis" proceeds as the protagonists, "[w]ithout saying a word" (215; 205), strip themselves bare aside from the lesbian phallus. Clothing, which serves both in the novel and in Butler as a signifier for the performance of identity (see the final line, cited above), vanishes, revealing the naked human form, a *tabula rasa* upon which meaning, sexual or otherwise, is projected. Even Korinna's initial libidinal attention to the erogenous zones on Vivian's body – sites of signification and gender determination that Korinna herself studies – seems to dissolve into the act of penetration, a performance of her maleness. The once fleeting traces of "I" from the previous paragraph are nowhere to be found. And like the "I" within the narrative, so too does the subject disappear from sight. What remains within the narrative are nothing but blank surfaces, instruments of the production of meaning through gesture and performance: "Divergent bodies" (216; 206).

As language struggles to come to terms with the difficulties of signifying gender in this sexual act, it points beyond itself to the act, to something beyond the pages of the text. Its medium for this deictic gesture is not simply description, but the same writing strategy employed by Judith Butler in formulating the problematic of performance: rhetorical questioning (here as eight unanswered interrogatives). The omniscient, anonymous narrator admits that the sexual act between Korinna and Vivian constitutes, with the help of "something supplementary," "a phantasmatic or perhaps phantasmagorical resignification" but alludes to the complexity, if not impossibility, of describing this redefinition of gender: "Would Vivian Atkinson later be able to describe this memorable sex act being consummated at this moment? And in whose words?" (216; 206). The narrator's query remains open-ended. Indeed, the text effaces Vivian's subjectivity by stripping her of signifiers and reducing her to a performing, signifying body. To pose such a rhetorical question – in whose words is a description of a sexual act and its attendant gender dynamic possible? – is thus to interrupt the narrative, to point beyond the narrative to a theoretical problem, and to refer self-reflexively to the narrative's own shortcomings. Theoretical discourse thus supplies literature with the means to surmount the obstacles posed by the insufficiencies of language.

What underlies and drives this passage, therefore, is a narrative performance of Butler's conception of performative gender identity. Theory, in other words, meets praxis. This shift towards practice nevertheless raises several important questions, the answers to which further deepen the understanding of the intertextual complexities at work in Meinecke's novel. First, by what means does the text effect this transfer? What discursive rules might govern the intertextual relationship and resonance between texts of ostensibly such a different nature? To what extent might we speak here of a literarization of theory? And in what ways might a Butlerian notion of performance, predicated on corporeal, social signification and a performance, be related through language and in literature, that is, with only narrative bodies?

The first of these questions is of particular importance here. In the foregoing, the morphological doubling – in paradoxical linguistic terms – illuminates the deficiencies of a binary model of gender identity while also alluding to signifying ambiguities irresolvable und ineffable in current language usage. A second textual practice, however, constitutes the most important means of formally structuring the text and inscribing it within a discourse of intertextuality: citation. Be it through direct quotation, indirect reference, footnote, attribution, allusion, second-hand information, hearsay, or repetition, *Tomboy* situates itself within a network of other texts and discourses against which it reacts and constructs its narrative. The novel is largely a narrative commentary and supplement to other texts that function as the condition for its own possibility.

Through this intertextual procedure of citation, which in turn enables a mimetic transfer from scholarly text to literary narrative, Meinecke sets in motion a jarring sex scene whose sober, ritualistic character occasions the insouciance that, one might argue, does not usually typify an assignation so far outside the realm of compulsory heteronormativity. Quotations of Judith Butler – via indirect speech, through recollection of her writings – and references to "[t]he lesbian phallus" (215; 205) interrupt the protagonists' rendezvous in the Judenwald and transport the physicality of the experience to a metalevel of theoretical reflection. "Don't be afraid, Viv, said Korinna Kohn as she pulled the dildo from her backpack, this here is also a sign of my personal acceptance of heterosexual paradigms" (215; 205). Korinna assuages Vivian's anticipated concern by bracketing the reality of "the permanently erect, clay-colored plastic penis" (215; 205) and interpreting it merely as a fetish object (in a psychoanalytic sense) – a comforting, familiar linguistic sign rather than a phallic symbol of power, oppression, and violence. Such sobering references underscore the signifying potential of all physical, sexual objects and simultaneously inserts them into the text. The seams and sutures of imported citations remain visible as evidence of an intertextual penetration, a discursive insemination occurring both on the narrative and metanarrative levels.

Such intertextual references open the passage and interrupt it twice more, introducing each time a semantic ambiguity between the novel and the original that is a relic of satiric praxis. The citational transfer adds a new contextual meaning to the original, which still resonates. In her attempts to calm Vivian by citing Butler "that the insertion of the lesbian phallus opens a discursive space" (215; 205), for example, Korinna both speaks of the subversive, revolutionary political value of this paradoxical sign and matter-of-factly reminds her of their impending sexual congress: Korinna's dildo as the lesbian phallus, Vivian's body as the discursive space it will open. This double-speak of the Butler references recalls the displacement and distortion of context in satire. In this instance, the original context of the scholarly reference (politics and the subversion of phallogocentric systems of meaning) dominates the practical meaning of the narrative context (actual sexual intercourse) by dint of its diction. In an unusual reversal, the latter is the palimpsest of the former. Meinecke's novel inverts the usual order, having poached the procedure of intertextual citation from satiric texts and discourses, which typically employ it to supply themselves with secondary contexts. In Meinecke, Butler is a primary ingredient, a quintessential narrative building block, not a secondary source. For this reason, among others, one cannot speak of *Tomboy* as a satire of *Gender Trouble* and Judith Butler. Instead, *Tomboy* is a satiric text because of its incorporation of *Gender Trouble* through satiric practices, that is, by virtue of the literary procedures it employs rather than any critical operation it performs.

This is not to say that the novel incorporates Butler wholesale. To be sure, the subjunctive of indirect speech marks the novel's invocation of other texts – Meinecke never uses quotation marks – and expresses a certain critical distance towards the cited material, one also present in ironic or satiric texts. Yet this contrast in verbal mood also guarantees a degree of textual independence for the fragments of Butler and other sources. Quotations play a constitutive role in shaping the narrative fabric and production of meaning in Meinecke's novel and also remain autonomous building blocks that the novel prominently displays without fully incorporating them. Instead of effacing the cited excerpts, the novel maintains and makes visible the seams that bind it to them; the text thereby proclaims itself a construct of multiple textual strata and is thus part of an economy of intertextual discourse. Because of this balance between the inherent claim to originality and debts to intertexts of varying provenance, the relationship of *Tomboy* to quotations is one of tenuous symbiosis, not parasitism. Juxtaposition trumps subsumption.

One cannot overlook the complexity of the discursive rules that facilitate and govern this symbiotic relationship between *Tomboy* and its intertexts. Three principles of intertextuality may be gleaned from the particular case of *Tomboy* and *Gender Trouble*. First, and perhaps most importantly, intertextual borrowings occur within and across different genres and media. The boundaries of such varied forms do not preclude or limit the trade or exchange of intertextual meaning. This claim stems from two basic assumptions undergirding intertextuality: namely, that multiple systems of meaning circulate within discourse and, further, that meaning does not inhere exclusively in any specific sign or sign system. The text of a novel may, therefore, participate in an intertextual dialogue with other novels, but also with nonfictional theoretical tracts, theatrical works, poetic fragments, or non-literary prose. As we have seen, this productive exchange is not confined solely to direct quotation. It also takes place on the level of intertextual semiotic strategies: textual citation, formal allusion, epistemological quotation, or any number of other intertextual operations that effect a transfer of signification from one narrative context to another.

Less evident is the discursive circulation that may occur among literary texts and those employing sign systems other than language. Literature and music, for example, may also enter into an intertextual relationship, but the discursive rules differ, operating under the sign of transmedial semiotic strategies. That is to say, transposition from one medium to another necessarily alters and distorts the signifiers involved in intertextual dialogue due to the variation in the concrete means of representation and signification among different media. In short, linguistically and non-linguistically semantic orders of meaning – literature and music, for example – employ different representational codes.[17] To transfer a signifier from one medium to another is in principle not impossible but, on account of these differing codes and means of expression, will entail a mapping operation from one system to another in which some meaning may be distorted, invariably altered, or lost.

Following the first premise that intertextual relationships may and do transgress formal borders, we come to a second axiomatic statement regarding the function of intertextuality in *Tomboy*. The transposition of meaning from one medium to another necessarily involves more than direct citation; it encompasses a broad range of semiotic properties of each medium and their deployment. Because each textual form, each genre, and each medium arguably engenders and shapes meaning uniquely, each therefore harbors a unique set of textual strategies to produce, represent, and express this meaning. Although the spectrum of these strategies spans a limitless array of possibility – and their combination further increases the panoply of textual results – the procedures enabling intertextual exchange are much more limited in scope.

Indeed, within the corpus of texts in this study, one may identify three dominant strategies that mediate between texts. Of these, two in particular have been discussed at length: epistemological inversion in Mikhail Bakhtin and Thomas Bernhard, and the mimetic creation of second-order myths in Roland Barthes and Elfriede Jelinek. By adopting and inverting commonplace textual epistemes and epistemological structures, Bernhard, for instance, cites extant models for ways of knowing while turning them on their head within the framework of his prose. The figure of inversion recalls the critical distance observed in works of satire. Such works derive their satiric bent from the dissonance produced by an out-of-place episteme nested in a new context. Bernhard's texts use this productive dissonance to analogous effect in reframing his era's and culture's ambivalence toward a dark past. Jelinek's texts draw upon formal and extratextual cultural paradigms and raise them to the level of a second-order semiological system. As in Barthes, whose theoretical speculations on myths she internalized and cri-

---

[17] It is this fact that makes me skeptical of attempts to read Meinecke's work through the lens of sampling. In spite of this reluctance, I mention Florence Feiereisen's important extensive study of Meinecke's indebtedness to the sonic worlds of the DJ, a monograph that also aptly demonstrates in Meinecke the intersection of the worlds of literature, theory, and popular culture. See *Der Text als Soundtrack, der Autor als DJ*.

tiqued, Jelinek uses mimetic strategies to mythify the quotidian signifiers of Viennese life. The irony that accompanies this mythification situates Jelinek's texts historically and positions them critically, even satirically, vis-à-vis a radical politics of identity that had increasingly stagnated amid the wave of New Subjectivity in the seventies.

Thomas Meinecke's mode of writing in *Tomboy* exemplifies citation as the third and arguably most common strategy of intertextual borrowing. Be it a direct quotation with attribution or an allusion vaguely familiar through phonology, morphology, or context, citation embodies one of the more general and richly productive strategies for linking texts together in a resonant, signifying relationship. Because it often manifests as a concrete snippet of text (i. e. as a direct borrowing), citation, likewise, is the most recognizable of intertextual strategies, belying any notion of textual solipsism. Citation reveals the text as a construction, a patchwork of heterogeneous discourses, source material, and contexts. And Meinecke employs it copiously and to great effect in *Tomboy*.

This intertextual strategy thus carries with it several ramifications for the novel. Citing a finite number of intertexts that it uses repeatedly – mostly scholarly texts like Judith Butler's *Gender Trouble* and Otto Weininger's *Sex and Character* [*Geschlecht und Charakter*], but also including the works of Silvia Bovenschen, Jacques Lacan, Michel Foucault, Luce Irigaray, and many others – *Tomboy* establishes an intertextual bibliography, providing itself with a seemingly intellectual foundation and shading itself as an academic work in its own right. Indeed, the scholarly studies of Vivian Atkinson, Frauke Stöver, and Korinna Kohn bleed from the narrative level into the formal structures of the text. The use of attributed citations to bolster hypothetical arguments and to create polemical camps on different sides of issues characterizes the university theses described within the novel as much as it does the novel itself. Within the fragmented narrative, Meinecke interweaves citations of every stripe: word-for-word appropriations with and without attribution, third-party requotations, hearsay, clichés, and stylistic allusions, to name but a few. While each type of citation has at its disposal disparate means and effects of signification – influenced in part by their varied ontological makeup – they nevertheless all operate under the sign of intertextuality.

Through an economy of intertextual exchange, texts like Meinecke's evince a grand historical shift in concepts of authorship, attribution, and originality since Jelinek's battles against the inward focus of the seventies and eighties. Indeed, employing citation as a strategy of textual construction amounts to applying it as a structural, formal methodology. Put differently, the prevalence of citational procedures in more recent literary texts points to an increased anonymization of discourse. The single author-subject yields, as it were, to the omnipresence of deafening textual background noise and thus to the ubiquity of productive intertextual relationships. The author functions no longer as a genius creator of texts *ex nihilo* but as a facilitator of meaning through the combinatorial mastery of extant texts. From this perspective, one might more easily understand the comparisons drawn between Meinecke's work as an author and his activity as a DJ (and the literary-musical connections of other authors within the literary establishment, often with a strong bond to pop discourse, such as Rainald Goetz).[18] The proliferation of these forms of citation marks a departure from ascriptions of authorship, instead embracing an understanding of authorial creation as inherently contingent upon other texts.

What ramifications does this intertextual episteme have for the processes and possibilities of textual signification? For one, the multiplication of textual sources amplifies the associative meanings of a particular text since it is, seen in this light, bound to a network of discourses and contexts that always resonate in concert with it. In fact, citational practices unsteady the primary text by "instead inevitably implementing [...] contexts that cannot and are not supposed to be controlled, that perpetuate and duplicate themselves, and can be processed further while reading."[19] This contextual and associative pluralism safeguards an understanding of the significatory potential and exuberance of language in the face of skepticism, for example, from the ranks of those who continually uncover its shortcomings and predestined failures. The accent thus shifts from the linguistic sign itself as the carrier of meaning to intertextual relationships as transmitters of associative significance. The self-reflexive signifier that bears meaning only through difference is superseded by "a gesture of pointing, of intentionally exposing, that marks differences and in this way produces meaning."[20] Ever pointing to shifting, unstable, temporary intertextual connec-

---

[18] To be sure, a common thread running through most Meinecke scholarship, be it scholarly article or newspaper interview, is the metaphor of writing as DJ-ing, of citation as sampling. For an overview of this spectrum of comparison, see Lenz and Pütz, "'Ich bin so ein Pop-Sommer-1982-Typ': Ein Gespräch mit Thomas Meinecke"; Schumacher and Meinecke, "Pop, Literatur. Ein Interview mit Thomas Meinecke"; Rüdenauer and Meinecke, "'Der Reiz des Rhizomatischen': Ein Gespräch mit Thomas Meinecke über Schreiben unter dem Vorzeichen von Techno, die Faszination für bestimmte Orte und hellblaues Frottee," 106–117; Schumacher, *Gerade Eben Jetzt*; Holger Noltze, "Literarische Fahrten im Meer der Verweise: ein Portrait des Erzählers und Musikers Thomas Meinecke," *Literaturen*, no. 10 (2004): 60–66; Dunker, "'Alle tanzen, doch niemand kennt die Platten'"; Feiereisen, "Identitäten im Remix: Literarisches Sampling im Fadenkreuz von Postmoderne und Postkolonialismus"; Feiereisen, *Der Text als Soundtrack, der Autor als DJ*.
[19] Schumacher, *Gerade Eben Jetzt*, 203–204.
[20] Schumacher, *Gerade Eben Jetzt*, 203. One might argue with Schumacher's contention that such gestural connections are intentional. For intertextuality, however, questions of intentionality do not obtain.

tions, this deictic gesture replaces the fixed linguistic sign as a progenitor of meaning. The referent cedes to the act of reference or referentiality *per se*. Curiously, the similarities that engender citation produce the difference from which meaning springs.

Seen also in Butler's conception of signification through performance, this displacement from referent to referentiality, from sign to gesture, brings to bear an important corollary for debates on the real. With an intertextual episteme, the search for the real leads inexorably to the phantasm of an originary text, of a concrete referent, of a terminus in the chain of references. Here a rift opens between theories of meaning that posit discrete carriers of signification and what one might deem an intertextual theory of signifying that seeks meaning in the act of reference, in gestural operations. From this perspective, such a theory of intertextuality bears a striking rhetorical resemblance and function to Judith Butler's notion of performance. The latter is formulated in sociological and political terms, the former from the frame of reference of texts, language, and semiotics. Nevertheless, both are predicated upon a conception of the production of (temporary) meaning through referentiality. Performance strips the signifier of its fixed meaning, envisioning an expansion of the paradigmatic scope of a sign's associative value through variations in its syntagmatic context. In other words, performative practices have the potential to unfix hitherto fixed metaphors and associations by altering the context in which they signify. They promise to introduce variability into a field of ossified signs. Intertextuality operates similarly but departs from an *a priori* claim to the permanent variation of meaning due to shifting referential contexts. Given this redistribution of emphasis from fixity to variability in both performative and intertextual practices, the real becomes increasingly elusive. Its existence depends in part on an essentialist notion of signification that the intertextual episteme suspends in favor of incessant contextual change. It is for this reason that simple inventories of intertextual references (and intertexts) in academic studies are moot. Abandoning the notion of a calcified catalog of citational references that determines a work's meaning is but the first step in comprehending the dynamism of intertextual discourse and its incommensurability with the real.

This brings us to our third property of intertextual connections; they are inherently dynamic and thus shift and change. When studies of intertextuality employ metaphors of historical continuum and anteriority to describe citational relationships between texts, they create a linear timeline. One text with a fixed contextual meaning historically precedes a later text that then draws upon the prior work. This conceptual model of intertextuality is predicated upon a dialectics of the production of meaning, wherein the newer text appropriates older source material and, within its own context, synthesizes new meaning from it. Here signification is a roughly additive process.

But two crucial realizations are lacking in this conception of intertextuality. First, the myth of anteriority postulates a timeline on which each text appears discretely rather than in conjunction with others, belying the epistemological model of intertextuality as a concurrent circulation of texts. According to this view, intertextuality would operate primarily through history and historical connections, and studies of intertextual relationships would necessarily plumb the temporal discursive stratifications within texts, following the lead of Foucauldian genealogy and archaeology. Significantly, these latter terms even retain the dominant temporal metaphor that proves insufficient in circumscribing intertextual practices.

Despite some spatial terms like palimpsest, the relative absence of a spatial component in metaphors of intertextuality numbers among the desiderata of a purely historically focused understanding of the phenomenon. Whether such figures of speech involve practices of citation, imitation, or pastiche, the relationship between two texts follows a generally schematic model. The mimotext, to use Genette's term, invokes a prior, older text. By virtue of its unquestioned object status – it functions, after all, as an originary source – the preceding text has mythological qualities. No longer a text in its own right, it is a second-order sign, having been redeployed as a sign of some anterior meaning or status. While intertextual referentiality necessarily operates to some degree within a temporal framework of before–after, first–second, or original–copy, the spatialization of time that occurs so tacitly in placing texts in a historical chronology fosters a certain thought pattern that imputes a petrifaction or fixity to prior discourses and meanings. By this thinking, the dynamism and interchange of intertextual discourse yields to a stagnation of fixed signs (texts) from which newer texts may draw meaning. This way of thinking intertextuality is insufficient insofar as it projects a one-way relationship from source to mimotext, a one-sidedness that smacks of parasitism or poaching. In setting up a historical hierarchy with textual separation, this untenable schema denies the discursive proximity that intertextual references engender among texts or that, conversely, engenders such references in the first place.

A model of intertextuality spanned uncomfortably between metaphors of time and space and oscillating between claims of distance and proximity hinders the ultimate aim: a deeper understanding of intertextuality itself. One possible solution embraces both the temporal and spatial aspects of intertextual metaphors simultaneously and conceives of shifting intertextual references as part of a discursive *hinc et nunc*. Their Protean shapes are neither exclusively subject to a historical continuum nor to spatial separation. Rather, this notion of intertextual discourse spatializes references to prior works through their accumulation and sedimentation in an ever-changing, mutable discourse and also temporalizes lateral connections by insisting on the specific historical contextualization of each citation. One might thus balance Foucault's archaeology and genealogy with the rhizome of Deleuze and Guattari as a counter-metaphor to help visualize this discursive model of intertextuality. Interlinked, interlocked, and intertwined, rhizomatic structures of meaning proliferate continually without recourse to an originary, deeper signification, effectively equalizing associative connections and leveling hierarchies. By conceiving of intertextuality in this way, one solves the problem of the parasitic one-way relationship by completing the intertextual circuit: that is, by asserting that intertextual connections have effects on the production of meaning in *both* texts, thereby eliminating a hierarchy between them.

11. Infinite Paradise of the Infinite Text: Thomas Meinecke's *Music* (2004)

The citational dynamic in Thomas Meinecke's novel *Tomboy*, which satirically deploys narrative and semiotic strategies gleaned from its theoretical intertexts to signal a new emphasis on the contingency of meaning through performance, resurfaces again in his 2004 work *Music*. While it would be misleading to speak of a refinement of this dynamic since *Tomboy*, the intertextual schema has undergone several transformations and displacements that bear examining and are more akin to those in the novel *Pale Blue* [*Hellblau*].[1]

Perhaps the most obvious difference between *Tomboy* and *Music* is the polyvocality of narrative voice in the latter. While *Tomboy* stages its citational play with a single unnamed omniscient narrator as its dramaturge, in his more recent work Meinecke pits the complexities of subjective first-person point of view against the complexities of intertextual referentiality. Narrative voices and citation proliferate explosively in *Music*, fragmenting the work into multiple narrative strands and smoothing the visible seams of its patchwork form as practices of citation become constitutive of "a manically and virtuosically formulated card catalog [*Zettelkasten*]."[2] The frequency and density of citation in *Music* has even prompted one critic to wonder whether "this whole thing is just a citation from the hive mind and the discourse in which we're all ensnared."[3]

The transparency with which the text exposes its debt to a circulating intertextual discourse of citations becomes clearer even as the discursive boundaries blur. Theoretical questions abound, as do references to academic works and theories, garnering the work the appellation of "narrated theory."[4] Although the performance of identity – and Judith Butler – continue to occupy the foreground in *Music*, quotations also stem from the works of Sander Gilman, Silvia Bovenschen, Hélène Cixous, Michel Foucault, and Georg Simmel, while juxtaposed with literary references to Rainer Maria Rilke, Elfriede Jelinek, and Gustave Flau-

---

1 Thomas Meinecke, *Hellblau* (Frankfurt am Main: Suhrkamp, 2001); Thomas Meinecke, *Pale Blue*, trans. Daniel Bowles (Las Vegas: AmazonCrossing, 2012).
2 Joachim Mischke, "Grübeleien über Gott und Groove: Thomas Meinecke kurvt in seinem meist spaßfreien, virtuosen Diskurswerk 'Musik' durch die Poptheorie," *Hamburger Abendblatt*, April 16, 2005, sec. Bücher im Journal.
3 Jörg Drews, "I Care 4 U oder vom Charme des Bauchredens," *Tages-Anzeiger*, September 25, 2004.
4 Sebastian Handke, "Wurm im Ohr," *Süddeutsche Zeitung*, October 16, 2004, sec. Literatur. Handke does not intend this as a compliment. He goes on to claim that "One has to be profoundly infected by these ideas to feel something akin to joy of reading as they march past."

bert and websites accessions from urbandictionary.com, MODELS.com, and cigaraficionado.com. Reproductions of theoretical arguments, literary citations, filmic analyses, musical allusions, internet trivia, newspaper articles, epistolary excerpts, wholesale textual appropriation, and of course second- or third-hand quotations comprise the ingredients of episodic narrative. Structure again takes precedence over plot.[5]

Like *Tomboy*, *Music* does not recount a teleological story, employing instead fragmentation and strategies of citation to chronicle and pursue a theoretical line of questioning. If in *Tomboy* intertextual strategies facilitated the adoption of theoretical models that toppled notions of gender binarism and gender identity, allowing a performative dynamic to develop both on the level of the narrative and on the level of language, *Music* does it one better. Not only does the open admission of its multiplicity of sources intensify the ambiguity between literature and theory at play in *Tomboy*, but *Music* doubles, splits, and inserts the guiding question of gender identity into the very formal structure of the text. Indeed, *Music* is a novel that does not speculate on gender identity from a third-person perspective. Rather, it incorporates into the formal structure of the text the hesitancy of assigning binary gender identity by effacing the identity of the narrator. Divided between two siblings, Kandis and Karol, the novel's narrative voice shifts surreptitiously from one to the other in each discrete section with no clear pattern. To ask who is speaking is to pose a troubling question that emerges from a tradition of political feminism to which Judith Butler was the heir. It amounts to asking whether a text is masculine or feminine or to what extent narrative language may be gendered. *Music* follows the traces of gender identity and performance in Butler to their historical predecessor, Cixous' *écriture féminine*, in speculations on gendered language.

By oscillating between narrators – a tactic the author used to a great, but somewhat less extreme degree in his 2001 novel *Pale Blue* – Meinecke's text employs a strategy that invites the reader to engage more critically with the narrative, a strategy with three key consequences. This procedure of shifting perspective, first, uncovers an epistemological precondition within the narratological convention the novel deploys (first-person narration): knowledge of the speaker's identity. By splitting the narrative into a seemingly epistolary (or novelistic) correspondence with neither salutation nor closing, Meinecke clouds narrative speech within a perspectival fog, making it both anonymous and plural. To

---

5 "Sometimes the suspicion creeps over you that, in *Music*, construction trumps content." Gerrit Bartels, "Lesen als Handlung," *die tageszeitung*, January 8, 2005, sec. Kultur. See also Handke, "Wurm im Ohr."

follow the story, the reader must identify when the shifts occur and thus when each narrator speaks.⁶

Second, because the novel erects a clear gender binary between Kandis and Karol, the shifts in perspective challenge the reader to rely on unquestioned, compulsory sexual dualism to identify the narrator despite the challenges the intertextual metanarrative may pose to it with citations of Butler, Bovenschen, or Cixous, among others. A productive dissonance thus erupts. Intertextual references that champion gender pluralism and the performance of gender identity, on the one hand, undermine the narrative dynamic, which is predicated upon a gender binary, on the other hand. That these two narratological aspects are at odds with one another plants hermeneutic obstacles for the reader.

The third ramification of the narrative shifting leads us back to Cixous and *écriture feminine*. The novel's structure compels the reader to seek identifying characteristics of the narrator in the stylistic features of the text. In short, identifying the gender of the narrator – and thus identifying the narrator – involves a game of bait-and-switch, wherein the reader must continually engage with the question of gendered text. What constitutes feminine writing? How might one contrast these traits with what comprises masculine writing? To what extent can we identify any stylistic differences between narrative perspectives and, moreover, impute these to gender differences? These queries provide the framework for the novel's exploration of the reality of gender identity, both in the subject and in narrative language.

---

6 This invitation to the reader to read differently has not won *Music* many fans among newspaper critics. Most negative reviews have maligned the novel for the narrative difficulty that stems from its combination of literature and theory. Their barely veiled charges of intellectual elitism stem from skepticism toward Meinecke's appropriation of academic, theoretical discourse in literature – the presumptuous notion, for example, "that academic studies can unlock the world" – while privileging plot at the expense of structure lays bare the one-dimensional expectation that a literary work toe the line of acceptable, non-experimental conventions and traditions. That Meinecke's work increasingly requires writerly reading, to use Barthes' term, is undeniable. For skepticism of academic studies and Meinecke's use of English, see Charlotte Staehelin, "Noch Literatur? Oder schon Wissenschaft? Die Geburt der 'Lola', ungeschnitten und live – Der Roman und sein Rezensent," *Basler Zeitung*, December 11, 2004, sec. Kultur. For reviews that criticize *Music* as "a reader-unfriendly collection of material" that confronts the reader "with a weirdly wired compilation of notes," see, respectively, Sabine Rohlf, "Sex mit dem Heiligen Geist: Thomas Meineckes Collagen-Roman über Keuschheit, Körper und Kirche," *Berliner Zeitung*, February 26, 2009, sec. Feuilleton; Wolfgang Lange, "Pop und Lakritz – Thomas Meineckes Roman 'Musik,'" *Neue Zürcher Zeitung*, December 29, 2004.

In this sense, *Music* is as much about gender identity as it is about reading: about reconstituting meaning from a fabric of fragmentary citations and intertextual contexts, about perceiving and interpreting gestural signs and cognizing performances. It is about penetrating through accumulated layers of discursive references, not to reach an unadulterated, originary signifying referent, but rather to uncover the stratification and plurality of meaning that exists in intertextual discourse. In essence, *Music* suggests a model of reading whereby the aim is less the instauration of a singular textual meaning, authorial intent, or worldview than the assemblage of meaning through intertextual practices.

To read under the auspices of an intertextual episteme amounts to an exploratory act of parsing and interpreting discursive associations and contexts and the contingent significations they engender. Whereas *Tomboy* displayed its intertextual weft more modestly, *Music* demonstrates an uncommon abundance and transparency of secondary sources in concert with a polyvocality of narrative voices. Intertextual citational strategies in *Tomboy* coalesced into a challenge to the gender binary, the representation of gender identity, and the division between literary and theoretical modes of writing. *Music* traverses this same fraught terrain, albeit with a shift in accent and an emphatic addition.

In the matter of accentuation, the text raises questions of gender identity, binarism, and representation not only on the level of the sign, but also on the level of form. In its update and redeployment of an epistolary novelistic structure, Meinecke's novel creates a semi-anonymous, dialogic text that impels the reader to provide solutions to the conundrum of gendered narration. In conjunction with this added formal complexity, *Music* features an unmistakable prominence of citational strategies and intertextual borrowings that saturate it with quotations and thereby doggedly interrupt and delay the narrative. Here the citational methodology amounts to an end in itself, if not the ultimate focus of the narrative.

This method prompts a fourth claim regarding intertextuality, which follows from the foregoing discussion of *Music* and the close reading of *Tomboy*. As an organizing principle of both narratological form and narrative content, intertextuality collapses yet another binary division: that between reading and writing. Given that reading in an intertextual episteme involves the active construction of meaning from fields of contextual associations and citations – a mode of writing – so too might writing in this vein be considered a mode of reading: the active work of assembling discursive fragments into a new signifying entity, analogous to Jean Paul's procedures of excerpting. Differences between reading and writing largely vanish when viewed through the lens of citational strategies and intertextuality; within the system of meaning-making, they operate identically. Indeed, it has not escaped notice that "'paths' of communication and reading determine how the storytelling advances," demonstrating how active reading might come to resemble a strategy of writing.[7] And in novels like *Pale Blue* and *Music*, this resemblance grows increasingly stronger and more pronounced within the narrative "insofar as it is no longer just individual characters working on dissertations and such things, but rather several characters pursuing a joint project for publication, exchanging material for it, and working up their own impressions of their readings for their communication partners within this fictional world."[8] Reading as the passive reception of written discourse no longer obtains. Instead, this antiquated and, one might argue, literary mode of reading is replaced by what might be termed a scientific or academic mode, in which writing explicitly predicates itself instead upon the reception of reading. The individual act of discursive consumption yields to a collective, social process of culling from and operating on discourse, a practice of constructing meaning and form from of a network of intertexts. If the former is a literary paradigm, the latter mode of reading more closely resembles scientific process. From this perspective, reading equals writing in its level of activity, and the circulation of discourse – the fact that citations both draw upon and become part of an intertextual network – ensures an intimate interdependence between them, stemming from the prominence of citational strategies.

Like *Tomboy*, *Music* adopts this strategy of incorporating features of an academic mode of writing and reading, which poses the question of the appropriateness of the clear binary between scholarly and literary styles. Effacing the differences between reading and writing has a history in twentieth-century semiology, paralleling, for example, the dynamic described by Roland Barthes in the "writerly text."[9] Indeed, in uniting literature and theory in this satiric mode, *Music* corresponds "exactly with what the seminar in German studies, with reference to Michel Foucault, imagines as the novel (and therefore literature in general)."[10]

Several citations in the novel that can be read as self-reflexive programmatic statements regarding the composition of the text allude to this conflation of reading and writing and, further, provide initial answers, however hesitant, to the question of the genderedness of discourse. One passage owes its debts to the cor-

---

[7] Andreas Geier, "Poetiken der Identität und Alterität: zur Prosa von Terézia Mora und Thomas Meinecke," in *Literatur der Jahrtausendwende: Themen, Schreibverfahren und Buchmarkt um 2000*, ed. Evi Zemanek and Susanne Krones (Bielefeld: Transcript, 2008), 131.
[8] Geier, "Poetiken der Identität und Alterität: zur Prosa von Terézia Mora und Thomas Meinecke," 131.
[9] See Roland Barthes, *S/Z*, trans. Richard Miller (New York: Hill and Wang, 1974); Roland Barthes, "From Work to Text," in *Image – Music – Text*, trans. Stephen Heath (New York: Hill and Wang, 1977), 155–164.
[10] Lange, "Pop und Lakritz – Thomas Meineckes Roman 'Musik.'"

respondence of Flaubert, an author who at once embodies the traditions of nineteenth-century literature as described in Roland Barthes' study, *Writing Degree Zero,* and yet whose narrative model in his unfinished, posthumously published novel *Bouvard and Pécuchet* presages the skepticism toward the sign in twentieth-century semiotics. "Literature," writes Flaubert presciently, whom Meinecke cites self-consciously, "increasingly takes on the demeanor of science; it will be especially explicative, which is not to say didactic. Science fiction, so to speak, taken literally."[11] What Flaubert recognized, and what Meinecke has taken up again, is the conflation of literary and theoretical modes of writing at the nexus of intertextuality. At the true zero degree of writing, one employs citations exclusively and constructs texts from extant sources.

In fact, Flaubert's letters betray the heavy reliance of his writing on the acquisition of discursive knowledge through reading. In *Music,* Meinecke cites the French author's correspondence with Madame des Genettes and others regarding the composition of *Bouvard and Pécuchet,* excerpts that mark reading as the condition for the possibility of writing and list the sheer number of books to be read for literary production. Indeed, in any thoroughgoing study "every work treated had to be read simultaneously or, as the case may be, beforehand" (359). As Barthes elaborated in his description of writerly reading, these two actions relate to one another more intimately than through complementarity. Writing and reading, as two sides of the same coin (the assemblage of meaning), converge in intertextuality. It is for this reason that Meinecke may write, tongue-in-cheek and self-reflexively, of both *Music* and *Bouvard and Pécuchet* with the ambiguous claim: "The characters in the novel read incessantly. Perhaps in no other book in literary history are so very many books consumed as in this one. Never before was reading depicted as action to such a degree" (358–359). To be sure, the text goes on to reference Flaubert's famous intellectual twosome, but to the extent the declaration holds for *Music,* too, Meinecke deals it an ironic twist; while the book essentially devotes its plot to active reading, it performs reading as writing, as an epistolary recollection of acts of reading.

In another programmatic passage, Meinecke quotes Hélène Cixous in an interview about her own writing process and the genesis of *écriture feminine.* Both her linkage of writing to reading and her telling descriptions of the form of a feminine text bear a striking resemblance to the intertextual dynamic and formal structure at work in Meinecke's novel: "Question: And how does writing

---

[11] Meinecke, *Musik,* 358. All subsequent references to *Music* will be made parenthetically in the body of the text.

unfold? Cixous: When I sit down to work on a book, I surround myself with a dozen other texts that I consult ceaselessly while working, confronting them up close and personal [*hautnah*], so to speak. Some, like the Bible in various editions, Shakespeare, and Kafka, I use constantly, others alternate according to the book I'm writing. A feminine text is not predictable. And it doesn't predict itself" (367). Like Flaubert, Cixous predicates writing on constant, concurrent reading while pointing to canonized works that always circulate in discourse and are invoked and made present during the reading process. She interrogates her sources, confronting them with a bodily immediacy that incorporates their meanings, formulations, or shapes. Intertexts, both in Cixous and in Meinecke, are palpably proximate and omnipresent. For the feminine text, intertextuality is a epistemological paradigm.

Of particular significance in this cited interview, too, is the contingency Cixous ascribes to each work, the unique and mutable compilation of texts that determine a work's composition. Drawing upon an ever shifting constellation of source material, each text unfolds differently and denies itself an internal teleology. No preconceived form attends to the creation of the feminine text; according to Cixous it comes about *sui generis*. As a citation of an interview within the framework of a literary text, this appropriation of Cixous may indeed read as an abbreviated poetics of writing for Cixous alone, recounted in the novel, but this reading neglects to contextualize the citation as part of the inner workings of its frame of reference. Owing to the continual slippage and relativity of the narrative subject in Meinecke's book, the deictic gesture of the first-person can be understood to have multiple targets. The reader may plausibly ascribe this self-referentiality to the "I" of the novel, for example, ignoring Cixous as a subjective, independent speaker and incorporating her voice into the fabric of the text. Taken then as a self-reflexive programmatic statement about *Music*, this double-pronged commentary on *écriture feminine* has deeper implications for the question of gendered writing in Meinecke's novel.

For one, it posits an intertextual mode of writing-as-reading as the basis of the development of writing and, further, alludes to an intertextual lattice unique to each text and within which each text operates. Operation within such an intertextual lattice lends further credence to understanding intertextuality as inherently rhizomatic, while denying a singular origin of the work in notions of originality or the author-subject. Such a corollary explicitly forbids the possibility of literary creation *ex nihilo*. Meinecke cites Cixous on the origin as a fallacy, as "a masculine myth depicted through Oedipus. A feminine text begins on all of its pages simultaneously. Proceeding from a feminine economy of libido, it also recognizes itself in the fact that it is without end" (366). The unpredictability of the feminine text that Cixous referenced in her interview thus results from its participation in this infinite libidinous economy.[12] Rather than mystify concepts of feminine writing through metaphysical references to infinitude and eternity, I maintain that this timelessness of the feminine text might be understood from the perspective of the intertextual episteme that governs it. As we have seen, combining temporal and spatial metaphors for intertextual relationships fashions a time-space for them, with the result that texts are subject to a kind of permanent but changing present; the intertextual lattice may shift and alter as discourse changes, but the text itself indeed has no beginning or end. The practicalities of a published work notwithstanding, Meinecke's novel *Music* bears the marks of a constant, mutable nexus of intertextual influences with a narrative that could in fact begin "on all of its pages simultaneously." The formal structure of the novel, consisting in discrete units of epistolary correspondence, often with only a passing reference to link one paragraph to the next, arguably allows for the beginning of the story at any point. The sparse reviews of the novel have recognized this lack of origin as well, although they ascribe it mostly to a perceived resemblance between the density and variety of intertextual references in Meinecke's novel and the far-ranging associations of internet hypertextuality.[13]

Narrative Uncertainties

That Meinecke's novel challenges the difference between writing and reading, and between literature and theory, with its narratological structure and intertextual strategies testifies to the ambivalence with which reviewers received his novel. In constructing a work that consists, to such a degree, of a discursive network of intertexts, Meinecke himself minimizes his claim to authorship and originality in the appraisal of his reviewers; he is "an excellent arranger, but not a gifted storyteller."[14] Yet *Music* depicts scenes and acts of citation, arranging, assembling, associating, fragmenting, and juxtaposing: not narrating. The means

---

12 One might counterargue that such feminine writing constitutes a feminine myth especially insofar as it resists definition much like the arch-myth of femininity: hysteria.
13 Reviewer Ulrich Kriest notes, for example, that "The point of origin of the textual movement seems random; at any point, one can access the hypertext and then see what the search engines spit out." "Mister DJ, schmeiß die Suchmaschine an!: Thomas Meineckes Buch 'Musik' ist Gegenwartsliteratur als Zeitmitschrift," *Stuttgarter Zeitung*, May 10, 2005, sec. Kultur; 27.
14 Rohlf, "Sex mit dem Heiligen Geist: Thomas Meineckes Collagen-Roman über Keuschheit, Körper und Kirche."

become an end; citational strategies gleaned from academic, theoretical writing occupy the foreground of the novel.

Ultimately, *Music* is about its own plot structure, about the unification of its narrative and metanarrative levels, the interrelation of writing and reading. Even the "hazily drawn"[15] characters, Kandis and Karol, operate within the text as nothing other than vehicles for the metanarrative; *Music* explores the nature of processes of reading and writing and is not a biographical enterprise, certainly not of conventional novelistic characters. Kandis and Karol function, on the one hand, as narrative voices of a *bricoleur* and, on the other hand, as a red herring that feigns traditional storytelling while functioning as an index for the text's underlying structure and intertextual character.

In *Tomboy* as in *Music*, Meinecke explores literature's capacity for intertextuality and for incorporating elements of its other. The result is a narrative, novelistic interrogation of cut-and-dry binaries, be they related to gender identity, literary or academic modes of writing, or practices of reading and writing. His means for achieving this aim stem from the intersection of varied discourses facilitated by intertextual citation: from the nexus of gender theory, performance, writerly reading, and academic citation. In three passages in particular, the reader may witness this varied conflation of content and composition and how the metanarrative assumes the position of – or, from a different perspective, suppresses – the narrative. Each demonstrates a different facet of Meinecke's intertextual strategy of citation.

The opening section erects an edifice of conventional novelistic narration by introducing an initially anonymous first-person narrator who describes the mountainous topography in which she is writing. However, the symmetric framing of the text by a series of associated characters – Meinecke has yet to identify their connection – threatens to overshadow the narrative "I" like the massive Schlern that towers over her alpine hut: "Ludwig I, King of Bavaria. Lola Montez. Ludwig II, King of Bavaria. Clara Bow. Ruby Keeler. Leonard Bernstein. Claudia Schiffer. And me" (7). Through the staccato inventory of eight seemingly only tangentially related names, most of some historical repute, the novel sets up a relation among the figures, if not a parity, without elaborating further what unites the entries on the list.

What follows nevertheless upsets the sense of equality in a surprising way. "*Seven* figures seek an author, male or female, seek to haunt me in my lonely log cabin" (7 [my emphasis, DB]). While convention might lead one to expect the narrative "I" to stand in a subject-object position with these figures, they instead

---

[15] Lange, "Pop und Lakritz – Thomas Meineckes Roman 'Musik.'"

disrupt the agency of the narrator insofar as they reveal themselves not as the objects of a story, but ironically both as coequal agents of narration in search of an author and as oppressors. They actively seek the possibility of their own inscription, embodying metaphorically the relation of active, writerly reading to writing as a prophetic, and thus receptive, undertaking. The beleaguered, as yet genderless, nameless "I" takes refuge from the torment in her Swiss cabin, delaying both the answer to the question of who is narrating as well as additional self-characterization by deferring narrative agency to her list of names.

The solitude and desolation depicted in what reads like a conventional beginning – a sweeping description of landscape and the narrator's topographical milieu – further underscore the isolation of the first-person voice. Does the narrator in fact enjoy subjectivity? Is she as removed from society as her description implies? Hers is not a place of creative abundance, but of ascetic self-denial. Indeed, she even denies this as a final scene of writing: "There is still no electrical outlet; once again I'll have to type out everything later at home" (7). Without a means for writing – her computer – the narrator reveals her enterprise as, foremost, one of reading. Books supplant plates on her shelves, and notebooks take the place of food on the table. Their contents amount to none other than the litany of names from the opening, repeated again here: "Ludwig I, Lola, Ludwig II, Clara, Ruby, Leonard, Claudia and Kandis, between black-and-white marbleized pasteboard covers" (8). Foreshortening the list and identifying herself as Kandis by way of parallelism, the narrator reinstantiates the parity invoked previously and identifies herself, like her list of names, as a textual object, not a subject.

It is here that Meinecke elevates the metanarrative level to that of plot. Kandis discloses her own textual constructedness and levels the conventional hierarchy between first-person subject-narrator and third-person object, relinquishing her subjectivity and injecting herself into a whirlwind of discursive connections. To emphasize the point, in a moment of irony, Meinecke borrows the rhetorical questioning of Judith Butler's writing while citing his own novel *Tomboy* and signaling through this reference the narrative focus of *Music*: "What stories will we have to tell each other up here, beyond the treeline, in the deathly Alpine silence?" (8). Two aspects of this passage are remarkable. First, the plural subject departs from the first-person singular, which had governed the rest of the passage, marking a shift from a single narrative subject to a multiplicity of narrating voices; Kandis as a narrating instantiation thus possesses the same narrative ability as her sources. Seen from this perspective, narration is not a solitary activity, but a dialogue: an intertextual conversation. Second, if this question is read programmatically, Meinecke's novel seeks to probe the possibilities of narration while making this heuristic experimentation the focus of the story itself.

What Meinecke accomplishes in this passage is the transformation of a stereotypical scene of writing into a scene of reading, a debunking of the myth of the solitary writing subject. The isolation of the author-subject, removed from society to be alone and channel creative energies, is subverted by the oppressive ubiquity of discursive associations and intertexts. The proverbial Emersonian retreat to the woods results not in the creation of a work *ex nihilo*, but in a clearer perception and reception of the incessant background noise of intertextual murmurings that essentially prefigure a work. To read actively is thus essentially to decide "what stories we will have to tell each other." Writing occurs in conversation – dialogically – with one's books.

As the female narrator of Meinecke's *Music* transforms her narrative objects into speaking subjects, these objects efface the narrative voice. In one later passage, the text channels its narrative voice through its intertexts, suppressing the narrator through a strategy of thick citation. One intertext after another is woven into the fabric of the story while the narrative "I" recedes into the background, either disappearing entirely from the story or relativizing itself with an indistinct third-person plural "we." Unleashed in response to a second-degree citation of Kandis' father's prom date, "You're not like me anymore" (296), this torrent of citations cascades forth in a rhizomatic frenzy of associative connection that reads like lecture or seminar notes. Impersonal imperatives ("Always to be differentiated") alternate with commands questionably addressed to the reader or to the narrator herself ("See also," "Note") and are then relieved by pure citations: "Judith Butler posed the question," "Andreas Kraß, editor of Queer Denken" followed by a deictic colon, and "Kraß summarizes" (297). Even the first occurrence of the first-person pronoun is linked through citation to Judith Butler's own narrative voice through a concluding "wrote Butler" (297).

Indeed, the warp and weft of the text's content and form reveal a union of narrative and metanarrative levels. The self-reflexive gesture that reveals the narrative enterprise embedded in this string of quotations likewise performs its own theoretical claims. From the initial comparison in the Marianne Rosenberg song title "I'm Like You [Ich bin wie Du]," the passage illuminates a particular mode of reading that it defines as an analytic means of discursive deconstruction: "Queer reading as a subtle cultural technique that aims to denaturalize normative concepts of masculinity and femininity, to destabilize the binarism of hetero- and homosexuality, to decouple the categories of gender and sexuality" (297). Meinecke's deployment of gender theory and queer discourse; his invocation of Judith Butler, Andreas Kraß, Jonathan Ned Katz, and Daniel Boyarin; and his insistence upon queer reading as an act of fundamentally reordering symbolic language – all structure the passage narratologically and refer the reader to a paradigmatic connection between queer reading and writerly reading. The former "takes into account the possibility of a textual desire that is coded in a subtextual symbolic order and is not coterminous with the desire that is articulated in the voices of the author, narrator, and characters" (297). In other words, queer reading seeks to unveil and unpack the dissonance between conscious and unconscious levels of speech; the deconstruction of familiar, self-evident discursive categories is perhaps its foremost aim. The mode of reading upon which Meinecke's novel is predicated likewise seeks to penetrate conventional artifice and uncover hitherto unread palimpsests that resonate with the primary text. Essentially, this passage offers the reader a roadmap for navigating its citational strategies and uncovering the false binarisms lurking within it, be they male–female, heterosexual–homosexual, subject–object, first- and third-person, or narrator and object of narration.

While Butler and her contemporaries struggle against the phallogocentric nature of written and spoken language in its proclivities towards binarism, Meinecke alludes to music as another semantic system predisposed to the complex signification that queer reading attempts to uncover in language. After erecting an edifice of theoretical citations that propounds a model mode of reading for itself, the text proposes musical works as utopian intertexts that configure within themselves the intricacies and complexities of citational dynamics and Deconstructionist rhetoric and reading. In Marianne Rosenberg's disco hit "I'm Like You," for example, "all this is already laid out" (297): Butler's challenge to the separateness of binaries, Kraß' description of queer reading, and Katz's and Boyarin's deconstruction of *a priori* assumptions about heterosexuality as an originary category. Relegated to a disco song by a laconic sentence, the very citations of Butler and Kraß that displaced and deferred the arrival of the narrative "I" cease their delay. The summation and insertion of these considerations into a non-linguistic semiological system momentarily sweep away the textual obstacles facing identity and subjectivity, ultimately prompting the appearance, for the first time in this passage, of the narrative "I."

A derivation from queer theory and Deconstructionist discourse, the destabilization, denaturalization, and decoupling that have hitherto unsettled a solid sense of novelistic, literary writing give ground to a preliminary, positive assertion of narrative subjectivity. The narrator, emerging if but for a fleeting moment from the thicket of citations, employs the first-person singular in a sovereign act that both reasserts her presence amid the other more dominant intertextual subjects and spins the very record – Marianne Rosenberg's – that seeks to deny her from saying "I": "I select the wavy, scratched-up 7-inch single and put it on" (297). As one might expect, the record proves to have the same effect on the narrator as the theoretical arguments inscribed in it have for subjectivity in general: the effacement of self. The narrative "I" vanishes as if having succumbed to the pressures of the preceding theoretical statements.

Instead, while listening to the "phenomenal disco hit" (297), the narrator's voice shifts from the specificity of the first-person singular to a vague, genderless "we": "we purchased our copy just a few weeks ago at a flea market" (297–298). The shift from singular to plural in this context is admittedly subtle but nonetheless peculiar. Who is speaking? Who inhabits this new plurality of voice? One possible reading might follow the indications of the novel's opening, in which the omniscient but scarce narrator allies herself with the subjects of her narrative. In this passage Kandis speaks in unison with Butler, Kraß, Katz, and Boyarin, and thus loses her momentary coherence in the multivocal "we." Indeed, aside from this sole instance of the narrative "I" here, one can hardly speak of a single, coherent narrator at all.

Given the purported powers of the musical medium to eradicate subjectivity and the frequency with which Kandis and Karol listen to music – and in particular to this oft-loved, well-worn tune – the negation of the self occurs regularly and precludes singular narrative coherence. And in truth, in Meinecke's novel the reader witnesses how citation frequently suppresses narrative specificity and, simultaneously, how the upsetting of binary norms reflects a preference for uncertainty. If in fact identity is created as "the effect of a certain repetition that produces the semblance of continuity and coherence" (299), one may read in *Music* the consistent interruption of and resistance to repetition and thereby the resistance to continuous, coherent identity.

What is nevertheless remarkable in this excerpt is the way various media – academic studies on gender identity, the music of a disco sensation and gay icon, a newspaper critique, and a risqué image of Kylie Minogue – impute identity formation onto their consumers. Particularly in the case of Marianne Rosenberg's song "I'm Like You" and the sexual posturing and posing of Kylie Minogue in photographs, these non-linguistic media seem to convey a clear meaning or set of inscriptions to their audience through a non-linguistic code of performance. On the one hand, Rosenberg's brief song captures the complexities and non-self-evidence of gender categories elaborated at length in Judith Butler, Andreas Kraß, and others (including Meinecke). And yet, Kylie Minogue – or more aptly, her image – "deludes young girls into wearing inappropriate clothing. The thirty-five-year-old likes showing herself with a bare midriff or bare legs and in tantalizing poses. In many videos, her backside and not her singing is in the foreground" (298). Meinecke's citation of British teachers in a newspaper article points to the signifying power of the image, the vast social capacity for the conveyance of encoded meanings in non-linguistic media – and thereby to the mediated process of signification, which is to say, to the filtering and manipulation of the signifying process by and through its medium. The dubious social effect on young girls noted by British educators, for example, results not from the singer's own statements supporting moral transgression, but from cryptic messages about self-presentation and self-representation perceived through the stylization of her image in print and video media (and facilitated of course by the social cachet of those media among young girls). In both music and image, Meinecke alludes to the power of the absent referent, or from a different perspective, to the enormous influence upon the signifying process of elements of staging, dramatization, gesture, and non-linguistic signs in conjuring absent meanings. He alludes, in short, to the power of performance.

What makes this excerpt emblematic of Meinecke's novel as a whole is less its stylistic character than its conspicuous, if not ostentatious use of the strategy of citation in deconstructing its own narrative. Conventional notions of authorship do not apply to a text in which the omniscient narrator shares the stage with the objects of narration to the extent that she employs a plural pronoun to encompass the breadth of narrative voices. Narrative incoherence, uncertainty, and polyvocality constitute Meinecke's novel in its turn toward an intertextual epistemology.

Similarly representative for this passage is how Meinecke redeploys gender theory to challenge implicitly accepted novelistic practices. By turning away from literary sources and drawing upon academic theories that question the integrity of the linguistic sign, the production of meaning, as well as absolutes, binaries, and *a priori* assumptions, Meinecke seizes upon a flexible template for structuring both the narrative and metanarrative levels of his literary text. In this way, *Music* repeatedly demonstrates its self-reflexivity by circulating continually around the question of its own capacity to signify and the results of that signification.

The symbiotic semiotic strategies of citation and of the epistemic dissonance resulting from the juxtaposition of these disparate cited ideologies both have a history within the discourse of literary satiric practices. As we have seen, citation is among the foremost procedures constitutive of satiric writing in general and in Judith Butler's *Gender Trouble* and Thomas Meinecke's *Tomboy* and *Music* in particular. The strategy of pitting contrary epistemes and ideologies against one another in a dialectical battle (which may account for antiquated definitions of satire as written aggression or invective) is made possible through the excerpting of citation. In Butler we observe the performative use of narrative procedures to denaturalize theory, analogous to the manner by which performance denaturalizes gender. Within Meinecke's novels, which use (Butler's) theory as a structuring element, satiric practices are redeployed in the framework of a literary narrative masquerading as – performing – theory. Having located and analyzed the citational procedures in Butler's and Meinecke's texts, we may thus trace the parallelism between the history of textual practices in postwar writing and the history of satire.

Conclusion | **Satire after Satire**

The chief guiding question of this study, to begin again, is a simple one: what *is* satire? Tenaciously resistant to fixed definition, the term has frequently provoked an intuitive response in the reader, who may identify its primary characteristics on the level of tone, topic, or socio-political function rather than on the level of form or semiology. Looking for a point of origin in genre is unhelpful because many of the satires of antiquity are lost to us. History has even obscured the etymology of the term, were that to persuade us of its nature. Satire, then, is a signifier without an origin. And yet it has a history.

The reconstruction of its recent history in these pages adopts a semiotic approach because semiotics offers an avenue toward a conception of satire unbounded by concerns of narrative tenor, genre, politics, and social context. Distilling from explicitly satiric texts a discrete set of semiotic practices in the postwar period – after satire as a genre has faded, after it had been declared aesthetically defunct – offers an opportunity to rediscover satire after satires as such are no longer being written as viable literary works. In essence, this synchronic perspective controls for the infelicities of vastly disparate historical contexts by focusing on the semiological constants among texts as case studies. Here, in this reassessment, the shifting accents on certain semiotic practices evince a history of their own, bringing the diachronicity of this narrative back into focus.

Certain ancillary questions have occupied the concerns of the foregoing chapters. What, for example, are the qualities of satire that constitute it as an aesthetic object? And to what extent are these specific qualities limited to literary writing? What are the ends of satire? As the starting point, Jean Paul was uniquely situated at a historical moment after which satire virtually vanished both from literature and from aesthetics. His early satires from the late eighteenth century contrasted favorably with his large-scale prose works from the first quarter of the nineteenth century. They demonstrated a semiotic and stylistic carryover from satire as genre to satire as a textual feature, just as the shifting tides of criticism debunked the notion of satire as genre. At this cusp of history, with Jean Paul, satiric practices enter into other modes of writing, particularly into novelistic prose. Jean Paul's unfinished novel, *The Comet*, served as a first case study from which to glean several dominant semiotic practices – epistemological dissonance from carnivalesque inversion, the establishment of a second-order sign system through mythification, and procedures of citation – whose history we might trace in postwar writings both fictional and nonfictional, literary and theoretical.

In distinguishing between these two modes of writing, one must tread a fine line. The opposition of literature to theory is, largely, an outmoded antinomy between narrative and non-narrative writing, between fictional and nonfictional prose. Because this distinction does not strictly hold under scrutiny – fictional prose of the postwar era incorporates non-narrative elements, and non-fictional writing often resorts to narrative strategies to provide structure for theoretical arguments – these two terms must be differentiated on the basis of their respective focus on narration and metanarration. At the same time one must not lose sight of the historical constructedness of the term literature and, by extension, its ostensibly scientific opposite, theory. As even a cursory reading will show, Roland Barthes' first large-scale work, *Writing Degree Zero*, makes the case that then-current (i. e. prestructuralist) conventions and conceptions of literature arose from a historical paradigm of realism in the nineteenth century. Barthes' diagnosis of a turn toward the zero degree in the *nouveaux romans* of writers such as Alain Robbe-Grillet – which is to say, a shift toward the Cartesian origin in the axial system of style and language, toward a purely semiotic mode of writing *[écriture]* – is thus predicated upon a notion of literature as a resultant construct of social and political history. Fuller elaborations of this work and Barthes' theories take place in other studies, but suffice it to say, the historicization of the term literature complicates any naïve opposition between the terms literature and theory. Indeed, such a complication aside, I have endeavored to demonstrate concretely how these categories become unstable when seen through the prism of the history of satiric practices and, further, how satiric practices in fact bring about this categorical instability. Sharing a common semiotic basis suggests a deeper relation by which literature may wax theoretical and theory become literary.

It is for this reason that both literary and theoretical texts are under discussion here: to recount a history of satiric practices of inversion, mythification, and citation that affects postwar prose in general. For in this age of the "new semiology," "the world is written through and through; signs, endlessly deferring their foundations, transforming their signifieds into new signifiers, infinitely citing one another, nowhere come to a halt: writing is generalized."[1] The opposition between theory and literature blanches in the face of "the science of the signifier."[2] Rather than advocate reading unidirectionally, from theory to literature, these pairings of theoretical writing with literary writing suggest a productive resonance between the two: that understanding literature through its shared history with theory in satiric semiotic practices might inflect the way we read theory.

The first nodal point continues a trend, in older satires, of narrating a clash between various modalities of perception, of suspending a hierarchical order of things. It speaks to the still ineradicable connection between satire and politics. A first theoretician of the carnivalesque who, through his reception in France (via

---

[1] Barthes, "Change the Object Itself: Mythology Today," 167–168.
[2] Barthes, "Change the Object Itself: Mythology Today," 166.

Julia Kristeva), helped bring about high structuralism, Mikhail Bakhtin composed his study *Rabelais and His World* as a dissertation in the late 1930s and early 1940s. Due to the political exigencies of censorship and the slow-rolling grist mill of Soviet academe, however, he only managed to publish it decades later. In this work, Bakhtin examines the French Renaissance writer and his ostensibly misunderstood text *Gargantua and Pantagruel* in light of its demonstration of a nearly extinct mode of folk humor that Bakhtin traces to medieval carnival practices and forms. To tell the story of this transfer of the carnivalesque from social practices to literary strategies, Bakhtin employs figures of inversion that position his work within a highly ambivalent context. On the one hand, Bakhtin exemplifies the inverting festivity of carnival while expressing a nostalgia for a culture in which the subversion of political hierarchies, however temporary, was still possible. On the other hand, the very suggestion of such an inversion – and one that, he contends, is a necessary condition for understanding Rabelais in the first place – casts a subversive shadow on Bakhtin's study in light of the Stalinist strictures under which and, arguably, against which he was writing. Political considerations, therefore, are not yet divorced from a conception of satire, and thus Bakhtin's use of satiric practices accords with earlier notions of satire as political, not literary writing (which is to say writing with an agitating, extraliterary intent rather than for its own sake or for aesthetics). In spite of this dichotomous split between satire as a political and literary mode of writing, Bakhtin's text shows a dialogism, as Kristeva points out, that is rooted in early Menippean satire, highly novelistic, and thus particularly literary.

The same could be said for Thomas Bernhard, whose two later novels, *Woodcutters* and *Extinction*, round off the discussion of the carnivalesque as a satiric practice here. As a perpetual gadfly for the Austrian literary, cultural, and political establishment, Bernhard published works whose polemical features and topical commentary frequently inspired the Austrian critical establishment to dismiss them as philippics besmirching the good name and reputation of the homeland. One cannot overlook Bernhard's undeniable role as a public intellectual and self-conscious *Nestbeschmutzer* [nest soiler], but in the satiric dimension of Bernhard's writing, he too combines an older political modality of satire with semiotic practices that are rooted in this narrative of satire's history since 1800. In the epistemological, syntactic, and lexical inversions; the hyperbole; and the repetition in his writings, Bernhard nevertheless demonstrates the viability of a conception of satire as a set of semiotic practices for which the critic needs no recourse to the extraliterary function of the work. As the political element of satiric writing begins to lose prominence, moreover, this analysis of satire shows a diachronic development in satire's relation to genre and politics. Such a focus on the semiology of satire helps account for shifts in the manifold guises of satire, whereas earlier conceptions of satire as political writing or as a fixed genre cannot keep pace with its Protean shapes.

Both *Woodcutters* and *Extinction* employ many of the same figures of inversion in their renderings of satire while evincing a shift towards a different set of practices. With Bernhard's archetypal hyperbole and repetition, *Woodcutters* dramatizes an inversion in first-person narrative perspective using syntactical and lexical inversions. In so doing, it relativizes the apodictic assertions of the narrator while juxtaposing two epistemologies: that of the carnivalesque, possibly mad observing narrator and that of the objects of his observations (the dinner party attendees). In a throwback to older conceptions of satire as political writing, the novel incited a publishing scandal through the links between its characters and real-life public figures who felt themselves libeled. *Woodcutters* thus came to represent the lingering political associations of satiric writing by embodying readers' assumptions of overlap between fiction and nonfiction, between represented reality and the real. The resolution of the lawsuits against Bernhard, however, landed in his favor and therefore implicitly in satire's favor. The verdict of the lawsuit against him might be thought of as a juridical ruling that affirms the viability of satire's literary and aesthetic character.

By comparison, Bernhard's last novel, *Extinction,* makes use of hyperbole and repetition with abundant linguistic inversions, but it shows a simultaneously inward and outward turn in its focus. Shuffling between multiple layers of narrative temporality, this novelistic swansong plays more consistently with the notion of narrative framing and, in its inward self-reflexive references to Bernhard's oeuvre, also shows an outward turn to the notion of satire as a mode of intertextuality. Its adoption of semiotic strategies from Bernhard's previous works and its incessant references to outside texts sets the stage for a more current and developed notion of satire as both a second-order semiological system and as a series of citations.

As the primary theorist of second-order semiological systems, Roland Barthes offers us a further example of the notion of satire as a semiotic construct. His early book *Mythologies* builds upon *Writing Degree Zero*, in which Barthes historicizes the notion of literature as a nineteenth-century mode of writing with both social and political origins. In *Mythologies*, Barthes scrutinizes objects of popular culture for the ways in which they conceal the history of their denotations and connotations and thus take on new commonplace associations as unquestioned layers of signification. From his shorter essays on Roman bangs in film and Billy Graham's Paris appearance, to the final assessment of the phenomenon of modern myths in "Myth Today," Barthes reveals his susceptibility as a theorist to the seduction of mythologizing his topics. Taken as short narratives, Barthes' essays betray a use of language in his narrative strategies – of metaphor, synecdoche, a mimetic use of forms, logical comparisons, etc. – that perpetuates the particular semiology of myth by which the first sign becomes the signifier of a second sign unto itself. The "metalanguage" of myth, he asserts, is the only weapon against the proliferation of trivial myths. To mythify myths, however, exposes their false ahistoricity while paradoxically establishing the procedure of mythification – and thereby the creation of new myths – as a constitutive element of modern, critical writing, a shift Barthes diagnoses later.[3] Barthes mythifies the media of representation and the conditions for his own critical perspective in exposing his objects of study as myths. His later conclusion "that the mythical is present everywhere *sentences are turned, stories told* (in all senses of the two expressions)"[4] underscores the tenacity of myth and its firm foothold in a concealed history of signification.

In responding to Barthes in her writing, Elfriede Jelinek shows, like Jean Paul, a nascent interest in a theoretical topic that later becomes a central feature of her own novelistic writings. Jelinek's direct reception of Barthes in her 1970 essay "Endless Innocence" attempts to carry his notion of myth further into the modern world of advertising, media, and (gender) politics. While he had viewed mythification apart from politics, Jelinek infuses her understanding of "trivial myths [*trivialmüten*]" with a politically charged notion of revolution. Having essentially written a short update of Barthes' *Mythologies*, Jelinek falls preys to the pitfalls of his own analysis; she creates new myths from old ones but tellingly makes a convincing case for the notion of myth as a catalyst for political change. Here, in Jelinek's repoliticization of myth, in "Endless Innocence" but especially in *Lust* and *The Piano Teacher*, literary writing inflects our understanding of Barthes' mythologies; Jelinek demonstrates how textual practices in literature can manipulate the process of mythification by ironizing it. In effect, Jelinek identifies a way to subvert the insidious naturalization of cultural violence by participating in it, a path untrodden by Barthes and one that alters our reading of theory.

With these two novels, Jelinek adapts from theory to novelistic practice the use of mythification as a satiric strategy – one that acts as an instrument for exposing dehistoricized significatory constructs. In *Lust*, myths form the basis for her narrative of an archetypal relationship of male domination over female docility. Peppering the text, references to paradigmatic myths of Austrian society reveal themselves through Jelinek's wordplay, repetition, and phonetic games as constructs that undergird the gender dynamic and violent discourse that suffuses the novel. Ultimately, however, Jelinek's satiric practice of mythification demon-

---

[3] Barthes, "Change the Object Itself: Mythology Today," 167–169.
[4] Barthes, "Change the Object Itself: Mythology Today," 169.

strates an ideological reliance upon myths of gender, desire, and sex, among others, which reveals the critical narrative stance toward both patriarchal discourse and the feminist rhetoric and writing that hopes to supplant it.

Jelinek's masterwork, *The Piano Teacher*, by contrast, deploys mythification to a similar effect – affirming Austrian society as a construct of nineteenth-century myths – while embedding it within a much less experimentally styled narrative. The narrative breakdown in *Lust* that shows identity to be a problem of language does not occur to the same degree in the earlier, more conventionally narrative, and yet more nuanced novel. Here Jelinek's satiric practices more directly involve the reader and present themselves as less political and ideological. The wordplay, repetition, and phonetic games we see later in *Lust* are present here too, but the primary narrative strategy in *The Piano Teacher* is that of its complex spatialization of narrative perspective. Jelinek adeptly hides her own myth of the reader as a voyeur beneath the weight of more obvious myths of psychoanalytic development, hysteria, musical patrimony, and gender imbalance. Only in the conclusive rape scene does the text expose the reader as a complicit agent in the sexualizing and sexual subjugation of the protagonist. This makes for a highly ambivalent mode of satiric writing; it is one that disavows the overt ideological position of earlier conceptions of satire in favor of a new use of satiric practices that position the *reader* within an ideological framework. Jelinek's satiric writing thus shows how the reader may project political and ideological import as a result of a series of semiotic practices. It also begins to suggest that satire after its demise as a viable genre may be linked as much to a particular mode of writing as it is to a mode of reading.

For Judith Butler and her text *Gender Trouble*, in fact, the issue of reading is fundamental. Based primarily upon a hermeneutic interpretation of signs as repetitions with contingent meanings, Butler's theory of gender performance takes the form of a text that employs citational practices as its central, structuring feature. Gender performance, she argues, parodies not a cited original but "the very notion of an original."[5] In essence, the performance makes use of citational practices that imitate what has always been nothing more than a citation itself. The essence of gender identity is revealed as a supplement – and thus a nonexistent falsehood – assumed by the reader of the performance on the (erroneous) basis that the citational chain is not infinite. What stands out in Butler's theory of performativity is this counter-suggestion that the citational chain has no origin. Subtly she shifts the emphasis of signification from referent to the procedure of referentiality, from the meaning of what is cited to the practice of citation itself. In

---

5 Butler, *Gender Trouble*, 175.

elevating the importance of citational practices, Butler simultaneously elevates her own text, which consists of a number of citational modalities, and reveals all textualities to be constructs of irresoluble referential practices. She performs her theory of performance with narrative strategies ranging from pure citation to an imitation of stock forms. As a strategy of satiric writing, citation thus repudiates the notion that satire must have an essential object, that satiric writing be functional or instrumental. Instead, this newer conception of satire sees in its set of semiotic practices an end in itself that dislodges satire from a dependence upon an intertext. Satiric writing may be thought of as an autonomous mode comprised of a discrete set of historical semiotic practices that illustrate the interrelation between writing and reading.

Thomas Meinecke's novels *Tomboy* and *Music* illustrate this relation between writing and reading virtuosically. His dominant citational practices presuppose an episteme of intertextuality that we saw inaugurated with Bakhtin's (and Kristeva's) theorization of the carnivalesque. Linking disparate discourses and texts, citation as a satiric practice positions the author at a liminal position between writer and reader; to be a writer of texts, the proposition states, one must be a reader of texts. Likewise, the reader of texts must also be, in a sense, a writer of them. In *Tomboy*, Meinecke implicitly describes this dynamic by way of the jarring juxtapositions effected by his citational practices. Confronted with a metanarrative of referentiality rather than a conventional novelistic story, the reader-as-writer must supplement the narrative connections omitted or only suggested by the narrator. In this way, the reader writes his own narrative, and for this reason, I refer to satire as a mode of reading or a mode of writing-as-reading. *Tomboy* illustrates this by narrativizing Butler's theory of performance and magnifying the citational dynamic in it. With his later novel *Music*, Meinecke further complicates matters for the reader by maintaining the abundance of citational practices in *Tomboy* and adding to them an ambivalence of narrative perspective that compels the reader to determine the gender identity of the unknown narrators (much as Jelinek's *The Piano Teacher* entangled the reader in the rape of its protagonist). Involving the reader as a complicit participant in the narrative, citational practices thus allow for the transformation of extraliterary discourses and objects into literary practices. Such a transformation amounts to a universalizing carnivalesque gesture in which ambiguities that result from the clash of epistemologies in intertextuality proliferate.

By divorcing satire from textual externalities like socio-political matters and polemical commentary, finally, the recent shift in satiric practices towards a citational dynamic for its own sake emancipates satire from the fetters of a purely operational understanding of it. According to this outmoded view, satire performs an operation on another text, is thus purely parasitic, and has no aesthetics of its own. To be sure, we have seen in the foregoing analysis how satiric writing may make reference to its historical context or to political conditions, but these are no longer limiting factors in its form or interpretation. Indeed, this analysis shows the necessity for reconsidering satire as a construct of semiotic practices, rather than as a fixed genre or form, or as a product of a particular tenor or operational impulse. In the shift from genre to practice, which we witness from Bakhtin to Meinecke, the disappearance of satire ironically becomes its proliferation as a ubiquitous element of written discourse.

Certain questions remain of course. What I have proposed here as a new conception of satire does not and should not, for example, suggest a recipe for it. For this would run counter to one key point: namely its blurring of the boundaries between writer and reader, between writing and reading. To argue, ultimately, that satire lies in the eyes of the beholder thus seems less like an admission of defeat in the face of a term that continues to defy formal definition than a clichéd truism. Indeed, the interpretive supplement of the reader coincides with a semiotic component of satire that blurs boundaries and subverts common conceptions of and divisions between writing and reading, between fiction and reality. In this age of the disappearance of satire from the landscape of literary and theoretical discourse, it is this prickly conundrum that has inspired an investigation of the afterlife of satiric practices in literature and literary theories, and, in the final analysis, that continues to allow us to locate satire after satire.

Bibliography

Arntzen, Helmut. "Nachricht von der Satire." In *Gegen-Zeitung: Deutsche Satire des 20. Jahrhunderts*, edited by Helmut Arntzen, 6–17. Heidelberg: W. Rothe, 1964.
Arntzen, Helmut. *Satire in der deutschen Literatur: Geschichte und Theorie*. Darmstadt: Wissenschaftliche Buchgesellschaft, 1989.
Bakhtin, Mikhail. "Discourse in the Novel." In *The Dialogic Imagination: Four Essays*, edited by Michael Holquist, translated by Caryl Emerson and Michael Holquist, 259–422. Austin: University of Texas Press, 1981.
Bakhtin, Mikhail. "From Notes Made in 1970–71." In *Speech Genres and Other Late Essays*, edited by Caryl Emerson and Caryl Michael Holquist, translated by Vern W. McGee, 132–158. Austin: University of Texas Press, 1986.
Bakhtin, Mikhail. *Rabelais and His World*. Translated by Hélène Iswolsky. Bloomington: Indiana University Press, 1984.
Bakhtin, Mikhail. "The 'Bildungsroman' and Its Significance in the History of Realism (Toward a Historical Typology of the Novel)." In *Speech Genres and Other Late Essays*, edited by Caryl Emerson and Caryl Michael Holquist, translated by Vern W. McGee, 10–59. Austin: University of Texas Press, 1986.
Bakhtin, Mikhail. *The Dialogic Imagination: Four Essays*. Edited by Michael Holquist. Translated by Caryl Emerson and Michael Holquist. Austin: University of Texas Press, 1981.
Bartels, Gerrit. "Lesen als Handlung." *die tageszeitung*, January 8, 2005, sec. Kultur.
Barthes, Roland. "Change the Object Itself: Mythology Today." In *Image – Music – Text*, translated by Stephen Heath, 165–169. New York: Hill and Wang, 1977.
Barthes, Roland. "From Work to Text." In *Image – Music – Text*, translated by Stephen Heath, 155–164. New York: Hill and Wang, 1977.
Barthes, Roland. *Le Degré zéro de l'écriture*. Paris: Éditions de Seuil, 1953.
Barthes, Roland. *Mythologies*. Paris: Éditions du Seuil, 1957.
Barthes, Roland. *Mythologies*. Translated by Richard Howard and Annette Lavers. New York: Hill and Wang, 2012.
Barthes, Roland. *S/Z*. Translated by Richard Miller. New York: Hill and Wang, 1974.
Barthes, Roland. *The Pleasure of the Text*. Translated by Richard Miller. New York: Hill and Wang, 1975.
Barthes, Roland. *Writing Degree Zero*. Translated by Annette Lavers and Colin Smith. New York: Hill and Wang, 1968.
Baßler, Moritz. *Der deutsche Pop-Roman: Die neuen Archivisten*. München: C. H. Beck, 2002.
Bataille, Georges. *Histoire de l'œil*. Paris: Gallimard, 1993.
Bataille, Georges. *Story of the Eye*. New York: Urizen Books, 1977.
Béguin, Albert. *Traumwelt und Romantik: Versuch über die romantische Seele in Deutschland und in der Dichtung Frankreichs*. Bern: Francke, 1972.
Bensmaïa, Réda. *The Barthes Effect: The Essay as Reflective Text*. Minneapolis: University of Minnesota Press, 1987.
Bergengruen, Maximilian. *Schöne Seelen, groteske Körper: Jean Pauls ästhetische Dynamisierung der Anthropologie*. Hamburg: Felix Meiner, 2003.
Bernhard, Thomas. *Auslöschung: Ein Zerfall*. Frankfurt am Main: Suhrkamp, 1986.
Bernhard, Thomas. *Der Italiener*. Salzburg: Residenz Verlag, 1971.
Bernhard, Thomas. *Der Stimmenimitator*. Frankfurt am Main: Suhrkamp, 1978.

Bernhard, Thomas. *Die Autobiographie*. Edited by Martin Huber and Manfred Mittermayer. Vol. 10. *Werke*. Frankfurt am Main: Suhrkamp, 2004.
Bernhard, Thomas. *Extinction: A Novel*. Translated by David McLintock. New York: Alfred A. Knopf, 1995.
Bernhard, Thomas. *Gehen*. Frankfurt am Main: Suhrkamp, 1971.
Bernhard, Thomas. *Goethe schtirbt: Erzählungen*. Frankfurt am Main: Suhrkamp, 2011.
Bernhard, Thomas. *Holzfällen: Eine Erregung*. Frankfurt am Main: Suhrkamp, 1984.
Bernhard, Thomas. *Meine Preise*. Frankfurt am Main: Suhrkamp, 2009.
Bernhard, Thomas. "Walking." In *Three Novellas*, translated by Peter K. Jansen and Kenneth J. Northcott. Chicago: University of Chicago Press, 2003.
Bernhard, Thomas. *Wittgensteins Neffe: Eine Freundschaft*. Frankfurt am Main: Suhrkamp, 1982.
Bernhard, Thomas. *Woodcutters*. Translated by David McLintock. New York: Alfred A. Knopf, 1987.
Betz, Uwe. *Polyphone Räume und karnevalisiertes Erbe: Analysen des Werks Thomas Bernhards auf der Basis Bachtinscher Theoreme*. Würzburg: Ergon, 1997.
Böck, Dorothea. "Die Taschenbibliothek oder Jean Pauls Verfahren, das 'Bücher-All' zu destillieren." In *Masse und Medium: Verschiebungen in der Ordnung des Wissens und der Ort der Literatur 1800/2000*, edited by Ingeborg Münz-Koenen and Wolfgang Schäffner, 18–37. Berlin: Akademie Verlag, 2002.
Böhler, Christiane. "Literaturskandal – Literaturtransfer: Eine Studie zur Rezeption von Skandalliteratur im Ausland am Beispiel von Thomas Bernhards Roman 'Holzfällen. Eine Erregung.'" In *Literatur als Skandal: Fälle, Funktionen, Folgen*, edited by Stefan Neuhaus and Johann Holzner, 513–523. Göttingen: Vandenhoeck & Ruprecht, 2007.
Brandist, Craig. *The Bakhtin Circle: Philosophy, Culture and Politics*. London: Pluto, 2002.
Brummack, Jürgen. *Satirische Dichtung: Studien zu Friedrich Schlegel, Tieck, Jean Paul und Heine*. München: Fink, 1979.
Brummack, Jürgen. "Zu Begriff und Theorie der Satire." *Deutsche Vierteljahrsschrift für Literaturwissenschaft und Geistesgeschichte* 45 (May 1971): 275–377.
Brune, Carlo. *Roland Barthes: Literatursemiologie und literarisches Schreiben*. Würzburg: Königshausen & Neumann, 2003.
Brunner, Maria Elisabeth. *Die Mythenzertrümmerung der Elfriede Jelinek*. Neuried: Ars Una, 1997.
Butler, Judith. *Bodies That Matter: On the Discursive Limits of "Sex."* New York: Routledge, 1993.
Butler, Judith. *Gender Trouble: Feminism and the Subversion of Identity*. New York: Routledge, 1999.
Calvet, Louis Jean. *Roland Barthes: A Biography*. Bloomington: Indiana University Press, 1995.
Clark, Katerina, and Michael Holquist. *Mikhail Bakhtin*. Cambridge: Harvard University Press, 1984.
Connery, Brian A., and Kirk Combe, eds. *Theorizing Satire: Essays in Literary Criticism*. New York: St. Martin's Press, 1995.
Dentith, Simon. *Bakhtinian Thought: An Introductory Reader*. London: Routledge, 1995.
Dentith, Simon. *Parody*. London: Routledge, 2000.
Didi-Huberman, Georges. *Invention of Hysteria: Charcot and the Photographic Iconography of the Salpêtrière*. Cambridge, Mass.: MIT Press, 2003.
Doppler, Bernhard. "Erregung gegenüber den fünfziger Jahren: 'Holzfällen' und der Tonhof." In *Thomas Bernhard: Traditionen und Trabanten*, edited by Joachim Hoell and Kai Luehrs-Kaiser, 207–216. Würzburg: Königshausen & Neumann, 1999.

Drews, Jörg. "I Care 4 U oder vom Charme des Bauchredens." *Tages-Anzeiger*, September 25, 2004.
Dunker, Axel. "'Alle tanzen, doch niemand kennt die Platten': Pastiche, Sampling und Intertextualität in Thomas Meineckes Roman 'Tomboy.'" *Weimarer Beiträge* 52, no. 1 (2006): 105–118.
Eco, Umberto, and Isabella Pezzini. "La sémiologie des Mythologies." *Communications* 36 (1982): 19–42.
Eickenrodt, Sabine. "Horizontale Himmelfahrt oder poetische 'ars volandi': Die optische Metaphorik der Unsterblichkeit in Jean Pauls 'Komet.'" *Jahrbuch der Jean-Paul-Gesellschaft* 35/36 (2001): 267–292.
Elliott, Robert C. *The Power of Satire: Magic, Ritual, Art*. Princeton, NJ: Princeton University Press, 1960.
Feiereisen, Florence. *Der Text als Soundtrack, der Autor als DJ: postmoderne und postkoloniale Samples bei Thomas Meinecke*. Würzburg: Königshausen & Neumann, 2011.
Feiereisen, Florence. "Identitäten im Remix: Literarisches Sampling im Fadenkreuz von Postmoderne und Postkolonialismus." In *Literatur der Jahrtausendwende: Themen, Schreibverfahren und Buchmarkt um 2000*, edited by Evi Zemanek and Susanne Krones, 281–293. Bielefeld: Transcript, 2008.
Fiddler, Allyson. *Rewriting Reality: An Introduction to Elfriede Jelinek*. Oxford: Berg, 1994.
Fischer, Michael. *Trivialmythen in Elfriede Jelineks Romanen "Die Liebhaberinnen" und "Die Klavierspielerin."* St. Ingbert: W. J. Röhrig, 1991.
Fleming, Paul. *The Pleasures of Abandonment: Jean Paul and the Life of Humor*. Würzburg: Königshausen & Neumann, 2006.
Fliedl, Konstanze. "'Echt sind nur wir!' Realismus und Satire bei Elfriede Jelinek." In *Elfriede Jelinek*, edited by Kurt Bartsch and Günther A. Höfler, 57–77. Graz: Droschl, 1991.
Foucault, Michel. *The Archaeology of Knowledge*. Translated by A. M. Sheridan Smith. New York: Harper & Row, 1972.
Fowler, Alastair. *Kinds of Literature: An Introduction to the Theory of Genres and Modes*. Cambridge, Mass.: Harvard University Press, 1982.
Gau, Sønke, and Katharina Schlieben, eds. *Spektakel, Lustprinzip oder das Karnevaleske?: Ein Reader über Möglichkeiten, Differenzerfahrungen und Strategien des Karnevalesken in kultureller/politischer Praxis*. Berlin: B_Books, 2008.
Geier, Andreas. "Poetiken der Identität und Alterität: zur Prosa von Terézia Mora und Thomas Meinecke." In *Literatur der Jahrtausendwende: Themen, Schreibverfahren und Buchmarkt um 2000*, edited by Evi Zemanek and Susanne Krones, 123–137. Bielefeld: Transcript, 2008.
Genette, Gérard. *Palimpsests: Literature in the Second Degree*. Translated by Channa Newman and Claude Doubinsky. Lincoln: University of Nebraska Press, 1997.
Gleber, Anke. "'Auslöschung. Ein Zerfall': Thomas Bernhards Poetik der Destruktion und Reiteration." *Modern Austrian Literature* 24, no. 3/4 (1991): 85–97.
Gräbe, Thorsten. "Thomas Meineckes Poetikvorlesung: Ausdenken ist verboten." *Frankfurter Allgemeine Zeitung*, February 9, 2012, sec. Feuilleton. http://www.faz.net/aktuell/feuilleton/buecher/autoren/thomas-meineckes-poetikvorlesung-ausdenken-ist-verboten-11642364.html.
Griffin, Dustin H. *Satire: A Critical Reintroduction*. Lexington, Ky.: University Press of Kentucky, 1994.
Grötzebach, Renate. "Humor und Satire bei Jean Paul: Exemplarische Untersuchungen mit besonderer Berücksichtigung des Spätwerks." Freie Universität Berlin, 1966.

Gürtler, Christa. "Die Entschleierung der Mythen von Natur und Sexualität." In *Gegen den schönen Schein. Texte zu Elfriede Jelinek*, edited by Christa Gürtler, 120–134. Frankfurt am Main: Verlag Neue Kritik, 1990.

Hackl, Wolfgang. "Unterhaltung und Provokation: Thomas Bernhard als Satiriker des österreichischen Kulturbetriebs: 'Holzfällen. Eine Erregung.'" *Germanistisches Jahrbuch DDR – Republik Ungarn* 9 (1990): 132–145.

Handke, Sebastian. "Wurm im Ohr." *Süddeutsche Zeitung*, October 16, 2004, sec. Literatur.

Hanssen, Beatrice. "Elfriede Jelinek's Language of Violence." *New German Critique*, no. 68 (1996): 79–112.

Harich, Wolfgang. "Satire und Polemik beim jungen Jean Paul." *Sinn und Form* 19, no. 6 (1967): 1482–1527.

Harris, Roy. *Saussure and His Interpreters*. Edinburgh: Edinburgh University Press, 2001.

Hartwig, Ina. *Sexuelle Poetik: Proust. Musil. Genet. Jelinek*. Frankfurt am Main: Fischer Taschenbuch Verlag, 1998.

Hegel, Georg Wilhelm Friedrich. *Aesthetics: Lectures on Fine Art*. Vol. 1. 2 vols. Oxford: Clarendon Press, 1975.

Hegel, Georg Wilhelm Friedrich. *Vorlesungen über die Ästhetik II*. Edited by Eva Moldenhauer and Karl Markus Michel. Vol. 14. Frankfurt am Main: Suhrkamp, 1970.

Helmreich, Christian. "'Einschiebeessen in meinen biographischen petits soupers': Jean Pauls Exkurse und ihre handschriftlichen Vorformen." In *Schrift- und Schreibspiele: Jean Pauls Arbeit am Text*, edited by Geneviève Espagne and Christian Helmreich, 99–122. Würzburg: Königshausen & Neumann, 2002.

Herzog, Andreas. "'Auslöschung' als Selbstauslöschung oder Der Erzähler als theatralische Figur." In *Thomas Bernhard: Die Zurichtung des Menschen*, edited by Alexander Honold and Markus Joch, 123–131. Würzburg: Königshausen & Neumann, 1999.

Heyl, Tobias. *Zeichen und Dinge, Kunst und Natur: Intertextuelle Bezugnahmen in der Prosa Thomas Bernhards*. Frankfurt am Main: P. Lang, 1995.

Hiebel, Hans H. "Elfriede Jelinek's Satirical Prose-Poem 'Lust.'" In *Elfriede Jelinek: Framed by Language*, edited by Jorun B. Johns and Katherine Arens, 48–72. Riverside, CA: Ariadne, 1994.

Highet, Gilbert. *The Anatomy of Satire*. Princeton, NJ: Princeton University Press, 1962.

Hoell, Joachim. *Der "literarische Realitätenvermittler": Die "Liegenschaften" in Thomas Bernhards Roman Auslöschung*. Berlin: VanBremen, 1995.

Hoesterey, Ingeborg. "Postmoderner Blick auf österreichische Literatur: Bernhard, Glaser, Handke, Jelinek, Roth." *Modern Austrian Literature* 23, no. 3/4 (1990): 65–76.

Höfler, Günther A. "Sexualität und Macht in Elfriede Jelineks Prosa." *Modern Austrian Literature* 23, no. 3/4 (1990): 99–110.

Höller, Hans. "Rekonstruktion des Romans im Spektrum der Zeitungsrezensionen." In *Antiautobiografie: Zur Thomas Bernhards "Auslöschung,"* edited by Hans Höller and Irene Heidelberger-Leonard, 53–69. Frankfurt am Main: Suhrkamp, 1995.

Höller, Hans, and Irene Heidelberger-Leonard, eds. *Antiautobiografie: Zur Thomas Bernhards "Auslöschung."* Frankfurt am Main: Suhrkamp, 1995.

Honegger, Gitta. *Thomas Bernhard: The Making of an Austrian*. New Haven: Yale University Press, 2001.

Hutcheon, Linda. *A Theory of Parody: The Teachings of Twentieth-Century Art Forms*. New York: Methuen, 1985.

Hutcheon, Linda. *Irony's Edge: The Theory and Politics of Irony*. London: Routledge, 1994.

Ingen, Ferdinand van. "Thomas Bernhards 'Holzfällen' oder die Kunst der Invektive." In *Literatur und politische Aktualität*, edited by Elrud Ibsch, Ferdinand van Ingen, and Anthonya Visser, 257–282. Amsterdam: Rodopi, 1993.

Jahraus, Oliver. *Das "monomanische" Werk: Eine strukturale Werkanalyse des Œuvres von Thomas Bernhard*. Frankfurt am Main: P. Lang, 1992.

Jahraus, Oliver. *Die Wiederholung als werkkonstitutives Prinzip im Œuvre Thomas Bernhards*. Frankfurt am Main: P. Lang, 1991.

Jameson, Fredric. "Postmodernism, or The Cultural Logic of Late Capitalism." *New Left Review* I, no. 146 (1984): 53–92.

Jameson, Fredric. *Postmodernism, Or, The Cultural Logic of Late Capitalism*. Durham: Duke University Press, 1991.

Jansen, Georg. *Prinzip und Prozess Auslöschung: Intertextuelle Destruktion und Konstitution des Romans bei Thomas Bernhard*. Würzburg: Königshausen & Neumann, 2005.

Janz, Marlies. *Elfriede Jelinek*. Stuttgart: J. B. Metzler, 1995.

Jean Paul. *Der Komet, oder Nikolaus Marggraf: Eine komische Geschichte*. Edited by Norbert Miller. Vol. 6. *Sämtliche Werke*, 1. Abteilung. Darmstadt: Wissenschaftliche Buchgesellschaft, 2000.

Jean Paul. "Die Taschenbibliothek." Edited by Norbert Miller. 3:769–773. *Sämtliche Werke*, 2. Abteilung. München: Wissenschaftliche Buchgesellschaft, 2000.

Jean Paul. *Horn of Oberon: Jean Paul Richter's School for Aesthetics*. Translated by Margaret R. Hale. Detroit: Wayne State University Press, 1973.

Jean Paul. "Studienhefte zu dem Roman 'der Komet.'" In *Jean Pauls Sämtliche Werke: Historisch-kritische Ausgabe*, edited by Eduard Berend, 412–507. Weimar: Verlag Hermann Böhlaus Nachfolger, 1996.

Jean Paul. *Vorschule der Ästhetik*. Edited by Norbert Miller. Vol. 5. Sämtliche Werke, 1. Abteilung. München: Wissenschaftliche Buchgesellschaft, 2000.

"Jean-Paul-Portal: Neue Werkausgabe." Accessed June 1, 2014. http://www.jean-paul-portal.uni-wuerzburg.de/neue_werkausgabe/.

Jelinek, Elfriede. "Die endlose Unschuldigkeit." In *Trivialmythen*, edited by Renate Matthaei, 40–66. Frankfurt am Main: März-Verlag, 1970.

Jelinek, Elfriede. *Die endlose Unschuldigkeit: Prosa, Hörspiel, Essay*. Schwifting: Schwiftinger Galerie-Verlag, 1980.

Jelinek, Elfriede. *Die Klavierspielerin*. Reinbek bei Hamburg: Rowohlt, 1983.

Jelinek, Elfriede. *Lust*. Reinbek bei Hamburg: Rowohlt, 1989.

Jelinek, Elfriede. *Lust*. Translated by Michael Hulse. London: Serpent's Tail, 1992.

Jelinek, Elfriede. *The Piano Teacher*. Translated by Joachim Neugroschel. London: Serpent's Tail, 1999.

Kaiser, Herbert. *Jean Paul lesen: Versuch über seine poetische Anthropologie des Ich*. Würzburg: Königshausen & Neumann, 1995.

Kämmerer, Harald. *"Nur um Himmels willen keine Satyren—": Deutsche Satire und Satiretheorie des 18. Jahrhunderts im Kontext von Anglophilie, Swift-Rezeption und ästhetischer Theorie*. Heidelberg: Universitätsverlag C. Winter, 1999.

Kaufmann, Sylvia. *The Importance of Romantic Aesthetics for the Interpretation of Thomas Bernhard's "Auslöschung. Ein Zerfall" and "Alte Meister. Komödie."* Stuttgart: Heinz, 1998.

Kayser, Wolfgang Johannes. *Das Groteske: Seine Gestaltung in Malerei und Dichtung*. Oldenburg: G. Stalling, 1957.

Kehlmann, Daniel. *Lob: Über Literatur*. Reinbek bei Hamburg: Rowohlt, 2010.

Kilcher, Andreas B. "Enzyklopädische Schreibweisen bei Jean Paul." In *Vom Weltbuch bis zum World Wide Web: Enzyklopädische Literaturen*, edited by Waltraud Wiethölter, Frauke Berndt, and Stephan Kammer, 129–147. Heidelberg: Winter, 2005.

Klappert, Annina. "Jean Paul intermedial: Phantasie und Exzerptsystem als Medien der Sichtbarmachung." *Zeitschrift für deutsche Philologie* 128, no. 2 (2009): 207–217.

Kögel, Annette, Jörn Hasselmann, and Ferda Ataman. "Heftige Diskussionen nach Kritik an CSD." *Der Tagesspiegel Online*, June 20, 2010. http://www.tagesspiegel.de/berlin/stadtleben/butler-auftritt-heftige-diskussionen-nach-kritik-an-csd-/1864540.html.

Kohut, Heinz. *The Analysis of the Self: A Systematic Approach to the Psychoanalytic Treatment of Narcissistic Personality Disorders*. New York: International Universities Press, 1971.

Kohut, Heinz. *The Restoration of the Self*. Chicago: The University of Chicago Press, 2009.

Kommerell, Max. *Jean Paul*. Frankfurt am Main: Vittorio Klostermann, 1957.

Köpke, Wulf. *Erfolglosigkeit: Zum Frühwerk Jean Pauls*. München: W. Fink, 1977.

Kovács, Edit. "Autor und Leser als Richter: Forensische und rhetorische Lektüren zu Thomas Bernhards 'Holzfällen.'" *Germanistische Mitteilungen* 60–61 (May 2004): 105–128.

Kriest, Ulrich. "Mister DJ, schmeiß die Suchmaschine an!: Thomas Meineckes Buch 'Musik' ist Gegenwartsliteratur als Zeitmitschrift." *Stuttgarter Zeitung*, May 10, 2005, sec. Kultur; 27.

Kristeva, Julia. "Bakhtine, le mot, le dialogue et le roman." *Critique* 17, no. 239 (1967): 438–465.

Kristeva, Julia. *Powers of Horror: An Essay on Abjection*. Translated by Leon S. Roudiez. New York: Columbia University Press, 1982.

Kristeva, Julia. *Semeiotike: Recherches pour une sémanalyse*. Paris: Éditions du Seuil, 1969.

Kristeva, Julia. "Word, Dialogue and Novel." In *The Kristeva Reader*, edited by Toril Moi, 35–61. New York: Columbia University Press, 1986.

Lacan, Jacques. "The Mirror Stage as Formative of the 'I' Function, as Revealed in Psychoanalytic Experience." In *Écrits: A Selection*, translated by Bruce Fink, 3–9. New York: W. W. Norton, 2002.

Lachmann, Renate. "Bakhtin and Carnival: Culture as Counter-Culture." Translated by Raoul Eshelman and Marc Davis. *Cultural Critique*, no. 11 (1988): 115–152.

Lange, Wolfgang. "Pop und Lakritz – Thomas Meineckes Roman 'Musik.'" *Neue Zürcher Zeitung*, December 29, 2004.

Lazarowicz, Klaus. *Verkehrte Welt: Vorstudien zu einer Geschichte der deutschen Satire*. Tübingen: M. Niemeyer, 1963.

Leitgeb, Christoph. *Barthes' Mythos im Rahmen konkreter Ironie: Literarische Konstruktionen des Eigenen und des Fremden*. Paderborn: Wilhelm Fink, 2008.

Lenz, Daniel, and Eric Pütz. "'Ich bin so ein Pop-Sommer-1982-Typ': Ein Gespräch mit Thomas Meinecke." *Neue Zürcher Zeitung*. August 23, 1999.

Lindhoff, Lena. *Einführung in die feministische Literaturtheorie*. Stuttgart: Metzler, 2003.

Lindner, Burkhardt. *Jean Paul: Scheiternde Aufklärung und Autorrolle*. Darmstadt: Agora Verlag, 1976.

Lindner, Burkhardt. "Satire und Allegorie in Jean Pauls Werk: Zur Konstitution des Allegorischen." *Jahrbuch der Jean-Paul-Gesellschaft* 5 (1970): 7–61.

Löffler, Sigrid. "'Ich mag Männer nicht, aber ich bin sexuell auf sie angewiesen': Gespräch über Pornographie, die Sprache des Obszönen, den Haß und das Altern." *Profil*, March 28, 1989.

Long, J. J. "'Die Teufelskunst unserer Zeit'? Photographic Negotiations in Thomas Bernhard's 'Auslöschung.'" *Modern Austrian Literature* 35, no. 3/4 (2002): 79–96.

Long, J. J. *The Novels of Thomas Bernhard: Form and Its Function*. Rochester, NY: Camden House, 2001.

Lücke, Bärbel. *Elfriede Jelinek: Eine Einführung in das Werk*. Paderborn: Fink, 2008.
Lukács, Georg. "Zur Frage der Satire." *Internationale Literatur* 2, no. 4/5 (1932): 136–153.
Luserke, Matthias. "Ästhetik des Obszönen: Elfriede Jelineks 'Lust' als Protokoll einer Mikroskopie des Patriarchats." *Text + Kritik: Zeitschrift für Literatur*, no. 117 (1993): 60–67.
Marquardt, Eva. "Die halbe Wahrheit: Bernhards antithetische Schreibweise am Beispiel des Romans 'Auslöschung.'" In *Wissenschaft als Finsternis?*, edited by Martin Huber and Wendelin Schmidt-Dengler, 83–93. Wien: Böhlau, 2002.
Marquardt, Eva. "Wortwörtlich: Formen der Wiederholung im Werk Thomas Bernhards." In *Dasselbe noch einmal: Die Ästhetik der Wiederholung*, edited by Carola Hilmes and Dietrich Mathy, 229–243. Opladen: Westdeutscher Verlag, 1998.
Meinecke, Thomas. *Hellblau*. Frankfurt am Main: Suhrkamp, 2001.
Meinecke, Thomas. *Holz: Erzählung*. Köln: Kiepenheuer & Witsch, 1988.
Meinecke, Thomas. *Ich als Text: Frankfurter Poetikvorlesungen*. Berlin: Suhrkamp, 2012.
Meinecke, Thomas. *Mit der Kirche ums Dorf: Kurzgeschichten*. Frankfurt am Main: Suhrkamp, 1986.
Meinecke, Thomas. *Musik*. Frankfurt am Main: Suhrkamp, 2004.
Meinecke, Thomas. *Pale Blue*. Translated by Daniel Bowles. Las Vegas: AmazonCrossing, 2012.
Meinecke, Thomas. *Tomboy*. Frankfurt am Main: Suhrkamp, 1998.
Meinecke, Thomas. *Tomboy*. Translated by Daniel Bowles. Las Vegas: AmazonCrossing, 2011.
Miller, Paul Allen. "The Otherness of History in Rabelais' Carnival and Juvenal's Satire, Or Why Bakhtin Got It Right the First Time." In *Carnivalizing Difference: Bakhtin and the Other*, edited by Peter I. Barta, 141–163. London: Routledge, 2001.
Millner, Alexandra. "Schreibtraditionen." In *Jelinek-Handbuch*, edited by Pia Janke, 36–40. Stuttgart: J. B. Metzler, 2013.
Minter, Catherine J. *The Mind-Body Problem in German Literature, 1770–1830: Wezel, Moritz, and Jean Paul*. Oxford: Clarendon Press, 2002.
Mischke, Joachim. "Grübeleien über Gott und Groove: Thomas Meinecke kurvt in seinem meist spaßfreien, virtuosen Diskurswerk 'Musik' durch die Poptheorie." *Hamburger Abendblatt*, April 16, 2005, sec. Bücher im Journal.
Mittermayer, Manfred. "Von Montaigne zu Jean-Paul Sartre: Vermutungen zur Intertextualität in Bernhards 'Auslöschung.'" In *Thomas Bernhard: Traditionen und Trabanten*, edited by Joachim Hoell and Kai Luehrs-Kaiser, 159–173. Würzburg: Königshausen & Neumann, 1999.
Müller, Götz. "Jean Pauls Privatenzyklopädie: Eine Untersuchung der Exzerpte und Register aus Jean Pauls unveröffentlichtem Nachlaß." *Internationales Archiv für Sozialgeschichte der deutschen Literatur* 11 (1986): 73–114.
Müller, Götz. "Nachwort." In *Jean Pauls Exzerpte*, by Jean Paul, 318–347. edited by Götz Müller. Würzburg: Königshausen & Neumann, 1988.
Mulvey, Laura. "Visual Pleasure and Narrative Cinema." *Screen* 16, no. 3 (1975): 6–18.
Noltze, Holger. "Literarische Fahrten im Meer der Verweise: ein Portrait des Erzählers und Musikers Thomas Meinecke." *Literaturen*, no. 10 (2004): 60–66.
Nussbaum, Martha C. "The Professor of Parody: The Hip Defeatism of Judith Butler." *New Republic* 220, no. 8 (February 22, 1999): 37–45.
Öhlschläger, Claudia. "'In den Wald gehen, tief in den Wald hinein': Autoerotische Phantasmen männlicher Autorschaft in Thomas Bernhards 'Holzfällen. Eine Erregung.'" In *Auto(r)erotik: Gegenstandslose Liebe als literarisches Projekt*, edited by Annette Keck and Dietmar Schmidt, 119–131. Berlin: Erich Schmidt, 1994.

Otto, Dirk. *Der Witz-Begriff Jean Pauls: Überlegungen zur Zeichentheorie Richters.* München: Utz, 2000.
Pail, Gerhard. "Perspektivität in Thomas Bernhards 'Holzfällen.'" *Modern Austrian Literature* 21, no. 3/4 (1988): 51–68.
Palmeri, Frank. *Satire in Narrative: Petronius, Swift, Gibbon, Melville, and Pynchon.* Austin: University of Texas Press, 1990.
Palmeri, Frank. *Satire, History, Novel: Narrative Forms, 1665–1815.* Newark: University of Delaware Press, 2003.
Pfabigan, Alfred. "Der Platz von 'Holzfällen' innerhalb der Ordnung des Gesamtwerks von Thomas Bernhard." *Études germaniques* 50, no. 2 (1995): 161–173.
Pizer, John. "Modern vs. Postmodern Satire: Karl Kraus and Elfriede Jelinek." *Monatshefte* 86, no. 4 (1994): 500–513.
Pommé, Michèle. *Ingeborg Bachmann, Elfriede Jelinek: Intertextuelle Schreibstrategien in "Malina", "Das Buch Franza", "Die Klavierspielerin" und "Die Wand."* St. Ingbert: Röhrig Universitätsverlag, 2009.
Proß, Wolfgang. *Jean Pauls geschichtliche Stellung.* Tübingen: M. Niemeyer, 1975.
Ramas, Maria. "Freud's Dora, Dora's Hysteria." In *In Dora's Case: Freud-Hysteria-Feminism*, edited by Charles Bernheimer and Claire Kahane, 149–180. New York: Columbia University Press, 1985.
Reiman, Erika. *Schumann's Piano Cycles and the Novels of Jean Paul.* Rochester, NY: University of Rochester Press, 2004.
Rétif, Françoise. "Die Lust am Obszönen bei Georges Bataille und Elfriede Jelinek." In *Elfriede Jelinek: Sprache, Geschlecht und Herrschaft*, edited by Françoise Rétif and Johann Sonnleitner, 107–118. Würzburg: Königshausen & Neumann, 2008.
Rohlf, Sabine. "Sex mit dem Heiligen Geist: Thomas Meineckes Collagen-Roman über Keuschheit, Körper und Kirche." *Berliner Zeitung*, February 26, 2009, sec. Feuilleton.
Rose, Margaret A. *Parodie, Intertextualität, Interbildlichkeit.* Bielefeld: Aisthesis, 2006.
Rose, Margaret A. *Parody: Ancient, Modern, and Post-Modern.* Cambridge: Cambridge University Press, 1993.
Rose, Margaret A. *Parody//Meta-Fiction: An Analysis of Parody as a Critical Mirror to the Writing and Reception of Fiction.* London: Croom Helm, 1979.
Rüdenauer, Ulrich, and Thomas Meinecke. "'Der Reiz des Rhizomatischen': Ein Gespräch mit Thomas Meinecke über Schreiben unter dem Vorzeichen von Techno, die Faszination für bestimmte Orte und hellblaues Frottee." *Sprache im technischen Zeitalter* 40, no. 161 (2002): 106–117.
Runte, Annette. *Lesarten der Geschlechterdifferenz: Studien zur Literatur der Moderne.* Bielefeld: Aisthesis, 2005.
Ryu, Eun-Hee. *Auflösung und Auslöschung: Genese von Thomas Bernhards Prosa im Hinblick auf die "Studie."* Frankfurt am Main: P. Lang, 1998.
Sasse, Sylvia. *Michail Bachtin zur Einführung.* Hamburg: Junius, 2010.
Scheitler, Irmgard. "Musik als Thema und Struktur in deutscher Gegenwartsprosa." *Euphorion* 92, no. 1 (1998): 79–102.
Scheu, Alexandra Barbara. "'Ich schreibe eine ungeheure Schrift': Sprache und Identitätsverlust in Thomas Bernhards 'Auslöschung.'" *Thomas-Bernhard-Jahrbuch*, 2005, 55–72.
Schierbaum, Martin. "'noch kein Schriftsteller hat die Wirklichkeit so beschrieben wie sie wirklich ist das ist das Fürchterliche': Literatur und Politik bei Thomas Bernhard am Beispiel von 'Auslöschung' und 'Heldenplatz.'" In *An den Rändern der Moral: Studien zur*

literarischen Ethik: Ulrich Wergin gewidmet, edited by Ulrich Kinzel, 150–171. Würzburg: Königshausen & Neumann, 2008.

Schiller, Friedrich. "Über naive und sentimentalische Dichtung." In *Theoretische Schriften*, 8:706–821. *Werke und Briefe*. Frankfurt am Main: Deutscher Klassiker Verlag, 1992.

Schindlecker, Eva. "Thomas Bernhard: 'Holzfällen. Eine Erregung': Dokumentation eines österreichischen Literaturskandals." In *Statt Bernhard: Über Misanthropie im Werk Thomas Bernhards*, edited by Wendelin Schmidt-Dengler and Martin Huber, 13–39. Wien: Edition S, 1987.

Schlich, Jutta. *Phänomenologie der Wahrnehmung von Literatur: Am Beispiel von Elfriede Jelineks "Lust" (1989)*. Tübingen: Max Niemeyer, 1994.

Schlichtmann, Silke. *Das Erzählprinzip "Auslöschung": Zum Umgang mit Geschichte in Thomas Bernhards Roman "Auslöschung, ein Zerfall."* Frankfurt am Main: P. Lang, 1996.

Schmidt-Biggemann, Wilhelm. *Maschine und Teufel: Jean Pauls Jugendsatiren nach ihrer Modellgeschichte*. München: K. Alber, 1975.

Schmidt-Hannisa, Hans-Walter. "Lesarten: Autorschaft und Leserschaft bei Jean Paul." *Jahrbuch der Jean-Paul-Gesellschaft* 37 (2002): 35–52.

Schmitz-Emans, Monika. *Schnupftuchsknoten oder Sternbild: Jean Pauls Ansätze zu einer Theorie der Sprache*. Bonn: Bouvier, 1986.

Schneegans, Heinrich. *Geschichte der grotesken Satire*. Strassburg: K. Trübner, 1894.

Schumacher, Eckhard. *Gerade Eben Jetzt: Schreibweisen der Gegenwart*. Frankfurt am Main: Suhrkamp, 2003.

Schumacher, Eckhard, and Thomas Meinecke. "Pop, Literatur. Ein Interview mit Thomas Meinecke." *Kritische Ausgabe* 5 (2000): 19–20.

Schweikert, Uwe. *Jean Pauls "Komet": Selbstparodie der Kunst*. Stuttgart: Metzler, 1971.

Shookman, Ellis. "Barthes's Semiological Myth of Brecht's Epic Theater." *Monatshefte* 81, no. 4 (1989): 459–475.

Simon, Ralf. "Das Universum des Schreibens in Kuhschnappel (Jean Paul, 'Siebenkäs' – Roman Jakobson)." In *"Mir ekelt vor diesem tintenklecksenden Säkulum": Schreibszenen im Zeitalter der Manuskripte*, edited by Martin Stingelin, Davide Giuriato, and Sandro Zanetti, 140–155. München: Fink, 2004.

Sinn, Christian. *Jean Paul: Hinführung zu seiner Semiologie der Wissenschaft*. Stuttgart: M & P, Verlag für Wissenschaft und Forschung, 1995.

Sprengel, Peter. *Innerlichkeit: Jean Paul: oder, Das Leiden an der Gesellschaft*. München: C. Hanser, 1977.

Sprengel, Peter. "Maschinenmenschen: Ein zentrales Motiv in Jean Pauls Satire." *Jahrbuch der Jean-Paul-Gesellschaft* 10 (1977): 61–103.

Staehelin, Charlotte. "Noch Literatur? Oder schon Wissenschaft? Die Geburt der 'Lola', ungeschnitten und live – Der Roman und sein Rezensent." *Basler Zeitung*, December 11, 2004, sec. Kultur.

Stevens, Adrian. "Schimpfen als künstlerischer Selbstentwurf: Karneval und Hermeneutik in Thomas Bernhards 'Auslöschung.'" In *Thomas Bernhard: Beiträge zur Fiktion der Postmoderne: Londoner Symposion*, edited by Wendelin Schmidt-Dengler, Adrian Stevens, and Fred Wagner, 61–91. Frankfurt am Main: P. Lang, 1997.

Todorov, Tzvetan. *Mikhail Bakhtin: The Dialogical Principle*. Translated by Wlad Godzich. Minneapolis: University of Minnesota Press, 1984.

Weidauer, Friedemann, Alan Lareau, and Helen Morris-Keitel. "The Politics of Laughter: Problems of Humor and Satire in the FRG Today." In *Laughter Unlimited: Essays on Humor,*

Satire, and the Comic, edited by Reinhold Grimm and Jost Hermand, 56–78. Madison, Wis.: University of Wisconsin Press, 1991.

Weinreich, Otto. *Römische Satiren: Ennius, Lucilius, Varro, Horaz, Persius, Juvenal, Seneca, Petronius*. Zürich: Artemis-Verlag, 1949.

Weiß, Gernot. *Auslöschung der Philosophie: Philosophiekritik bei Thomas Bernhard*. Würzburg: Königshausen & Neumann, 1993.

Weiß, Wolfgang. *Swift und die Satire des 18. Jahrhunderts: Epoche, Werke, Wirkung*. München: C. H. Beck, 1992.

Wenzel, Jan, and Thomas Meinecke. "Vielleicht kann man ja immer wieder dasselbe Buch schreiben: Thomas Meinecke spricht mit Jan Wenzel über Hedy Lamarr, Paul Gilroy, Kodwo Eshun, Hubert Fichte und den Atlantik." *Edit*, no. 26 (2001): 60–65.

Wieland, Magnus. "Parasitärer Paratext: Die 'Hand in margine' in 'Des Feldpredigers Schmelzle Reise nach Flätz.'" In *Am Rande bemerkt: Anmerkungspraktiken in literarischen Texten*, edited by Bernhard Metz, Sabine Zubarik, and Thorsten Bothe, 191–208. Berlin: Kulturverlag Kadmos, 2008.

Wilhelm, Frank. *Literarische Satire in der SBZ/DDR 1945–1961: Autoren, institutionelle Rahmenbedingungen und kulturpolitische Leitlinien*. Hamburg: Kovač, 1998.

Will, Michael. "Jean Pauls (Un-)Ordnung der Dinge." *Jahrbuch der Jean-Paul-Gesellschaft* 41 (2006): 71–96.

Winkels, Hubert. "Lob der Kybernetik: Thomas Meineckes Popprogramme und Prosaminiaturen." In *Einschnitte: zur Literatur der 80er Jahre*, 201–220. Köln: Kiepenheuer & Witsch, 1988.

Index

abjection 127, 129, 149, 167
aesthetics 6, 13, 15, 16, 20, 49, 52, 173, 209, 212, 215
alienation effect 104
anteriority 190
apodictic claims 60, 69, 81, 112, 212
archetype 124, 126
artificiality 152, 167, 174, 176, 177
Austria 10, 119, 136, 153, 211

Bach, Johann Sebastian 129, 149
Bakhtin, Mikhail 10, 19, 186
– opposition to Stalinism 56, 211
– *Rabelais and His World* (1965) 10, 42, 211
Barthes, Roland 36, 138, 174, 186, 196
– *Camera Lucida [La Chambre clair]* (1980) 101
– *Mythologies* (1957) 42, 212, 213
– infinite text 98, 101, 172, 177
– *Mythologies* (1957) 11
– *Roland Barthes by Roland Barthes* [Roland Barthes par Roland Barthes] (1975) 101
– *S/Z* (1970) 101
– *Writing Degree Zero [Le Degré zéro de l'écriture]* (1953) 11, 109, 113, 197, 210, 212
Barth, Hans 115, 116
Bataille, Georges 119
Beauvoir, Simone de 162, 164
Bernhard, Thomas 159, 172, 186
– *Correction [Korrektur]* (1975) 85
– *Extinction [Auslöschung]* (1986) 10, 42, 211
– *Goethe schtirbt\Erzählungen* (2011) 98
– *My Prizes [Meine Preise]* (2009) 62
– politics 57
– "The Italian" ["Der Italiener"] (1971) 98
– *The Lime Works [Das Kalkwerk]* (1970) 85
– *The Loser [Der Untergeher]* (1983) 85
– *The Voice Imitator [Der Stimmenimitator]* (1978) 98
– *Wittgenstein's Nephew [Wittgensteins Neffe]* (1982) 62
– *Woodcutters [Holzfällen]* (1984) 10, 42, 211
body 59, 137, 150, 167, 176, 183
borrowing 170

Bovenschen, Silvia 187, 192, 194
Brecht, Bertolt 104
Breuer, Josef 142
Butler, Judith 157–159, 170, 184, 202, 204
– *Bodies That Matter* (1993) 160
– *Gender Trouble* (1990) 12, 42, 170, 205, 214
– performance 14
– rhetorical questions 14, 174, 181

capitalism 119
carnivalesque 10, 45, 47, 48, 54, 58, 60, 70, 77, 211, 215
Cervantes, Miguel de 26, 51
Charcot, Jean-Martin 136, 139, 142–144
citation 9, 12, 86, 136, 158, 160, 166, 167, 168, 176–179, 183, 185–191, 192, 199, 203, 209, 215
Cixous, Hélène 192, 193, 194, 197–198
classicism 16, 22
compulsory heterosexuality 160, 181
conservatism 136
cosmogony 118, 162, 168

Deconstruction 10, 167, 203
deixis 27, 51, 85, 178, 183, 189
Descartes, René 32
diachronicity 169, 176, 209
dialectics 189
dialogism 45, 47, 48, 59, 61, 81, 96, 97, 195, 202, 211
Didi-Huberman, Georges 143
digression 39, 69, 166
distortion 31, 32, 36, 58, 83, 98, 113, 123
Douglas, Mary 167

Eco, Umberto 101
écriture 11, 210
– écriture feminine 193, 194, 197, 198
Ellrodt, Theodor Christian 17
Entwicklungsroman. See novel of development
episteme 18, 30, 32, 56, 186, 195
epistemological dissonance 41, 48, 71, 81
excerpting 23

feminism 10, 125, 142, 157, 158, 162–164, 173, 193, 214
Fichte, Hubert 170
fictionality 63, 67, 106, 121, 143, 176, 179, 209, 212
Fischart, Johann 50, 60
Fischer, Kuno 50, 52
Flaubert, Gustave 193, 197, 198
– *Bouvard and Pécuchet* (1881) 197
Flögel, Carl Friedrich 50
Foucault, Michel 119, 157, 158, 160, 162, 164, 165, 166, 167, 168, 169, 187, 191, 192
fragmentation 104, 105, 195, 199
frame story 84, 85
Freud, Sigmund 136, 139, 142, 151, 158, 160

gender 13, 14, 117, 121, 125, 126, 127, 131, 137, 160, 162–164, 165, 170, 173, 179, 181, 214
– hierarchy 127
– identity 174, 182, 193, 195, 200, 204, 214, 215
– in language 127, 164, 180, 193, 194, 196, 198
Genette, Gérard 11, 15, 47, 161
genre 11, 161
gesture 59, 189, 195, 205, 215
Gmelin, Otto 115
Goethe, Johann Wolfgang von 21, 92, 152
– *Faust* 152
Goetz, Rainald 171, 188
Grimmelshausen, Hans Jacob Christoffel 50
grotesque 8, 35, 48, 50, 52, 58, 71, 78, 84

Hanswurst 50, 60
Haraway, Donna 175
Hegel, Georg Wilhelm Friedrich 6, 15, 50, 52
Heine, Heinrich 22
heteroglossia 61, 195
Hofmannsthal, Hugo von 119
homophony 27, 121, 125, 132, 134, 213
humor 8, 23, 211
Hutten, Ulrich von 50
hyperbole 35, 58, 60, 72, 80, 88, 93, 95, 211
hypertextuality 199
hysteria 136, 142–144, 214

identity 29, 31, 32, 34, 39, 80, 85, 131, 142, 166, 174, 181, 203, 204
imitation 12, 161, 166, 190
infinite regression 160
infinite text. *See* Barthes, Roland
inquit 87, 91
intertextual episteme 12, 13, 15, 16, 25, 177, 188, 189, 195, 199, 205, 215
intertextuality 5, 8, 9, 13, 47, 59, 95, 158, 173, 176–179, 183, 185–191, 197, 200
– infinite text. *See* Barthes, Roland
inversion 9, 10, 19, 30, 32, 41, 47, 53, 59, 67, 69, 74, 77, 81, 87, 88, 124, 131, 209, 211
Irigaray, Luce 119, 162, 164, 187
irony 8, 38, 85, 101, 172, 201, 213

Jameson, Fredric 6, 12, 160
Jean Paul (Johann Paul Friedrich Richter) 9, 95, 152, 159, 209, 213
– digression 25
– excerpting 21, 41, 195
– *Greenlandic Trials [Grönländische Prozesse]* (1793) 26
– *School for Aesthetics [Vorschule der Ästhetik]* (1804) 16
– *The Comet, or Nikolaus Marggraf: A Comical Story [Der Komet, oder Nikolaus Marggraf: Eine komische Geschichte]* (1822) 25, 209
– *The Invisible Lodge [Die unsichtbare Loge]* (1793) 23
– "The Pocket Library" ["Die Taschenbibliothek"] (1795) 17
Jelinek, Elfriede 159, 172, 174, 186, 192
– "Endless Innocence" ["Die endlose Unschuldigkeit"] (1970) 12, 102, 114–118, 213
– *Lust* (1989) 12, 42, 102, 213
– *The Piano Teacher [Die Klavierspielerin]* (1983) 12, 42, 102, 129, 213, 214, 215
Jung, Carl 139, 141

Kafka, Franz 95, 147, 198
Kayser, Wolfgang 50
Kohut, Heinz 139
Kraß, Andreas 202, 204
Kraus, Karl 119, 172
Kristeva, Julia 45–47, 49, 59, 61, 96, 130, 160, 162, 164, 167, 211, 215

Lacan, Jacques 136, 139, 141, 158, 160, 166, 187
Lampersberg, Gerhard 62
language crisis 119
laughter 50, 52, 58, 82, 86–89
Lévi-Strauss, Claude 110, 115, 160
literature as theory, theory as literature 14–15, 101, 173, 183, 196, 197, 199, 210, 216

Mann, Thomas 10
Mauss, Marcel 110
McLuhan, Marshall 115
media 115, 175, 176, 186
Meinecke, Thomas
– *Beating around the Bush [Mit der Kirche ums Dorf]* (1986) 170
– Frankfurt Lectures on Poetics 170
– *Music [Musik]* (2004) 14, 42, 159, 170, 215
– *Pale Blue [Hellblau]* (2001) 192, 193, 196
– rhetorical questions 174, 181, 183, 201
– *Tomboy* (1998) 14, 42, 159, 170, 215
– *Wood [Holz]* (1988) 170
Menippean satire 47, 61, 211
Mering, Christian Friedrich August von 37
metalanguage 113, 124, 213
metanarrative 14, 25, 37, 78, 127, 131, 179, 194, 200, 201, 202, 205, 210
metaphor 28, 32, 90, 108, 113, 114, 123, 125, 127, 145, 174, 189, 212
metonymy 29, 30, 83, 179
mimesis 36
mimotext 12, 190
minimal pairs 121, 125, 127
Minogue, Kylie 204
mode of reading 77, 81, 103, 177, 195, 203
mode of writing 195. *See also* satire as a mode of reading
modernism 136
Möser, Justus 50
music 136, 138, 150, 204, 214
mystification 117, 123
myth 102
– acquiescence [*Einverständnis*] 105
– as depoliticized speech 105
– as second-order semiological system 30, 120
– as type of speech [*parole*] 112

mythification 9, 11, 12, 36, 42, 105, 106, 108, 110, 122, 130, 135, 150, 209, 213

narrative perspective 10, 66, 68, 82, 84, 89, 98, 121, 131, 137, 139, 141–145, 146, 147, 192, 193, 200, 203, 214, 215
neologism 128
New Subjectivity 187
nouveau roman 117, 210
novel of development 160, 162, 169
Nussbaum, Martha 157–158, 163, 165

originality 14, 16, 177, 185, 198, 214

palimpsest 27, 47, 129, 169, 190, 203
paradigm 11, 12, 19, 36, 74, 119, 152, 172, 178, 184, 196, 198, 210
parasitism 114, 138, 185, 190, 215
parody 6, 8, 52, 97, 161, 172
pastiche 6, 11, 111, 160–162, 172, 175, 190
pathology 59, 76, 137, 138, 142
patriarchy 117, 120, 126, 131, 149, 214
performance 12, 142, 151, 157, 174, 176, 177, 182, 205
performativity 35, 169, 170, 176, 181, 182, 194
periodization 22
phallogocentrism 13, 134, 140, 148, 160, 162, 184, 203
poetics 19, 51, 80, 105, 175
poetology 19, 20, 90, 171
polemic 23
politics 12, 57, 135, 152, 157, 173, 179, 184, 210, 211, 214
polysemy 27, 37, 40, 181
popular culture 101, 115, 174
postmodernism 161
postsatiric age 6, 41, 216
poststructuralism 45, 173, 177
power 119, 162, 179
proairetic 65
psychoanalysis 117, 125, 126, 136, 139, 150, 166, 214
– Freudian 139
– Lacanian 116
– mirror stage 141, 150–151
pun 119, 128, 151

Qualtinger, Helmut 119
queer 174, 203

Rabelais, François 26, 46, 49, 50, 51, 58, 60, 211
real 189
reality 32, 84
referent 28, 30, 34, 39, 83, 107, 186, 189, 195, 205, 214
referentiality 13, 28, 34, 65, 138, 149, 150, 167, 176, 189, 192, 214
relationship between reading and writing 195, 215, 216
relationship between writing and reading 15, 18
repetition 11, 33, 59, 68, 74–79, 87, 90–94, 149, 175, 204, 211, 213, 214
– of myths 136
– of signifiers 76, 93, 129, 149
– of syntax 77, 91
representation 28, 30, 31, 32, 78, 84, 138, 148, 186, 213
rhizome 175, 191, 198, 202
ridiculous 8
Rilke, Rainer Maria 192
Robbe-Grillet, Alain 210
roman à clef 66
Romanticism 22
– and the end of carnival 51, 60
– deliterarization of satire 20
Rosenberg, Marianne 202, 203, 204
Rousseau, Jean-Jacques 32

Sachs, Hans 50
sampling 171
satire
– alternate history 9, 49, 205, 209–216
– and postmodern writing 6
– as aggression 3, 205
– as a mode of reading 8, 15, 215
– as a mode of reading and writing 97, 214, 215, 216
– as a mode of writing 3, 82, 171
– as an *Empfindungsweise* 3
– as criticism 3, 24, 29, 51, 93, 109, 119
– as genre 3, 51, 209, 211
– as negation 3, 51, 53, 61, 80

– historical shift 20
– problems of definition 3–5, 24, 209
– "satiric impulse" 161
satiric effect 7, 13, 21, 121, 169
Schiller, Friedrich 3, 21, 64
– *Wallenstein* 152
Schlegel, Friedrich 50
Schneegans, Heinrich 50, 58
Schnitzler, Arthur 136
Schubert, Franz 148, 149, 152
scopophilia 73, 137
self-referentiality 27, 38, 121, 176, 205, 212
semantic satiation 94
semiology 12, 102, 115, 123, 196, 209, 210, 211
semiotic practices 8
semiotics 5, 8, 29, 101, 103, 113, 145, 176, 197, 209, 210, 216
sexuality 124, 146, 162, 181, 183
Shakespeare, William 51, 198
sign 34, 39, 107, 182, 189, 214
signification 9, 19, 46, 61, 82, 114, 138, 150, 167, 169, 175, 180, 186, 191, 203, 204, 213
signified 105, 148, 210
signifier 13, 28, 29, 34, 36, 83, 105, 122, 148, 209, 210
simulacrum 29, 33
stasis 10, 68, 71, 78, 93, 97, 169, 175, 190, 195, 199
Sterne, Laurence 39, 48, 51
structuralism 45, 110, 211
style 11
subjectivity 22, 34, 84, 130, 131, 132, 133, 183, 201, 203
Swift, Jonathan 32, 39, 111
synchronicity 169, 209
synecdoche 104, 106, 108, 212
syntagma 126, 181, 189
syntax 67

teleology 10, 59, 93, 175, 193
transmediality 5, 49, 171, 172, 185
trivial myths 30, 105, 116, 117, 121, 213

unreliable narration 73, 76, 81

Vienna 10, 12, 65, 128, 139, 187
violence 119, 120, 121, 124, 127, 131, 133, 135, 136
voyeurism 66, 67, 73, 137, 143, 144, 146–148, 214

Wedekind, Frank 136
Weininger, Otto 177, 187
Wieland, Christoph Martin 26

Wiener Gruppe 119
wit 8, 23
Wittig, Monique 158, 160, 162, 163, 164, 165, 167
wordplay 26, 31, 40, 123, 124, 127, 128, 132, 213

zeugma 121, 125, 126

www.ingramcontent.com/pod-product-compliance
Lightning Source LLC
Chambersburg PA
CBHW030620230426
43661CB00053B/2087